Terence Armstrong

SCOTT POLAR RESEARCH INSTITUTE
SPECIAL PUBLICATION NUMBER 3

TERENCE ARMSTRONG

RUSSIAN SETTLEMENT
IN THE NORTH

CAMBRIDGE

AT THE UNIVERSITY PRESS LIBRARY

1965

PUBLISHED BY
THE SYNDICS OF THE CAMBRIDGE UNIVERSITY PRESS
Bentley House, 200 Euston Road, London, N.W. 1
American Branch: 32 East 57th Street, New York, N.Y. 10022
West African Office: P.O. Box 33, Ibadan, Nigeria

©

CAMBRIDGE UNIVERSITY PRESS
1965

Printed in Great Britain at the University Printing House, Cambridge
(Brooke Crutchley, University Printer)

LIBRARY OF CONGRESS CATALOGUE
CARD NUMBER: 65–12496

CONTENTS

Contents

PART III

SETTLEMENT SINCE 1917

PLATES

MAPS

INTRODUCTION

It is perfectly clear today that there is no nation with a better knowledge of, or more interest in, the development and exploitation of Arctic lands than the Soviet Union. Soviet specialist knowledge has recently been applied with marked success in the Antarctic. These are important facts, because pressure of world population is demanding, and will continue to do so with increasing insistence, that use be made of all marginal land areas, of which the largest remaining are in the polar regions. The use that will be made of them will not necessarily be to accommodate the overspill, but to exploit their resources. Among the causes for the Soviet interest, the historical one must come high. For Russians have settled in the north and become familiar with its problems over a long period, and on a larger scale than any other people now exercising sovereign rights in the polar regions.

The object of this book is to follow the Russian advance into the north, and examine its causes and effects. The book cannot be a fundamental work of scholarship, because the archives which contain the records have not been at all extensively published. There have been editions of some of the more important manuscripts bearing on the early part of the period, but the documents have been selected in order to illustrate primarily the history of exploration rather than that of settlement, so their usefulness is limited. The standard published collections of historical sources, such as the editions of Russian chronicles, are also of little use in an enquiry as far removed from political history as this one. The archives themselves are in effect inaccessible to non-Soviet scholars, not because access is necessarily forbidden, but because the work demands much longer periods of time than a visitor is permitted to spend in the country. Moreover, some of the material for the Soviet period is still highly sensitive politically and is therefore not likely to be made available in full until there is a radical change of government policy.

But much has been published in Russia, both before and after the Revolution, by scholars who have studied these archives. In the last decade especially, very substantial contributions have been made. The interpretation shows the influence of Marxism-Leninism, and is often strongly nationalist, but the scholarship is generally good. It therefore seems reasonable to use this material, even if secondary, in order to fill a rather considerable gap. The justification for filling it at something less than the highest level of scholarship is for the reader to judge.

The story which will be told is, of course, part of the history of Russia. But its points of contact with the diplomatic and even social history of the country are remarkably few. The north of Siberia was so utterly remote from St Petersburg that this is perhaps not to be wondered at. Life on the fringe, not only of the Russian Empire but of the habitable world, might be expected to be little affected by the words and deeds of rulers so very far away—the more so when the rulers displayed little interest in their northern subjects. It is as part of the history of man's relation to his environment that this story is mainly interesting. For this reason the term settlement has been preferred to the term colonisation. Either might have been used, but settlement stresses the practical aspects of living, while colonisation stresses the political annexation of the territory.

The period to be covered will be from the first appearance of Russians in the north to 1959. Data for the Soviet period are far from complete, but it is essential that some indication should be given of the tremendous advances made since 1917, and the results of the census of 1959 are of the first importance in this respect. As regards limits in space, there is no generally agreed definition of 'the north' in Russian geographical literature, either before or after the Revolution. For the present purpose, the main factors are remoteness from population centres and communications, combined with an Arctic or sub-Arctic environment. There is little to be gained from choosing the boundaries of administrative areas, because most of these keep changing. Since any solution will be to a large extent arbitrary, it has seemed best to draw the southern boundary along the Arctic Circle to the west of the Ural mountains, and along latitude 60° N. to the east, dipping southwards at the western end to include the whole of the peninsula of Kola (Kol'skiy Poluostrov), and at the eastern end to include almost all the Yakut administrative area, the north coast of the Sea of Okhotsk, and Kamchatka (see Map 1 on p. 2). But this boundary is only to be regarded as a rough guide, and will not be rigidly held to.

Introduction

The word 'Russian' in the title is also to be interpreted very loosely. 'Slav' conveys more of the connotation required, but even that is not accurate. For the purpose of this book the word should be taken to mean any inhabitant, or the descendant of an inhabitant, of the states of Novgorod, Muscovy, or the European part of the Russia of Peter the Great; in other words, primarily a person of Russian, Ukrainian, Belorussian or Polish national origin, but including some of Finnish, Baltic, German and other origins. The important thing is that it excludes the indigenous inhabitants of the north; although one must bear in mind that intermarriage between Russians and natives was frequent, so that the Russian blood was diluted and sometimes finally rendered unrecognisable. This study is concerned with the penetration into the north of a group which is not necessarily an ethnic unity, but which has a culture sharply differentiated from that of the natives.

North America presents an interesting parallel. There also representatives of technologically advanced peoples moved into the sparsely inhabited sub-Arctic, and for motives which were closely similar. The parallel is not exact, as no historical parallel ever is. The distances were less and, for various historical reasons, the density of settlement was lower and the period later. But many of the same problems have arisen in each case, and there is obviously value in seeing if, and how, the solutions differed. Detailed comparison along these lines would be material for another book, but occasional points are mentioned here in the hope of stimulating interest among Canadians and others working in the North American Arctic. With Scandinavia there is also a parallel, but a much less exact one. There the climate is less severe, and history has caused many differences.

Place-names have been rendered according to the system approved by the British Permanent Committee on Geographical Names and the United States Board on Geographic Names, so that they can be found with the minimum of difficulty in all officially produced maps and gazetteers in the English-speaking world. Where places have had more than one official name, the earlier forms are also given. The names of native peoples are in general given in the form currently used in the Soviet Union, but again earlier forms are given as well to help identification (see Appendix I). Transliteration of all Russian words, whether place-names or not, has been done according to the system approved for place-names, in order to avoid using more than one system.

In a work of this nature the credentials of the author are relevant. I was born in England in 1920, educated at Winchester College and Cambridge University, where Russian was one of my subjects, and have been a student of Russian polar activities since 1947, working at the Scott Polar Research Institute in Cambridge. On two visits to the Soviet Union, in 1956 and 1960, I have made friendly contacts with many Soviet specialists in various fields, and I have worked also on earlier Russian material in Finland and Czechoslovakia. The northern regions of the Soviet Union have not, however, been accessible to foreign visitors since before 1939, so that I lack first-hand experience of those regions. But I have spoken to some who have had that experience, and I have some knowledge of the equivalent situation in other parts of the north from journeys in the North American Arctic and Greenland.

I wish to thank the following organisations and individuals who have helped me in connection with this book: the Leverhulme Trustees, whose award of a travelling fellowship made possible a visit to Moscow and Leningrad in 1960; the staff of the Arctic and Antarctic Research Institute in Leningrad, where the Acting Director kindly made arrangements for use of the Institute's library; a number of Soviet colleagues, who helped with valuable advice, and Dr E. J. Lindgren, Miss J. Mitchell, Mr C. T. Smith, and my wife, who read the manuscript and made many useful suggestions (but none of these are in any way responsible for the opinions expressed); and to the Director and staff of the Scott Polar Research Institute, whose cooperation, although taken for granted, was fundamental to the whole enterprise.

T.E.A.

July 1963

PART I

BACKGROUND AND BEGINNINGS

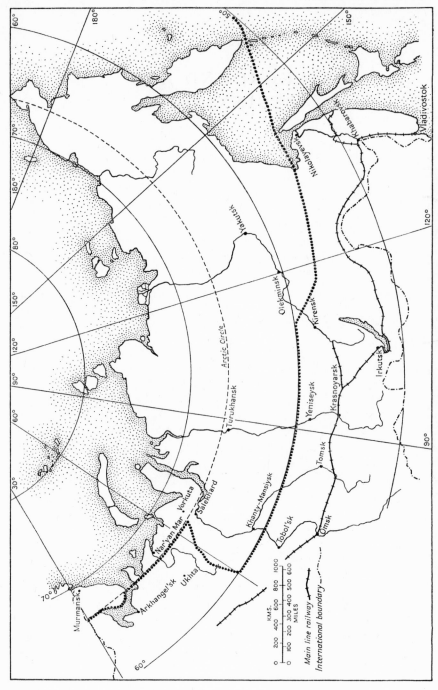

Map I. The north as defined for this book. The heavy dotted line marks the southern boundary.

1

THE ENVIRONMENT

From the point of view of supporting human life, conditions in the Russian north are almost everywhere severe. In places, they are among the most severe of any inhabited part of the earth's surface; only in the Antarctic are they surpassed. A detailed climatological study would not be in place here,[1] but a summary of the principal factors is necessary.

The southern limit of the region, as defined on Map 1, runs for the whole of its length through forest. In Asia, it traverses the heart of the *tayga*, the great virgin coniferous forest which spreads across the whole country from Scandinavia to the Pacific, while in Europe it lies near the northern edge of the forest, in the transitional zone where the trees start giving way to tundra. True tundra, which typically is flat and treeless, supporting only lichens, sphagnum moss and occasional shrubs, begins when the north coast is approached. In the European sector the coastal strip of tundra is generally not more than 80 km. deep, but further east, round the Ob' and Yenisey estuaries and Taymyr, it reaches 500 km. inland. The islands are all tundra, with some of the more northerly largely ice-covered. Settlement took place in both forest and tundra, but to a greater extent in the forest. The settlers therefore found vegetation, sometimes quite abundant, and a fauna, on land and in water, which was very abundant, but not so varied as in temperate regions.

The wild life is the most favourable factor. The flora, apart from the lichens, mosses and dwarf shrubs of the tundra, includes many species of conifer, some birches and some alders. There is a good supply, therefore, of fuel and building materials. In the forest zone there are meadows, commonly in the flood plains of rivers but also elsewhere, and these are important to agriculture and stock farming. But the fauna provides the real riches of the environment. In the tundra in summer there are reindeer, a source not only of food and clothing, but, when domesticated, of transport; the whole economy of many native peoples is constructed around the reindeer. There are

[1] It can be found, for instance, in Alisov (1956). (All references are listed on pp. 198–217.)

also lemmings, Arctic fox, Arctic hare, ptarmigan, ducks, geese, and many salmonid fish, to name only the commonest species. Most of these are also found in the forest, where in addition there are the small fur-bearers, such as sable, ermine and squirrel, more birds, such as grouse, capercaillie and many others, and more fish. Obviously, the food potential of all these is great.

The less favourable factors centre on the climate. In general, temperatures in the greater part of the territory are comparable with those in the Northwest Territories of Canada. Certain coastal regions are better compared with the Alaskan coast, both north and south, and the most temperate region is Kamchatka, where the analogy is with Labrador, and even, at its southern tip, Newfoundland.[1] Almost everywhere the annual mean temperature is below 0° C. (32° F.). The mean for the coldest month is generally between −10 and −30° C., and that of the warmest month between 10 and 20° C. Within the area there are quite wide differences. In the Murmansk region, the Gulf Stream has a big influence (Murmansk almost alone in the whole Russian north has a positive annual mean, of 0·1° C.); but the summers are cool, and the number of frost-free days so small that agriculture becomes very difficult. To the east, the influence of the Gulf Stream soon disappears, and an increasing continentality becomes apparent. The coldest regions in the northern hemisphere are in the vicinity of the upper Yana (Verkhoyansk), the upper Indigirka (Oymyakon), and some other upland areas, where the mean for the coldest month is below −50° C. In some frost hollows, where the cold air collects in still conditions, absolute minima of almost −70° C. have been recorded. These regions are far south of the Arctic Ocean coast, and that round Oymyakon is even south of the Arctic Circle. Summers in these inland areas are short but warm, with quite frequent temperatures of over 20° C., and in the Verkhoyansk area 35° C. has been recorded. The coastal regions to the north are less extreme because of the moderating influence of the sea. Further east, the influence of the Pacific is felt, but this is much less marked than the Atlantic influence at the western end. In all parts, snow lies for a long time and the number of frost-free days in summer is small. The general picture is of long cold winters and short cool summers, with the extremes heightened

[1] Nuttonson (1950), p. 58.

in the inland areas in Siberia. Table 1 shows these data for certain selected points in the north, with some more southerly points added for comparison. These last show that southern Siberia also has a severe climate, but has the advantage of a longer summer.

Table 1. *Some climatic characteristics of selected points*[1]

	Mean temperatures (° C.)			Mean no. of days with snow	Mean no. of frost-free days
Place	Annual	Jan.	July		
Murmansk	0·1	− 9·9	12·8	195	104
Nar'yan Mar	− 3·8	−17·1	12·2	219	92
Salekhard	− 6·7	−24·4	13·8	233	94
Berezov	− 4·0	−22·4	15·9	208	100
Dudinka	−10·7	−29·5	12·0	248	77
Turukhansk	− 7·6	−28·4	15·4	229	81
Pevek	−10·4	−27·1	7·5	228	Not known
Seymchan	−11·9	−39·5	15·5	221	55
Yakutsk	−10·2	−43·2	18·8	206	95
Nizhnekolymsk	−12·4	−35·8	11·8	235	74
More southerly points for comparison					
Vologda	2·4	−11·7	17·1	166	118
Perm'	1·3	−15·4	18·0	176	118
Tyumen'	1·2	−16·7	18·6	164	123
Novosibirsk	− 0·5	−19·3	18·3	169	123
Krasnoyarsk	0·8	−17·4	19·9	150	119
Khabarovsk	1·5	−22·25	19·21	Not known	165

[1] Information from Shcherbakova (1961), pp. 254–83; V. V. Orlova (1962), p. 342; and from various *Klimatologicheskiye spravochniki (Climatological handbooks)* published between 1948 and 1950, quoted by Slavin (1961 *a*), pp. 20–1.

Wind is not a remarkable feature of the climate of the Russian north. The Arctic does not generate the extraordinary high and sustained velocities common in parts of the Antarctic. But it is worth noting that whereas the coldest period in central and southern Siberia is associated with calm weather, and the really low temperatures occur only in such conditions, winds become more frequent as the coast is approached. A temperature of − 40° C. in still air is bearable and not unduly unpleasant, but when there is a wind of 30–40 km./hr., as is not at all uncommon in the tundra, then the temperature becomes quite unbearable. At − 40° C., a wind of only 6 km./hr. is sufficient to cause exposed flesh to freeze.

Precipitation is very light, varying from 20 to 40 cm. of water equivalent a year. One effect of the low precipitation is the difficulty it causes for any sort of agriculture, rendered difficult enough already by the shortness of the summer and the infertility of the soil.

Almost the whole of the region lies within the permafrost zone. This means that below the top few cm. or metres which freeze in winter and thaw in summer there lies a layer of permanently frozen soil, or permafrost, which may be hundreds of metres thick. The practical effects of this are considerable. Drainage is very bad, and the summer melt water, unable to soak away, forms shallow pools on the surface. These provide an ideal breeding ground for the insects which are the major irritant to human beings in the summer. More important now, but less important in earlier times, are the complications caused by permafrost to the construction of any heavy building. Heat is conducted down from the building through the foundations to the frozen layer, which thaws and ceases to support the load. Distortions may take many forms, and houses have often been rendered uninhabitable as a result. Other engineering problems arise also. Roads, railways and bridges may upset the permafrost balance and suffer damage in consequence. Wells cannot be sunk. But the full complexity of these problems was certainly not apparent to the early settler, whose peasant's *izba* of simple wooden construction cannot have provoked much reaction from the permafrost, and was flexible enough to accept small movements. Only in the last 30 years or so has the desire to undertake major engineering works stimulated detailed study of the problems and a search for solutions.

It may be objected that the climatic data on which the preceding paragraphs are based are taken from comparatively recent observations, made mainly in this century and only in a few cases going back to the second half of the last century, and that they may not reflect the climate of earlier centuries. This is a valid objection, because climate can change considerably in that time. Evidence about the climate in the sixteenth to nineteenth centuries is not plentiful. Search in the cossacks' reports of the seventeenth century reveals almost no direct comment on the climate, presumably because this was something altogether too well known to demand any comment. Indirect indications, such as dates of break-up or freeze-up on the rivers, might be thought likelier to occur, but here again little is to be found. The accounts are highly condensed, the doings of months and years being recorded in a few lines. Many dates are mentioned, however, and these often permit one to see whether travel was by boat or sledge at that time. The conclusion from these is that the ice and open water periods were broadly the same as now. The same impression is received from a study of ice conditions in the Kara Sea from 1580 to the present.[1] A big change can be ruled out, but small changes, which are more likely, are just what the evidence is too inexact to show. The same sort of conclusion is also reached by consideration of climatological theory. For here it is difficult to see what mechanism could have caused any substantial change over the last three or four centuries, at least in northern Siberia (the shores of the Barents Sea and of the North Pacific are a different matter, and could well have changed). So it is reasonable to suppose that in general, and over most of the area, the climate has been as described for the whole period of Russian settlement.

But not all the factors controlling the environment and its habitability are climatic. Another important one is the changing length of night and day. It is the long period of darkness in winter (rather than the compensating daylight in summer) which constitutes the main disadvantage to human beings, but it is to some extent offset by reflection from snow. In all parts of the region darkness is marked, although only north of the Arctic Circle, of course, does the sun actually fail to appear. The most northerly settlements, in the vicinity of latitude 70° N., do not see the sun from the end of November to the end of January, while the most southerly, on the 60th parallel, have short days in December. The darkness tends to affect minds rather than bodies, and immigrants rather than natives, but it is a serious limiting factor to many activities.

Remoteness from established centres of human habitation is not a part of the natural environment, but it was clearly one of the major factors for those who went to live there. The remoteness of northern Siberia can be seen at once on a map, but it is perhaps not fully comprehended unless a comparison is made with known territory. It was not at all uncommon for a group of Russian pioneers to set up their small headquarters 800 km. from anywhere that could be called a town, and for individuals to be out in the forest another 500 km. beyond that. This was as if they had started out from Calais (but their town would have been very much smaller), trekked

---

[1] Nazarov (1947).

through almost unknown and uninhabited country, built a hut or two to operate from near Turin, and had struck off in ones and twos as far as Rome—the whole of this in country without roads of any kind. And indeed these distances were sometimes exceeded.

Impressions of what it was like for Russians to live in these conditions are not hard to find in the literature. This one, by a missionary, describing the Nizhnekolymsk region in about 1850, is typical.

Winter, with all its blizzards, accompanied by unrelieved dampness, and at the same time unrelieved deep cold (a most unfavourable combination), lasts nine months. Then come two and a half months of just dampness, like a bath, with thick marshy emanations; in the air there is a ubiquitous fog of minute bloodthirsty insects, for such are midges and gnats there. From these insects the native has no peace, inside or out, day or night. Furthermore, in summer the sun does not set, which is very picturesque to see described, but is extremely tedious to experience in fact. Average temperature for the year is − 10° C., and it is below − 37° C. in December and January. In winter it is cold, damp and gloomy, and the sun does not rise. Vegetation is poor. You do not even find fir and pine; birch has become a dwarf, alder a low-growing shrub, the majestic Siberian cedar has also turned into a dwarf.[1]

And yet, as will be seen, many were able to overcome all these difficulties. The settlers had before them, it should be emphasised, the example of the natives, who had long before succeeded in coming to terms with the environment. This was a tremendous advantage, even if the settler had to modify or even give up his accustomed mode of life in order to benefit by that example. Probably the cold, which is apt to be thought the major obstacle, was the one noticed least. For no Russian is unfamiliar with deep cold, and Arctic winter temperatures are not a very great extension of what he knows well. But without any doubt a remarkable degree of toughness, both physical and mental, was required. The pioneers—and the pioneering stage lasted a long time—had to clear forest and make the timber into huts, build boats, sail down unknown rivers for weeks on end; they were often caught by the freeze-up far from their base and compelled to winter wherever they were. At any time there might be fights with natives, or equally likely with Russians under another leader. And it was impossible to lead this life for just a short while; it had to be for years, and was often for a lifetime.

[1] Argentov (1876), p. 388.

2

THE COMING OF THE RUSSIANS

The conquest by the Russians of the northern parts of Eurasia was carried out more by a process of infiltration than by military action. There were some battles, it is true, but these were rare, and in any case involved only a few hundred men at most. The reason for this relatively bloodless taking over of a vast area of land was, of course, the small scale and unorganised nature of the resistance. Some thousands of widely scattered inhabitants of the boreal forest—hunters and fishermen of a dozen or more tribes—were all there was to be overcome. Furthermore, they lacked firearms, which the Russians possessed. But even taking this into account, the pace of the main advance was astonishing: from the Urals to the Pacific, a distance of nearly 5000 km. ,was covered in just 60 years. The Pacific was reached, it may be noted, before Moscow gained an outlet to either the Baltic or the Black Sea.

This movement eastwards from the Ural mountains across northern Siberia is the most important phase of the advance, and it is reasonably well documented. But it was preceded by the movement towards the north coast of European Russia, and here there is much less certainty about the pattern and the dates. The beginning of the story of the advance into the north therefore lacks conciseness and is somewhat conjectural. What follows (both the European and the Asiatic phases) is taken largely from the historians Bakhrushin and Belov, who have made detailed studies of this subject.[1]

EUROPEAN RUSSIA

There is indirect evidence of Slav contact with the north before the tenth century A.D. For instance, the sixth-century Gothic writer Jordanes mentions trade between Slavs and Yugria (roughly, the plain on either side of the northern end of the Ural mountains), and the Arab geographer Ibn Ruste, writing about 912, refers to a Slav

---

[1] Bakhrushin (1955 *a* and *b*) (a posthumous edition of his collected works written between 1915 and 1950) and Belov (1956). Two compilations of archive material have also been used: Belov (1952) and Orlova (1951).

9

trade in sables, an essentially northern fur bearer. This early mention of fur is interesting, for it provided the main motive for incursions by southerners into the north over a period of many centuries. It is likely that the White Sea littoral was the first region actually occupied. But it is not clear just when the Slavs, represented by the then dominant state of Novgorod, obtained effective sovereignty over it. The code of Svyatoslav Olegovich, Prince of Novgorod, compiled in 1137, lists among the state's possessions the northern territories of Onega, Mosha, Pinega, Ust'-Yemtsy, Vel', Vekshenga and Tot'ma— all rivers draining into the White Sea. Access to these rivers must have led to voyages down them and across the sea to other shores. Belov[1] feels that Kola may have been Novgorod territory in the twelfth century because Gulathing's Law (1200) states that the Norwegians in the region had to be on guard against the Russians. The whole of the area was in fact quite well known to the Norsemen, who had conducted expeditions into it for some 300 years. The Bjarmeland of the Norse accounts is identified by Nansen with the southern shores of the White Sea, the Bjarmas, or Beormas, being probably Karelians, an agricultural people related to the Finns and speaking a language very similar to Finnish. The peninsula of Kola (Kol'skiy Poluostrov) was apparently thought by the Norsemen to be uninhabited.[2] But a list of the fallen in the battle of Lipitsa (1216) mentions one Sem'yun Petrilovets, a tribute collector (*dannik*) of T'r.[3] T'r, Ter, or Tre may be taken to mean the eastern part of the peninsula, known today as Terskiy Bereg (compare the Norsemen's 'Land of the Terfinnas'), or perhaps even the peninsula as a whole.[4] This evidence therefore tends to show that the area was inhabited, and that the inhabitants were dependent upon Novgorod. They were presumably Lapps, fishers and reindeer herders at that time, probably established in much the same regions of northern Scandinavia as they are today. The position of the Norwegian frontier is given in a surviving part of the first Novgorod-Norwegian treaty of 1251, and it ran substantially where it runs now, with the peninsula wholly on the Novgorod side. A treaty between Novgorod and Tver concluded in 1264 mentions Tre among Novgorod's lands. Between 1271 and 1323 there were no fewer than six campaigns

---

[1] Belov (1956), pp. 29–30.   [2] Nansen (1911), vol. 2, pp. 135–40.
[3] Belov (1956), p. 29.   [4] Shaskol'sky (1962), p. 272.

undertaken by Novgorod in defence of this north-western frontier, so it is to be assumed that the land behind it was by then highly valued. The historian Platonov[1] maintains, however, that Novgorod at no time made a formal claim to the peninsula. This may be true, but does not necessarily contradict what has just been said. Novgorod's interests were in colonisation and trade, and these could be furthered in the remote Kola area by the plain exercise of force, without the need for any legal justification.

The whole of this coastal region in what became northern European Russia—primarily the White Sea littoral, but by extension a much larger area—was known as Pomor'ye, 'the sea shore'. It was here that the Slavs had most of their early experience of the sea, and its inhabitants later played a prominent part in Arctic seafaring, and in settlement also, further east.

In the thirteenth century, too, peasant settlement started in the White Sea area. The peasants who came were mostly fugitives, either from the Tatars who were raiding the Rostov-Suzdal' lands, or from the lords of Novgorod itself. They settled along the big rivers (Severnaya Dvina, Onega, Pinega). The peasants were followed by monastic foundations. These played a large part, here as elsewhere, in spreading Slavonic culture in distant regions. In 1417 the Nikolo-Korel'skiy monastery was founded on the southern shore of the White Sea, near the mouth of the Severnaya Dvina, to be followed later by the Arkhangel'skiy and Antoniyevo-Siyskiy monasteries in the same locality. Most important in its later history was the Solovetskiy monastery, founded by the monk Zosima in 1425 on the Solovetskiye Ostrova, islands in the White Sea. It was from here that the two most northerly monasteries were founded in the middle of the sixteenth century: one on the Kola, the other on the Pechenga, both rivers flowing into the Barents Sea close to the Norwegian frontier. The monasteries became centres not only of religion and of culture in general, but of trade and industry: hunting, fishing, sealing, and even whaling were undertaken from them.

The earliest indication of the advance through the Pechora basin to the sea may be found in an account by a man of Novgorod named Guryat Rogovich, in a manuscript collection put together in the early twelfth century, in which he mentions that the road through the

[1] Platonov (1924), pp. 11–12.

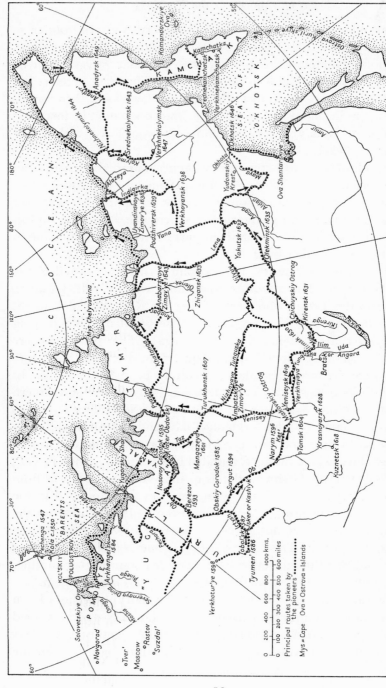

Map 2. The Russian advance across Siberia. The date shown after a town-name is the date of foundation. Many settlements started as a *zimov'ye* or *ostrog* (see Glossary of Russian Terms), but this was later dropped from the name. Main sources: Belov (1956), Bakhrushin (1955a).

Pechora region was known. The vicinity was at that time called by the vague and elastic term Yugria, after the Yugry who lived there (Bakhrushin believes the Yugry were in fact Khanty, also called Ostyak, a hunting and fishing people whose language is related to Finnish, and who then lived between the Pechora and the Ural mountains). Yugria, like Pechora—if indeed there was any real distinction between the two —probably became a colonial possession of Novgorod in the twelfth century, but the link binding them to the mother state was weak, and how far north in either the men of Novgorod penetrated is not clear.[1] Pechora was mentioned as a Novgorod possession, together with Tre, in the treaty with Tver of 1264. The whole region was a source of fur, and the traders and adventurers from Novgorod no doubt went more or less where they wished in it. There was little strongly organised opposition to make the region a battleground, and largely for that reason, perhaps, the chronicles say little about it. One of the few events recorded is a five-week siege of a Yugrian settlement by a Novgorod force in 1198, resulting in the death, through a ruse, of the Novgorod commander and his subordinate leaders.[2] At all events, there were no outsiders to dispute ownership, and by the fourteenth century it was certainly in Russian hands.

There were, however, insiders to dispute it, in the shape of the other principalities of the north Russian plain—Ust'yug, Suzdal', and finally Moscow. The Pechora trade was lucrative enough to be a frequent cause of conflict between them in the fourteenth and early fifteenth centuries. But the fifteenth century saw the rise of Moscow and the eclipse of Novgorod. In 1476 Ivan III of Moscow absorbed virtually all Novgorod's possessions, including the northern ones, and thereafter Russian progress in the north was the progress of Moscow.[3]

Although the advance across Siberia is normally dated from Yermak's sally in 1581, the lower Ob' region, to the east of the Ural mountains, was known not only to the Muscovites, but also to the men of Novgorod long before. As already mentioned, Yugria, along with Pechora, was probably tributary to Novgorod in the twelfth century. This could be taken to refer to that part of Yugria on the European side of Ural. But Bakhrushin[4] believes that even at that

---

[1] Platonov (1924), p. 26.   [2] Tomilov (1947), pp. 22–3.
[3] A list of rulers in Moscow, with their dates, is given in Appendix V.
[4] Bakhrushin (1955*a*), pp. 74–5.

13

time parties may have crossed over from the Pechora. In the mid-fourteenth century they were using this route, and going on to the lower Ob', where the natives offered stubborn resistance. After Muscovy had taken over, there were further moves to strengthen the position here. Campaigns were undertaken in 1485 and again in 1499–1500, but the result was only the most nominal hold of the Moscow princes over the population of the lower Ob'. None of this amounted to occupation of the area, but it does constitute knowledge of, and contact with, a sizable trans-Ural region a long time before Yermak.

It is clear, then, that the Slavonic people of Novgorod established themselves firmly, although no doubt in very small numerical strength, in the Arctic part of what became European Russia, roughly between the twelfth and the fourteenth centuries. The feelers of the advance even reached over the Ural mountains at their northern end and out into Siberia. The impetus behind the movement was the search for fur, which had great importance in the external trade of Novgorod, one of the principal world centres of the fur trade. It seems unlikely that the movement started as the result of any deliberate policy on the part of the state, although these territories and their rich product became an asset well worth guarding. The initial settlement was almost entirely concerned with the fur industry, and in that sense was industrial. Peasants followed later and consolidated the gain. Then, after a pause during which leadership passed from Novgorod to Moscow, there began the next and most spectacular stage of the advance.[1]

SIBERIA

Kazan', the Tatar stronghold at the junction of the Volga and the Kama, from which Moscow had so long been dominated or threatened, fell to the army of Ivan the Terrible in 1552. This opened the way for an advance eastwards along a more southerly route than that which crossed the Ural mountains from the Pechora to the lower Ob'. The merchant family of Stroganov asked in 1558 to be allowed to occupy and exploit large estates on the upper Kama. The family were energetic entrepreneurs and were soon establishing settle-

[1] The best account in English of the Russian advance into Siberia is to be found in Baddeley (1919).

ments to man their various enterprises. Their eye was already on the far side of the Urals, and a Dutch employee of theirs, Oliver Brunel, made two journeys to the lower Ob' and beyond in the 1570's. In order to protect their employees and the settlements in which they lived from attacks by natives, the Stroganovs sought and obtained permission to employ cossacks. The leader they found was Yermak Timofeyevich, who came from the Don, and it was under his command that a force of about 800 men, also largely from the Don, set out from the Stroganov estate in September 1581. Wintering in the mountains, they descended the next year on the Tatar khanate of Sibir' (Siberia), defeated the khan, Kuchum, and seized his capital, Isker or Kashlyk, on the Irtysh. The west Siberian Tatars, descendants of the warriors who served Genghis Khan in the thirteenth century, were Moslems, spoke a Turkic language and lived a semi-nomadic life as cattle farmers. Yermak himself was killed in later fighting in the vicinity (1584), but the Tatars never drove the Russians out of the khanate. The fame achieved by Yermak as 'the conqueror of Siberia' was thus, broadly speaking, justified; but the Siberia he conquered was a very much smaller area than that which the name connotes today. This campaign, which was strictly a private one financed by the Stroganovs and designed to protect and extend their own private empire, was followed at once by others undertaken by the government in Moscow. When Yermak started off, the policy of the government was not in harmony with Yermak's objectives, for it had granted a measure of protection to some of the northern peoples (although not the Tatars) beyond the Urals. But when his successes were evident, the policy changed. Prince S. D. Bolkhovskiy was sent with a force of 500 men to the Irtysh in 1584. He was followed by Ivan Mansurov, who built the first Russian town in Siberia, Obskiy Gorodok, at the confluence of the Irtysh and the Ob', in 1585.

Kuchum and the Tatars were defeated, but not routed, by Yermak and Bolkhovskiy. Kuchum's son even re-occupied the old capital, Kashlyk. But the Russians, now committed to action in Siberia, built more towns: Tyumen' (1586), and, close to Kashlyk, Tobol'sk (1587). From the latter a force under the cossack Danilo Chulkov defeated the Tatars in 1588 and drove them southwards into the steppe. Kuchum was still alive, however, and remained a threat for another ten years. To counter it, an outpost was established in 1594 at Tara, 400 km. up the Irtysh. But an effect of the continuing resistance, which came not only from Kuchum, was to channel the next stage of the advance into the north-easterly quadrant.

Tobol'sk was the administrative centre for the newly acquired territory. From it the Russians now moved downstream, and also came over the Ural mountains by their old route from the Pechora, into the regions known to their forebears. The native princelings agreed to pay fur tribute (*yasak*)[1] to them. In 1593 the town of Berezov (or Berezovo) was founded on the lower Ob', at the point where the Pechora route emerged into it, on the site of the Khanty (Ostyak) town of Sugmutvash. Two years later Nosovoy Gorodok (later Obdorsk, and now Salekhard) was founded at the mouth of the Ob', and also on the site of a Khanty town, Pulnovatvash. Moving eastwards at a more northerly latitude, too, the Russians went up the Ob' to found Surgut in 1594 (the nearby Obskiy Gorodok was then abandoned), and Narym in 1596. The advance in this direction might have stopped here if a native prince had not asked for a Russian town to be built in his land, and thus Tomsk came into being in 1604. From here the outpost of Kuznetsk was founded in 1618, and this remained for a century the high point of Russian advance into the territory of the Kirgiz, a Turkic-speaking nomadic people and then the most active opponents of the Russians. At the same time the invaders looked backwards and secured their lines of communication by building Verkhotur'ye on the eastern slopes of the Urals to command a new passage across the mountains close to that pioneered by Yermak. Although the route from the Pechora continued in use well into the seventeenth century, Verkhotur'ye became, and remained for a century and a half, the main gateway into Siberia.

From the lower Ob' region the fur seekers moved eastwards again, pushing forward into a district which was certainly known to their predecessors from forays fifty years and more before. This was the district of Mangazeya, east of Obskaya Guba, rich in sables. Hakluyt mentions Molgomsey or Molgomzaia in the 1550's, and quotes Giles Fletcher as commending the furs of Momgosorskoy (certainly the same place) in 1588.[2] The journey to it from the Ob' was by water,

---

[1] See Glossary of Russian Terms on pp. 194–6.
[2] Hakluyt (1809), vol. 1, pp. 377, 538.

PLATE I

'The conquest of Siberia by Yermak.' A painting made in 1895 by V. I. Surikov, now displayed at the Russian Museum, Leningrad.

PLATE II

(*a*) Mangazeya in its prime, from a volume of views of Russian towns [*Vidy gorodov*] by Makayev, undated but probably eighteenth century.

(*b*) Yakutsk, probably in the early eighteenth century, from the same volume by Makayev.

through nearly 800 km. of the open and often stormy estuaries of the Ob' and Taz. Early Russian visitors came most of the way by water, leaving the White Sea and coasting north-eastwards, passing through Yugorskiy Shar and then cutting across the peninsula of Yamal by rivers and portages. This was a much quicker route than the overland one, although its use was limited to the two or three months in the summer when the ice was absent. In 1600 the government decided to set up a firm base in the district of Mangazeya, and a force sent out of Tobol'sk built, in 1601, the town of Mangazeya, situated on the Taz and occupying the site of one of the traders' wintering cabins (*zimov'ye*) which already existed in the region.

The founding of Mangazeya was important. To quote Bakhrushin[1]

Mangazeya town, a desolate fort deep in the frozen tundra, almost on the Arctic Circle itself, amid the warring tribes of 'bloodthirsty Samoyed' and other 'unpeaceful natives', cut off from Rus and even from neighbouring Siberia by the storms of the Mangazeya Sea—notwithstanding all the disadvantages of its position, it was for five decades of the 17th century one of the most important centres of Russian activity in Siberia.

The government's reason for establishing Mangazeya seems to have been both to supervise the collection of customs duty and fur tribute, and also to control the native Nentsy, the 'bloodthirsty Samoyed' of the old accounts, who were nomadic reindeer herders, hunters and fishers in the tundra between the White Sea and Taymyr. Belov[2] urges in addition the need to counter the threat of foreign infiltration. The Dutch, and to a lesser extent the English, were active in the sea approaches to north-western Siberia about this time: Nai, Tetgales, Barents, Pet and Jackman. Would not this have provided a strong incentive to Boris Godunov to assert Russian sovereignty? It is an interesting theory, but Belov does not produce much evidence to support it, beyond showing that certain military measures were taken.

The town grew quickly. Its centre was a walled enclosure, within which were the houses of the *voyevoda*, or military governor, the traders, and the cossacks. Apart from a few russianised natives, the whole population was Russian. In the first decades of the century, there were said to be 500 dwelling houses in the town. Each autumn the boats arrived from Russia with supplies. In early spring the

---

[1] Bakhrushin (1955a), p. 297.   [2] Belov (1956), p. 111.

hunters went out, and returned in June when there was a great
gathering and a fair. This was attended also by the hunters who had
wintered in the forest at outlying cabins. For the fair there would be
as many as 2000 people in the town.

But less than twenty years after its foundation, the town received
a severe blow. In 1619 Tsar Mikhail Fedorovich decreed that the sea
route to Mangazeya from the White Sea should be used no more. His
object in doing this was apparently to eliminate the possibility either
of foreigners trading directly with Mangazeya, or of Russians
trading directly into foreign ports, in either case causing loss of
considerable income to the state. Belov again stresses the threat of
foreign annexation of these northern regions. Now he is on rather
firmer ground, for there is good evidence that James I of England,
acting through the Russia Company in London, had designs on
north Russian territory in 1612. But the end of the 'time of troubles'
and the accession of Mikhail Fedorovich effectively prevented any
action, and there is no evidence that the Russian government ever
knew anything about it.[1] All that can be said is that great care was
taken in the years 1619 to 1626 to patrol the area and make certain
no foreigners got through, and perhaps these measures reflect more
nervousness than infringement of customs regulations would call for.[2]
Belov makes a good point in showing that various interested parties
in the Tobol'sk region were well aware that the sea route was in
direct competition with their own more southerly routes into Siberia,
and that these people were doing all they could to hinder the one
in order to promote the other.

This prohibition did not have any immediate effect on Mangazeya.
The commerce in furs continued, but it was purely Russian, and
communications were now exclusively by way of the lower Ob'. In
November 1629 there were still 1270 people in the town, and several
hundred arrived and departed each summer. Traders had for some
time been feeling out further eastwards. Indeed, the Yenisey was
probably reached by some when the town was being built, but the
first settlements on it were not established until 1607. They were
Turukhanskoye Zimov'ye, less than 300 km. from Mangazeya, and
Imbatskoye Zimov'ye, further upstream. This link with the Yenisey
permitted a new route of access to Mangazeya, and in due course this

[1] Lubimenko (1914).   [2] Orlova (1951), pp. 55–73.

became a standard alternative to the lower Ob' route. But at the same time the movement eastwards continued, with the main line of advance now following waterways in lower latitudes, and fur began to get scarcer in the Mangazeya region, so that trade started to fall away. In 1638 the number of winterers was down to 542, and further decline followed.

In the early 1640's a number of ships going to Mangazeya by way of the Ob' estuary were shipwrecked, and this had a discouraging effect. On the other hand, there was little falling off in the number of hunters passing through the town right up to 1660.[1] But what seems to have been the final blow was the decision by the *voyevoda* of Tobol'sk in 1667 to stop sending the usual supplies of grain and salt by this route, sending them instead by the Yenisey. This virtually stopped traffic through the Ob' estuary, and Mangazeya was quite isolated from the main Siberian arteries. In 1672 the garrison was withdrawn. A small *ostrog*, or fortress, was built to replace the all but dead town, but this too later disappeared. Today there is almost no trace of either. Confusingly, however, the name lived on for some time. As Mangazeya declined, the name Novaya Mangazeya was applied to Turukhanskoye Zimov'ye. 'Novaya' (New) was often dropped, and there was much ambiguity for over a century. But in 1782 Novaya Mangazeya was renamed Turukhansk.

Mangazeya was, in Bakhrushin's words,[2] 'in essence a large fortified trading post, serving as a centre for the main bulk of Russian fur traders on the way to the hunting grounds, and one of the chief tasks of the little government outpost, with its wooden towers and inappropriate cannon, was the defence of traders and hunters and the collection of tithes from them'. It is clear that Mangazeya follows the pattern already noted of early Russian activity in Siberia; the pioneering was done by private individuals, out for what they could get, and when it was apparent that they were on to a good thing, the state followed up with the formal framework of administration. The state, too, was out for what it could get, in this case taxes from Russians and fur tribute from natives; but it was also aware of the larger issues. The traders, although undoubtedly benefiting from the state's protection against hostile natives, were also at times angered by the taxation. The *Mir*, or town council, of Mangazeya, has been

[1] Aleksandrov (1960), p. 18.   [2] Bakhrushin (1955a), p. 334.

studied in detail by Bakhrushin, and he reports that it rose in revolt in about 1631 because those concerned directly with the fur trade thought their products overtaxed—this after they had overcome so many natural difficulties. Such antipathy between authority and private enterprise arose on many subsequent occasions.

The movement eastwards continued by two routes. The first, through Mangazeya to the Yenisey, has already been mentioned. The second was some 800 km. further south, by way of the Ket', a tributary of the Ob'. By this route the Yenisey was reached at Yeniseysk, where a settlement was founded in 1619. Not long afterwards, Krasnoyarsk was established further upstream (1628), and here, as on the upper Ob', resistance was met from the forces of the Altyn-Khan, the Mongol leader. Continuing eastwards, where resistance was negligible, again two routes were followed. The southern one, out of Yeniseysk, went up the Verkhnaya Tunguska and Ilim (Ilimsk was founded in 1630), whence by a short portage to the Muka, a tributary of the upper Lena, the route continued down the Lena, and at the bend where the river turns due north Yakutsk was founded in 1632 by the cossack commander (*sotnik*) Petr Beketov. The northern route also terminated at Yakutsk, reaching it by way of the Nizhnyaya Tunguska, with a portage to the Churka, a tributary of the Vilyuy. This was the route followed by Mangazeya hunters in search of new fur areas, and notably also by a large party of 40 cossacks led by Shakhovin in 1633, which came into conflict with fur-tribute collectors from Yeniseysk. But the creation of Yakutsk and the decline of Mangazeya tended to take traffic away from the northern route. Yakutsk, made an independent *voyevodstvo* in 1642, became the new focal point, and the Yeniseysk–Ilimsk waterway became its principal line of communication. In that year 3000 people travelled to Yakutsk.

But men from Mangazeya also took a more northerly course still, to the mouth of the Yenisey and on to the peninsula of Taymyr. The sea was reached soon after the foundation of Turukhanskoye Zimov'ye (1607). In 1611 there was already mention in a fur-tribute book of the river Khatanga, which reaches the sea at the eastern end of the peninsula. Meanwhile two merchants, Kurochkin and Shepanov, had sailed in 1610 out of the Yenisey into the Pyasina, the next river to the east. There is archaeological evidence that a group of unknown Russian seafarers rounded Mys Chelyuskina, the most northerly point of the peninsula, and of Asia, about 1619; the dating is deduced from a collection of coins found among the remains of a camp site on the north coast.[1] No settlement was established on Taymyr itself, which is north of the tree line and not inhabited by natives. But to the east of it Anabarskoye Zimov'ye, on the river Anabar, was established in 1643 by Vasiliy Sychev, a hunter travelling overland from Mangazeya. This journey became common as the better hunting offered by the Anabar valley became known.

The advance from the Yenisey to the Lena is considered by Belov to have been pioneered by *sluzhilyye lyudi*, or government servants (in this case cossacks), and not by hunters and traders. He advances this view against Bakhrushin, who took the opposite line, on the grounds that the hand of the central government is everywhere apparent as organiser and administrator. The further east the advance went, the more difficult it is to imagine that private individuals could afford at their own expense and risk to travel the enormous distances involved. When the far north-east was finally reached, it must have been the government which planned and carried out the journeys. The change-over from privately stimulated exploration to state-organised exploration occurred somewhere, and the Yenisey–Lena phase of the advance is perhaps the likeliest place.

The agents through whom the government acted were military. At the head of the hierarchy, at the Siberian level, was the *voyevoda*, the military governor. As Russian power was extended into Siberia, so each administrative centre, starting with Tobol'sk, was put under the charge of a *voyevoda*. Under him were two kinds of troops. First, there were the regular forces, or *strel'tsy*. There were not many of these in Siberia, since they were normally more urgently required elsewhere. But the garrison of Mangazeya, for instance, was composed of *strel'tsy*. More important was the second kind: the irregular forces, or cossacks. From Yermak onwards, they played a most important part in the whole conquest of Siberia, and indeed in its subsequent history.

It is not easy to determine just who the cossacks were.[2] They are first found in the Middle Ages acting as a frontier force protecting

[1] Okladnikov (1951).
[2] Czaplicka (1918) elucidates many of the confusions. See also Gagemeyster (1854), tom 2, pp. 74–96.

Kiev, and later Muscovy, from the south. There were cossack communities on the Dnepr and the Don, and although independent they generally allied themselves to the Slavs. Their origins are obscure. The word itself seems to come from the Turkic *kiz* or *kez*, meaning to wander. The original groups are likely to have been Kipchak or Polovtsy who escaped destruction by the Mongol invaders in the twelfth and thirteenth centuries through being in inaccessible swampy land. Their numbers were enlarged by fugitives and deserters. There was, therefore, no ethnic unity. The Don cossacks were a well established group by the mid-sixteenth century, and it was largely from them that the Siberian cossacks stemmed. Yermak was from the Don, where he had a price on his head for indulging in the common cossack practice of attacking traffic on the river. In Siberia, of course, there was no 'homeland' for the cossacks (although cossack villages were set up there later), but their traditional occupation as frontiersmen continued. They were very loyal to their Russian masters—a curious thing, as Czaplicka points out, when the Don had produced so many movements of liberation. Once in Siberia, recruiting was not restricted to 'genuine' cossacks from the Don, but on the contrary was open to any local Russians and even in some cases to non-Russians. In this way hunters and traders often became cossacks in order to obtain the advantages of the status (not the least of which was not being ordered about by cossacks).[1] Thus the first garrison of Krasnoyarsk were 303 'foot cossacks' selected in 1630 by the *voyevoda* Akinfiyev from among the hunters and vagrants at Yeniseyskiy Ostrog.[2] Siberian cossacks received a very small annual money payment, a much more considerable payment in kind (food), and in return had to obey orders and render service to the Tsar whenever necessary. The basis of service of the Siberian cossacks was retained for the cossack regiments (*voiska*) of the Imperial army, which were formed very much later (1816 in Siberia). During the advance they were employed as leaders of pioneer detachments, as soldiers, and as frontier guards; in territory already secured they came to act as a kind of police force, and later took charge of all communications. They were therefore a colonising element of some importance, and this aspect will be considered later.

In the movement across Siberia, then, the cossacks were playing

[1] Maydel' (1893–96), vol. 2, pp. 442–4.   [2] Bakhrushin (1959), p. 62.

a more and more important part. The advance posts did not remain long on the Lena. Already in 1633, the year after Yakutsk was founded, Il'ya Perfir'yev with a large hunting party sailed down the Lena to the sea, and, coasting eastwards, reached the Yana. A detachment of his party under Ivan Rebrov, another cossack, sailed westwards into the Olenek. Later, Rebrov turned eastwards and entered the Indigirka, where a *zimov'ye* was built, together with a small *ostrog* (1638). This settlement was called Uyandinskoye after the Yukagir chief on whose land it was, the Yukagir being a predominantly hunting people whose territory then stretched from the Lena to the Anadyr'. Meanwhile the cossack Yelisey Buza had established a *zimov'ye* on the Olenek in 1637, and Posnik Ivanov Gubar', travelling overland to the Indigirka in 1636, had built one on its middle reaches, called the Sredneindigirskoye Zimov'ye. All these were primarily bases from which fur tribute could be collected, the motive behind all this further pushing eastwards being still the same, the search for more fur.

Only shortly after the Arctic Ocean had been reached by way of the Lena, the Pacific Ocean itself was attained. A cossack group under Ivan Moskvitin left the Lena and followed the Aldan and the Maya to reach the Okhota and thence the Sea of Okhotsk in 1641. Here he turned south, discovered the Ostrova Shantarskiye, islands in the south-west corner of the Sea of Okhotsk, and continued to the Amur. His route was followed two years later by Vasiliy Poyarkov. But although the sea had been reached, the extremity of the land had not by any means been attained yet.

Further parties explored eastwards along the coast of the Arctic Ocean. The cossack Dmitriy Zyryan, sailing out of the Indigirka in 1642, established a *zimov'ye* on the Alazeya. The following year he and two other cossacks, Mikhail Stadukhin and Semen Dezhnev, sailed on together to the Kolyma, and built a *zimov'ye* twelve days sail up the river. This was the place that came to be called Stadukhino in the nineteenth century; but Zyryan and his companions moved their base a year later to the site of what subsequently became, and still is, Nizhnekolymsk. These were the first known travellers in this area, but they were quickly followed by many others. By 1647 there were no less than 396 Russians on the Kolyma, and fur returns were already large.

As the map shows, the end had still not been reached. There was more unknown land to the east, and it was Dezhnev who was the first to navigate to the end of the Eurasian land mass. A party of 50 fur seekers wanted to leave Nizhnekolymsk in order to seek the river Anadyr', reputed rich in fur. Fedot Alekseyev Kholmogorets, a successful trader, was the leading spirit. He asked the authorities at Nizhnekolymsk if a cossack could be made available to lead the party. They agreed, and Dezhnev was appointed. Their first attempt, in 1647, was unsuccessful, evidently because of unfavourable ice. The next year Dezhnev sailed again, in six *kochi* (a type of open boat) with 60 companions, and was joined on leaving by another group of 30 men under Gerasim Ankudinov. This time the ice was favourable, but the weather was not. The most north-easterly point of the continent was rounded—it bears today Dezhnev's name—and the Anadyr' was reached; but two severe storms struck the flotilla, and as a result only 24 men of the 90 reached their destination. Alekseyev and Ankudinov, separated from Dezhnev in the second storm, apparently reached Kamchatka, where they later died of scurvy. Dezhnev built a *zimov'ye* on the middle Anadyr' in 1649, and this, known as Anadyrsk, became the focal point of Russian influence in the peninsula. He remained ten years in the region, levying fur tribute and hunting walrus at the mouth of the river. When he did return, it was by the overland route, by then travelled by others, to Nizhnekolymsk, and thence by sea to the Lena. Dezhnev's achievement was great. He demonstrated, and, it seems, realised the full significance of the fact, that Asia and America were separate. His voyage was not repeated for a long time, since the overland route was easier, and by an unfortunate chance his own report lay buried in the archives at Yakutsk for many years. The historian G. F. Müller (Miller) found it in 1736, and by the time he published the facts and the voyage became generally known, more than a century had passed since its accomplishment.

Russians had now reached the furthest extremity of Asia. Small settlements had been established, and administration of a sort provided. The natives were nowhere so numerous as to be able, even if they had wished, to put up serious opposition, although local conflicts could and did occur. Only in the far north-east, where Dezhnev had pioneered, could it be said that the Russians had no control. They were still very few, and what was known of the Chukchi, the reindeer herders and sea mammal hunters whose territory it was, showed that they were likely to be tough opponents. But there was no question of any outside power seeking to dispute sovereignty with Russia.

Although the far north-east does not seem a likely stepping-stone to anywhere else in Asia, it did in fact provide the base from which Kamchatka was first reached by Russians. The beginnings are somewhat hazy. Fedot Alekseyev probably got there about 1650. It is said that the river Fedotovshchina, or Fedotikha, a tributary of the Kamchatka between Verkhnekamchatsk and Srednekamchatsk, was named after him.[1] Perhaps a more solid indication of Russian knowledge of the area is the fact that several maps of the second half of the seventeenth century show a river Kamchatka, the first of them being that produced by Petr Godunov, the *voyevoda* of Tobol'sk, in 1667–68 (see Pl. IV). In the 1680's and 1690's there is evidence of a number of journeys by cossacks southwards from Anadyrsk at least to the northern marches of Kamchatka. The first *zimov'ye* was built in 1695 or 1696 by the cossack Dmitriy Potapov at the junction of the 'Tobon and Kylega rivers' (exact location unknown, but presumably in the north of the peninsula). But the date from which the attachment of Kamchatka to Russia is reckoned is 1697. In that year the Lena cossack Vladimir Atlasov led a party of 60 men to the peninsula expressly for that purpose, and made a considerable exploratory journey. Atlasov was a cruel and avaricious man, and on his return he was arrested for robbery. He went back later to Kamchatka, was deposed by his own cossacks, and finally was murdered. But his expedition laid the foundation of continuous Russian occupation of this territory. All these travellers approached Kamchatka from the north. The very much more direct route, across the Sea of Okhotsk from the west, did not come into use until 1716.

The Russians had now flowed on until the sea was reached on all hands. The whole of Arctic and sub-Arctic Asia was theirs, and they have never lost it. The native peoples, worsted in such skirmishes as there had been, paid fur tribute to the conqueror with relatively little show of resistance. In 1700, the hand of the conqueror was light.

[1] Krasheninnikov (1949), pp. 473–4, 749. Ogruzko (1953) adheres strongly to this theory.

He did not want to displace the native from his territory; he wanted to join him in it, and the territory was wide enough, and the numbers of intruders small enough, for this to make very little difference. The Chukchi alone were actively resisting. Their country had been reached almost last, it is true. But their unity and national pride was such that it was to take a considerable campaign by the Russians, later in the eighteenth century, to break them.

ALASKA

Although the Russian conquest of the Asiatic north was practically finished by the end of the seventeenth century, there remains another, and less successful, stage. This is the extension of the eastwards movement across the North Pacific to North America.[1]

There was, as might be expected, a pause before the next onwards surge. During this pause the Russian Government, under the initial stimulus of Peter the Great, undertook what remained until the twentieth century the largest exploring expedition ever mounted, the Great Northern Expedition. It lasted from 1733 to 1743 and employed at various times 977 people. One of the main functions of this expedition was to explore the North Pacific, and Vitus Bering, the Danish-born leader of the squadron assigned to that task and the nominal head of the whole expedition, made a great circuit during which he sighted many of the Aleutian Islands and part of the mainland of Alaska. This part of the expedition is also known as Bering's second expedition, or the second Kamchatka expedition. These discoveries stimulated a number of Russian merchants into setting out, in the second half of the century, to see what fur they could get from the Aleutians and beyond. At this same period also Russian imperial expansion towards the north-east encountered for the first time competition from other European powers, in particular Britain. The voyages of Cook in 1776 and of others later—Meares, Portlock, Vancouver—made plain the British interest in the region, an interest which the loss of the American colonies increased. This clash of interests was quickly followed by another over markets: both countries sold fur in China.

[1] Okun' (1951) gives a good general account from the Soviet viewpoint, and this has been the main source for what follows.

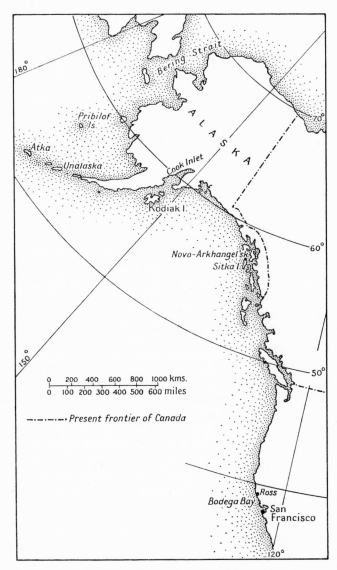

Map 3. Alaska on the same scale as Map 2, showing
the principal Russian settlements.

Catherine the Great, therefore, in 1786 approved the memorandum submitted by Count A. R. Vorontsov and Count A. A. Bezborodko, which claimed for Russia the American coast north of latitude 55° 21′ N., the off-lying islands, the Aleutians, and the Kurils, on the basis of Bering's discoveries, which antedated Cook's. But an essential part of this policy had clearly to be the maintenance of a naval squadron in the North Pacific, and her plan to send one from the Baltic for this purpose came to nothing because of war with Turkey and then with Sweden. Another approach was therefore tried: commercial penetration, without any direct state support. England had done this sort of thing with the East India Company, so why not beat her at her own game? This was the thinking which led, after much manoeuvring among interested merchants, to the Imperial charter signed by the Tsar Paul in 1799 setting up the Russian-American Company. The company was given a monopoly of hunting and mining on the islands and on the North American mainland north of latitude 55° N., and the right to make discoveries beyond these areas. There was no government subsidy, although the company in fact became an agent through which government policy was carried out. For half a century the Russian Government strove for mastery in the North Pacific, and even waged war, while all the time masking its operations under the name of the company.

Grigoriy Shelikhov had been one of the most active merchants in the area before the company was formed. After successful fur trading in the Aleutians, he established the first Russian settlement on Kodiak Island in 1784. He died in 1795, and it was his manager on Kodiak, Aleksandr Baranov, who became the company's Governor in Alaska. In 1799 he was in command at the building of the fortress of Mikhaylovsk on the island of Sitka (now Chichagof Island), which was to be the main base of the company. Mikhaylovsk was stormed in 1802 by Tlingit Indians, with, it is said, British assistance. But in 1804 Baranov recaptured it, and this time built a new fortress on a nearby hill. Novo-Arkhangel'sk was the name given to the new centre, and it was thought to be impregnable. Meanwhile, the business of the company was prosecuted at the various settlements, where sea otter, fur seal, walrus and small terrestrial fur-bearers were hunted. By the early 1820's, there were perhaps 600 Russians and people of mixed Russian-native blood distributed between fifteen permanent settlements. These were on the Komandorskiye Ostrova (islands off Kamchatka), Atka and Unalaska in the Aleutians, the Pribilof Islands, Kodiak (the original Russian centre), Cook Inlet on the mainland, Sitka, and finally Ross Colony in California, near San Francisco. The biggest were Sitka (Novo-Arkhangel'sk) and Kodiak, which between them accounted for 80 per cent of the Russian and mixed population. More must be said, however, about the Ross Colony.

It had always been the intention of the company (that is, of the Russian Government) to move southwards. Shelikhov had even had markers buried on shore at various points, inscribed 'land belonging to Russia'. The Government hoped at the right moment to claim the whole of the Californian coast. The reason for this hoped-for expansion southwards was not only the desire to enlarge the territory. There was also the need to find a source of food for the Alaskan settlements. Round-the-world voyages from St Petersburg by way of the Cape of Good Hope and Australia had become the normal supply route, and they could be upset by the slightest diplomatic trouble. Long-term operation of the northern outposts was contingent upon expanding southwards. In 1811, therefore, a settlement was established at Bodega Bay, in latitude 38° N., and named the Ross Colony. It was chosen precisely because it was a good jumping-off place for further southwards movement. In 1818 there were 27 Russians there, and perhaps 100 others.

It was now time to match this *de facto* expansion with some legal declaration. When the company's charter came up for revision in 1819, the southern boundary was extended from latitude 55° N. to 51° N.—a far cry from 38° N., but a move in the right direction. But, in spite of this, when conventions were signed a few years later with the United States (1824) and Britain (1825), the boundary was pushed back to latitude 54° 40' N., and the Ross Colony was simply not mentioned. The reason for this was that Alexander I did not want to antagonise Britain at a time when he was hoping to intervene in the Balkans and partition Turkey. By the same conventions British and American traders and fishermen were permitted free entry to the Russian settlements. This, as some Russians saw at the time, in fact made it likely that the British and Americans would become the real masters, because of their closer proximity and greater numbers, leaving Russia only the empty legal title to the land.

But these conciliatory gestures did not prevent Alexander from still trying to win California. Force of arms was out of the question, but D. I. Zavalishin, his intelligent and resourceful representative at Ross, tried to persuade the Californians to secede from Mexico. But it became clear that both Americans and British realised that an independent California would increase Russian influence, and they could be expected to oppose this. From that time, therefore, any real prospect of the Russians achieving their aim was at an end. Later Baron F. P. Vrangel', who was Governor of the American colonies in the 1830's, proposed to win California by agreement with Mexico, in exchange for recognition by Russia of Mexican independence from Spain. This, however, the Tsar would not agree to, and in 1836 California declared itself independent. No longer was this advantageous to Russia, as it would have been fifteen years earlier, because the United States was now strong enough to penetrate California in force. The Ross Colony had thus by now lost all usefulness. In 1833 it had a population of 199, among them 41 Russians, and the desertion rate was high. It was just self-supporting for food, but had failed completely to supply the northern settlements, and was costing the company 10,000 roubles a year. In 1839, therefore, Ross was abandoned. The high-water mark of Russian expansion in the North Pacific had been reached, and the tide began to recede.

The ebb continued quite rapidly. In the same year that Ross was abandoned, the company agreed to lease the Alaskan 'pan-handle' (the coastal strip between latitude 54° 40′ and 59° N.) to the Hudson's Bay Company, with which there had been bitter rivalry up to then. The reason for this concession was again to be found in events on the other side of the world. Russia was striving to eliminate causes of friction with Britain, because negotiations on the government of the Black Sea straits were under way. And increasingly, in the 1840's, the Russian-American Company came to be regarded as a convenient bargaining counter for Russian diplomacy—an area where concessions could be made without serious loss in order to make gains elsewhere. At the same time the hunting returns fell, the price of fur also went down, rendering operations still more unprofitable, and the long-standing difficulty of food supply found no solution; in 1849, grain was being imported to Alaska from the Baltic provinces of Russia. At this time Count N. N. Murav'yev, the Governor-General of Siberia, was asked by the Tsar to report on the company's activities, and his report implicitly recognises the uneconomic functioning of the company. He supported the idea of a government subsidy, partly because he himself planned to use the company as a cloak for regaining for Russia the lower Amur region—a plan that he later successfully realised. But by the late 1850's even this usefulness had disappeared, and it was now generally agreed that the time had come to sacrifice the no longer required pawn.

The best price would probably have been obtainable from Britain, because the British would not want to see the Americans getting this natural extension of Canada, but Russia now wanted to win American support against Britain in the matter of the abrogation of the Treaty of Paris and the partition of Turkey. Negotiations had been started in 1857, before these considerations were operative, but had been delayed by the American Civil War. The deal was finally completed in 1867, when the Russian colonies in Alaska were sold to the United States for $7,200,000. The purchase was not popular in America, where many felt that too much good money had been spent on a wilderness of 'ice and snow'. But in fact, quite apart from the strategic advantages to America which became apparent subsequently, the income from the salmon fishery and gold mining very quickly surpassed the cost price.

So ended the unique example of major Russian expansion overseas. Its failure, as will be seen later, could be ascribed as much to a failure to settle Russian peasants as to any other single cause.

Thus the Russians came into possession of their northern territory. The conquest was largely a matter of filling in a vacuum. Fur was always the lure, attracting at first individuals, and later, as the distance from European Russia increased, government enterprise. The advance continued until it came up against opposition of a more serious nature than that offered by primitive, if fierce, native peoples. When that happened, there was a falling back to the point at which the serious threats no longer operated—in fact, to the shores of Asia. Within those continental confines there never has been, before or since, any determined challenge to Russian authority.

NORTH SIBERIAN TRAVEL IN THE SEVENTEENTH CENTURY

First-hand accounts by Russian administrators, cossacks and traders give some idea of what living conditions were like during the seventeenth-century advance across Siberia. Environment and climate are seldom referred to, no doubt because they were familiar to men from northern and eastern European Russia. Such accounts help towards an understanding of the period. The physical appearance of a report of this sort is shown in Pl. III.

First, some idea of a pioneer journey down the Lena may be derived from this report by Petr Beketov, the cossack who founded Yakutsk, to Tsar Mikhail Fedorovich.[1]

In 1627 Sire, I, your slave, was sent, and with me some service men, up the Verkhnyaya Tunguska river to the Rybnaya and the Chadobchya, to the Tungus, and these Tungus, righteous Sire, were not obedient to you, gave you no fur tribute and beat the service men and traders. . . .

I, your slave, was sent in 1628 for a year on your royal service to collect your royal fur tribute below Bratsk rapids. And, Sire, I performed this year-long service, and went from Bratsk rapids up the Tunguska, and the Oka, and the Angara, as far as the mouth of the Uda, and collected fur tribute from the Buryat princes and from the people in the villages, and brought the Buryat people under your exalted rule, Sire. And at this time those Buryat people bring in your royal fur tribute to Yeniseyskiy Ostrog. And before me, Sire, no Russian person visited those places.

And in 1630, Sire, I, your slave, was sent on your royal service from Yeniseyskiy Ostrog with service men to the great river Lena. And from below the Lena portage I went up the great river Lena and reached the Buryat lands and those of other peoples. And these Buryat people, not wishing to pay fit tribute to you, righteous Sire, collected together and surrounded me. And with service men I was besieged in my Buryat lands. And near these Buryat people, Sire, lived Tungus of the Nalyaskiye lands, and they gave fur tribute to the Buryat people. And I, your slave, brought the Nalyaskiye lands of those Tungus under your exalted rule, and again collected your fur tribute, Sire, from the Tungus, and at that place, the Nalyaskiye lands, the Tungus pay fur tribute to you, righteous Sire.

And from the Bratsk lands, Sire, I went, your slave, to the Lena portage, and at the Lena portage I wintered. And from the Lena portage I, your slave, sent out service men to collect your royal fur tribute along the tributary rivers Ilim and Ringa [Kirenga], and obtained more fur tribute

[1] Orlova (1951), pp. 93–5. In this excerpt, as in the later ones, translation is literal, but the years have been changed to modern usage. Not all the place-names mentioned have been traced.

PLATE III

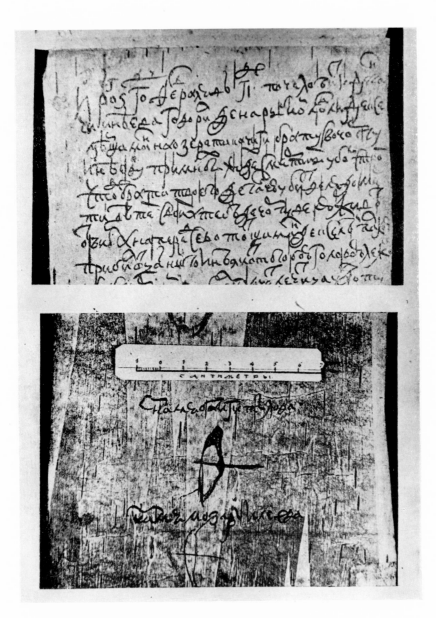

A cossack report written on birch bark in 1668 (Al'kor & Grekov, 1936).

PLATE IV

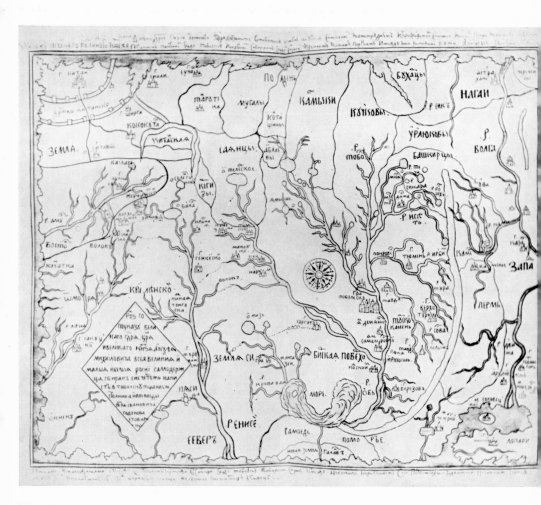

The first general map (*obshchiy chertezh*) of Siberia was that made by the *voyevoda* of Tobol'sk, Pe[
Godunov, in 1667. Russian, German and Swedish copies of this map have come down to us. Th[
one is a Russian version, probably of 1672, as reproduced in Baddeley (1919). North is at the botton[
and the rivers Ob' and Yenisey are the most prominent features. River systems and portages are th[
principal items of information conveyed. The river Kamchatka is marked half-way down the left-han[
edge of the map (see p. 25).

PLATE V

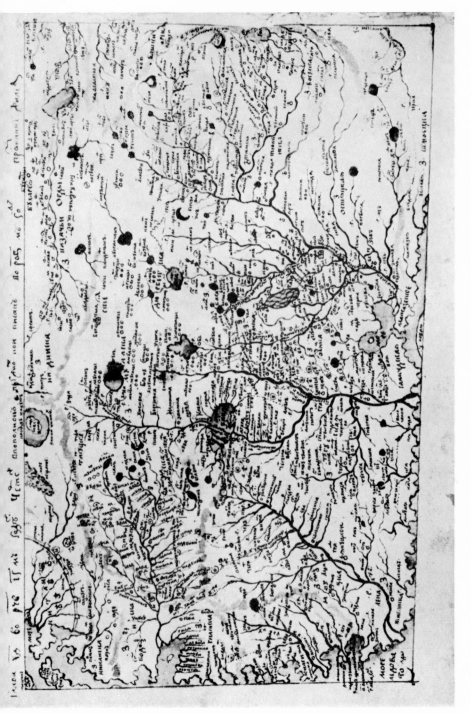

This is a corrected and augmented version of the Godunov map of Siberia (see Pl. IV), and was made 17 years later, in 1684, by Semen Remezov. It was reproduced by Bagrow (1947), where the date is wrongly given as 1687. In the 17 years since Godunov, much new material had come in, especially for the north-east (bottom left).

PLATE VI

(*a*) An overnight stop in the woods in eastern Siberia (Boulitchoff, 1856).

(*b*) A halt on the Tauy, near Okhotsk. These two pictures of Siberian travel relate to a period 200 years after the journeys described on pp. 32–8, but the methods changed little in that time.

for you, Sire, than in former years. And in the spring of that year, Sire, when the ice went out, I, your slave, and the service people sailed down the great river Lena, and having arrived at the Yakut lands, built an *ostrog*, and made all necessary defences for the *ostrog*.

And at Yakutskiy Ostrog I, your slave, spent a year with the service people, and for your royal contentment brought under your exalted rule many Yakut princelings and their villagers...and for you, righteous Sire, collected much fur tribute from the Yakut lands and Yzhiganekh, and from the Tungus on the surrounding streams. And I, your slave, at that time collected again for you, Sire, on the great river Lena 6—[text deficient] roubles in ship tax. And before me, Sire, no one spent a year on the great river Lena, and no one built an *ostrog* anywhere on the Lena, nor collected ship tax, nor tithes from service and trading people....

The tone of this report is typical of most of its kind. All emphasis is on pleasing the autocrat, with the writer hoping to justify many years of service during which he has not reported at all. The report quoted above includes in its peroration

And while in your service, Sire, in distant parts, I shed my blood for you, Sire, and suffered hunger and every sort of hardship, and defiled my spirit, and ate mare's meat and roots and fir bark and all kinds of filth, and many times had scurvy.

Apart from such general indications, there is very little information on day to day life, and the narrative is highly condensed. As to the peoples mentioned, the Tungus (now called Evenki in the Soviet Union) were reindeer nomads who wandered over much of eastern Siberia, the Buryat were Mongol-speaking cattle farmers and tillers of the soil, and the Yakut were Turkic-speaking cattle and horse farmers of the Lena valley.

A good idea of the difficulties that could arise, and of the risks of travel in these northern regions, is conveyed by a report of the Tobol'sk esquire (boyar-son) Dmitriy Cherkasov on a journey he made to Mangazeya in 1643. The object of the journey was to bring grain and other supplies to the town. It was made by the standard route of that time—down the Irtysh and Ob' to Obskaya Guba, thence up Tazovskaya Guba to the Taz—a total of some 2000 km., water all the way. The time taken was six months.[1]

On 13 July last year, 1643, two boats were sent out from Tobol'sk to Mangazeya with the government grain supplies for Mangazeya service

[1] Orlova (1951), pp. 80–2.

men, and also the boat of the clerk Grigoriy Teryayev, and a traders'
boat with grain supplies and all sorts of other goods. They reached Berezov
on 1 August, left Berezov on the following day, 2 August, and put out to
sea from among the islands on the 15th [the head of Obskaya Guba].
At sea they met contrary winds and made no progress for two days and
two nights, and then proceeded under sail for two days to the turning [at
the entrance to Tazovskaya Guba]. And at the turning the wind began
to lash the boats, and the government boats and the traders' boat capsized,
and the government stores and the traders' stores were scattered over the
sea and the shore, and the people floated and struggled to the shore on oars
and planks and in rowing boats. But Grigoriy Terayev the clerk's boat
was thrown bodily on shore, and the stores were swept out, and the boat
was filled with sand on the beach, and there they stood, and it took them
two weeks to dig out the sand and get the boat back into the water. And
from this disaster the clerk Grigoriy Teryayev sent to Tobol'sk two of the
Tobol'sk service men, Petrushka Ostaf'yev and Sozonko Volodimerov, and
five traders; they went in a rowing boat and took news of the shipwreck.

Fifteen men, Bogdashka Kochevshchik and his companions, remained to
winter at the site of the shipwreck with their goods and the supplies of the
traders.

From this disaster all the other people, numbering 70, set out in Grigoriy
Teryayev's boat for Mangazeya. They sailed on for a day. And when they
were opposite the black rocks of the Stolbovaya river, they encountered a
north wind on the beam. And this wind threw the boat on shore, and
they could not get it off again.

And they remained on that shore for eight weeks, and the Samoyed
were round about. And from that shipwreck they set off by sledge along
the shore towards Mangazeya, reaching Filipov's hut in ten days. And
the Samoyed began to approach them and began to fight with them.

And after the fight, they and Dmitriy spent the night there. And after
that all day the Samoyed began to find them, and fought, and would not
let them pass. And when they were opposite Yapanshin Shar, the Samoyed
took from them eight sledges with supplies and goods, and with weapons.
And at the same place Ivan Pleshchiyev was wounded in the head by an
arrow, and Nadezhka Sidorov, an officer of the Taz *Strel'tsy*, and Sameyka
Ivanov of Mezen', a trader, were killed, and a serving boy was captured
from the sledge of Grigoriy Teryayev the clerk. And from there the
Samoyed followed them to Purovskiy Ostrov, and at Purovskiy Ostrov
fought long with them. And at that fight they wounded Yefremko, a
member of the staff of the *voyevoda*, Prince Petr Mikhaylovich Ukhtomskiy, and of that wound Yefremko died.

The Tobol'sk service man Fed'ka Volkov killed a reindeer of the
Samoyed. And from there they went on to the mouth of the Taz, and to
the mouth of the Taz from the black rocks took them eight weeks, and
hunger overtook them, because the Samoyed would not let them through

and stole their supplies, and the service men and traders began to die from hunger, and about 50 people died, and Grigoriy Teryayev's two daughters and nephew died. And from the mouth of the Taz the clerk Grigoriy Teryayev sent news to the town by the Mangazeya service man Okinka Kharitonov and his companions. And these service men scarcely reached the town because of hunger, and when they had got there the service man Fomka Mikhaylov died from hunger. But the clerk Grigoriy and his men went on in hunger and continued for ten days along the Taz, and hunger wore out the clerk and them, and the clerk Grigoriy, together with Ivan Pleshchiyev, reached a point opposite Ledenkin Shar. And Dmitriy Cherkasov with the Tobol'sk service men went on ahead, and travelled one day ahead of the clerk Grigoriy. And in that camp the Tobol'sk service man Kost'ka Galkin stopped, could go no further, and later died. And from that camp they went on for three days in hunger, and ate leather and reindeer hide from their snowshoes.

And at that camp a Tobol'sk service man, the *Pyatidesyatnik* Grishka Prokop'yev, and the Taz soldier Grishka Romanov, stopped from hunger, and they later died. And from there they went on for three days to Sukharevo Zimov'ye, and ate dogs on the way, and at Sukharevo Zimov'ye they stayed for three days. And as a result of the message received from the clerk Grigoriy Teryayev, the *voyevoda* Prince Petr Mikhaylovich Ukhtomskiy sent out to meet him his son Prince Fedor with soldiers and traders and with food supplies. And they found them and Dmitriy at Sukharevo Zimov'ye.

And from Sukharevo Zimov'ye Prince Fedor sent Dmitriy ahead to the town with the trader Krenko Davydov. And to search for the clerk Grigoriy Teryayev he sent his own men, Taz *Strel'tsy* Os'ka Shutov and Pyatko Savin, and the Tobol'sk soldiers Fed'ka Volkov, Fed'ka Kuznets, and Vas'ka Kulakov. And they found Grigoriy at the camp opposite Ledenkin Shar, and with him his wife, and his people: his man Fil'ka with his wife and daughter, and also Ivan Pleshchiyev with his man Oleshka, and Makar Negodyayev the trader from Kolmogory with his son Yakun'ka....

And they took them all, Grigoriy and his wife and people and Pleshchiyev, and put them on sledges, and came to Sukharevo Zimov'ye. And at Sukharevo Zimov'ye Pleshchiyev died. And from Sukharevo, coming to Shchuch'i Kur'i, only a day and half from the town, the clerk Grigoriy died on the road. And his wife, and his man Fil'ka with his wife and daughter, were brought to Mangazeya town on 14 January. And of all the service men and traders, there came to Mangazeya town about 20....

It was a nightmare journey, clearly enough; but in its hardships it was certainly not unique, and probably not even very exceptional.

Comments going beyond simple narrative, for instance on the nature of the country passed through, or the human beings encountered, are in general found only in the much rarer accounts written by more educated people. Such a man was Nikolay Spafariy, who was sent by Tsar Aleksey Mikhaylovich on an embassy to China in 1675. He reported in some detail on those parts of Siberia he traversed. In a letter from Yeniseysk to his protector at the court in Moscow, he says:[1]

...By God's mercy and through the Great Tsar's good fortune, I, thy servant, reached Yeniseysk on the 9th day of July, with all my people, though with the greatest difficulty—for, the river Ket' was in flood, below, so that neither with oars nor with poles, but only by towing could we make any way, while, above, the water was so low that we spent many a day on shoals—this with great cold and much snow. Then we were assailed by one of Pharaoh's plagues, mosquitoes and flies, by which we are still, and will be, tormented, they tell us, right up to winter again—pests that allow us neither to eat nor to sleep....

This Yenisey country, my lord, is very fine, reminding me of Wallachia —and the Yenisey river of the Danube, a very great river and a merry one. And God has given abundance of corn of all kinds, and cheap; and all else; and a numerous population.

Again on the subject of the Khanty or Ostyak:[2]

...All the Ostyaks catch great quantities of fish. Some eat it raw, others dry it and boil it, but they know neither salt nor bread, nothing but fish and a white root *susak*, of which they collect a supply in summer, dry it, and eat it in winter. Bread they cannot eat; or if any do eat their fill of it, they die. Their dwellings are yourts; and they catch fish not merely for the sake of food, but to make themselves clothing out of the skins—also boots and hats, sewing them with sinews of the fish. They make use of the lightest possible boats, built out of wood, holding five or six men, and even more. They always carry with them bows and arrows, to be ready to fight at any moment. Wives they have in plenty—as many as they wish, so many do they keep.

The predominance of water travel has been emphasised before, and these excerpts all bring it out. There were several types of vessel in use in the seventeenth century. The stoutest was the *kochmara*, or *koch*, a wooden vessel perhaps 30 feet long, decked, capable of carrying, say, ten men and six or seven tons of cargo, with one sail and oars. It was flat-bottomed and drew little, and was not too difficult for a group of men to haul over a portage. There was a

[1] Baddeley (1919), vol. 2, p. 258. Baddeley's translation.
[2] Baddeley (1919), p. 254.

larger version, used when the ships had to go downstream to the sea, and this could be up to 60 feet long, had more than one sail and a keel, and could carry 34–40 tons. The boats mentioned in the report on the Mangazeya voyage by Cherkasov just quoted were *kochi*, probably of the larger type. Those used further south were probably the smaller ones, and indeed must have been so if a portage was involved. The *koch* is first mentioned in the sixteenth century in the White Sea area, and seems to be a design of Russian origin, long preceding the western European influences introduced by Peter the Great. For purely river work, however, the flat-bottomed *doshchanik* was more commonly used. It was not unlike the smaller *koch*, decked, with a sail as well as oars. This was the type of vessel Spafariy used on the Irtysh and Ket'. Besides these sizable craft, there were also, of course, ordinary small rowing boats (*karbasy*).[1]

It is interesting that the designs were quite different from those in use in Canada at the comparable stage in that country's exploration by Europeans. The *voyageurs* used canoes of birch, and later cedar, having copied the design from the natives. Only after a hundred years and more, at the end of the eighteenth century, did the use of bigger boats become common. The difference is no doubt mainly due to the Russians' long familiarity with large-scale inland water-ways, and the absence of this background in the French and English. It is also true that in Canada there were fewer long rapids-free stretches, and nowhere did a traverse of the open sea form part of a journey. But the argument against use of bigger boats in Canada rested mainly on the difficulties at portages, so the Russians must have credit for successfully overcoming these.

At the portages, the boats were manhandled by the pioneers and those immediately following them, and then, once the routes became established arteries, there were enough boats to permit a travelling party to change boats rather than haul them across. Transport between the two rivers was assisted by pack horses or horse-drawn vehicles. This degree of organisation was achieved quite quickly, often within a few years of the first discovery of the route.

In winter there was less travel, but when it had to be done, sledges were used. They were pulled most commonly by horses. This does not mean that the Russians had to bring in all the horses needed,

[1] Belov (1956), pp. 188–215.

37

for the Yakut, for instance, kept horses themselves. Reindeer were used in some northern regions, and dogs in parts where the natives were dog-drivers (the Nentsy, Chukchi and Kamchadal, for instance). Winter travel could often be faster than in summer.

The normal rate of travel by waterways was decidedly slow, the average for a journey being generally between 15 and 30 km. per day. Bakhrushin has made a study of the routes across Siberia, and the rough times given below are his (see Map 2).[1]

From the confluence of the Irtysh and Ob' to Makovskiy Ostrog, 11½–13½ weeks (1350 km.).
From Yeniseysk to the Lena portage at Ilimsk, 13 weeks (950 km.).
From Tobol'sk to Mangazeya, 8–13 weeks (2100 km.).
From Mangazeya to Turukhansk, 2½–4 weeks (250 km.).
From Turukhansk to Chichuyskiy Ostrog, 11 weeks (1800 km.).
From Yakutsk to the Kolyma overland, via the Yana, Indigirka and Alazeya, 13–14 weeks (1800 km.).

The most northerly routes from the Lena included a section of open sea between river mouths, and the time required for these is more variable owing to the need to take account of the weather and ice situations. The route from Yakutsk to the Sea of Okhotsk at first followed the Aldan and the Maya and took 13 weeks, but later a more direct overland route by way of Yudomskiy Krest was preferred, and this took only five weeks.

[1] Bakhrushin (1955a), pp. 111–36.

PART II

SETTLEMENT UNDER THE TSARS

3

CONSOLIDATION:
THE NUMBERS OF SETTLERS

The central question is now reached. How was this enormous region settled? Before considering the types of settlement and the motives behind them, it is desirable to try to establish in general terms how big the movement of population was. It will be convenient also to restrict the scope of this and the succeeding chapters to the period up to 1917, and to deal with the Soviet period separately.

There is considerable difficulty in finding population figures for these northern areas. There were censuses of a kind—the so-called 'revisions' of the eighteenth and nineteenth centuries—but these were not only inaccurate,[1] but also, being designed to obtain information relating to a capitation tax, fell far short of providing the information that a census usually provides. There was, in fact, only one complete census ever held in the Russian Empire, that of 1897, and the available results of this do not distinguish between Russian and non-Russian population in particular administrative areas.[2] Moreover, most of the administrative divisions into which Siberia was broken up do not fit neatly into the north as defined for the purpose of this book. They have always tended to be shaped round a north–south axis, with the centres of population in the south, and separate results for the sparsely populated northern portions were not issued. Similarly with immigration figures. Plenty are available for Siberia as a whole, but it is not at all easy to establish what proportion of immigrants went to the north. This is a difficulty which will recur in many different forms; it is that of ascertaining to what extent trends observed in Siberia as a whole are apparent in the north. There is also the difficulty of interpreting population figures. The revisions expressed their results in 'souls', these being males in the taxable classes. To convert 'revision souls' into population, Lorimer[3] multiplies by 2·2. But in remote northern areas there are

---

[1] Shvetsov (1888), p. 18; Kabo (1949).
[2] Naseleniye gorodov (1897); Naseleniye Imperii (1897); Troynitskiy (1899, 1905).
[3] Lorimer (1946), p. 203.

likely to have been fewer Russian women than elsewhere,[1] so for the purpose of this chapter the number of souls has been doubled in order to obtain rough total population figures. In view of all these possible causes of error, the figures quoted below, even when apparently exact, should not be taken as more than a rough guide.

The area can be divided into a series of subdivisions based chiefly on river valleys, since settlement followed the waterways.

KOL'SKIY POLUOSTROV

Novgorod established dominion during the twelfth and thirteenth centuries over the Pomor'ye, or White Sea region, including the peninsula of Kola (Kol'skiy Poluostrov). Although the mention of Sem'yun Petrilovets, the tribute collector of Tre, provides evidence that Novgorod asserted rights over the peninsula from at least the early thirteenth century, there is nothing to indicate any permanent Russian occupation. The settlement of Kola is often referred to as being in existence in 1264,[2] but it has recently been shown that this is quite unlikely, and the result of misinterpretation of chronicles. In fact, there is no reliable mention of it until 1565, when it was said to have three houses.[3] Meanwhile, however, the north coast of the peninsula—the Murman coast—was probably becoming familiar to some of the more daring seafarers, who may have been finding their way out of the White Sea, and small groups from time to time no doubt went inland.

The first certain knowledge of Russians living on the Murman coast relates to the missionary activities of monks, and in particular to the establishment of two monasteries in the middle of the sixteenth century.[4] This was followed by defensive measures against the Swedes, with whom Moscow went to war in 1575 over possession of Estonia. *Ostrogi* were built in the early 1580's along the Kola river, and Kola itself became an *ostrog* in 1583. Ivan the Terrible obliged the Stroganovs to undertake this in return for granting them permission to build facilities ashore for their fishing fleet, and a small garrison thus came to be maintained. Roughly from this time on, the inlets and coves of the Murman coast must have become quite well known

---

[1] Population figures given in Sbornik istoriko-statisticheskikh svedeniy (1875–76), relating to the period 1863–73, show that the proportion of men to women in small towns of north-eastern Siberia, such as Vilyuysk, was about 55:45.

[2] For example, Tomilov (1947), p. 27. [3] Shaskol'skiy (1962). [4] See pp. 88–9.

to a number of Pomor'ye sailors, who were by now fishing and hunting sea mammals here. English voyagers of the second half of the century, such as Stephen Burrough, mention meeting many Russian fishing parties along the coast.[1] This industry became well established, but it remained a seasonal one. The fishermen came up from the White Sea in spring and returned in the autumn. Apart from the garrison on the Kola, there was no permanent fishing settlement along the coast.

In the first quarter of the eighteenth century anything between 40 and 355 boats were active each year off the Murman coast.[2] Peter the Great encouraged the industry, fortifying the Kola *ostrog*, and in Catherine the Great's reign it continued to flourish. During the period 1787–89, for instance, the annual traffic between Arkhangel'sk and the Murman coast was of the order of 150–200 ships and 1500–2000 men.[3] Meanwhile, however, the garrison at Kola had been withdrawn to Arkhangel'sk and the little settlement declined. A proposal by Ye. Golovtsyn, the Governor of Arkhangel'skaya Guberniya, to settle 400 peasant families on the peninsula was not approved, on the grounds that any settlement must be voluntary.

In the nineteenth century the fishery continued, but there was interference from outside. The British navy attacked the fishing fleet and some of its installations ashore, and burnt the settlement of Kola. This took place in 1810, when Russia was operating the continental blockade against Britain. A very similar attack, from the same quarter, was sustained again in 1854, during the Crimean War. It was only after this, in the second half of the century, that serious attempts were made to settle the region. The establishment of permanent fishing villages was what was in mind, but it was hoped that the settlers would cultivate the soil too. The Governor of Arkhangel'skaya Guberniya in 1860 tried to attract Norwegian settlers, who he thought would have the necessary agricultural knowledge—after all, there were plenty of permanent Norwegian settlements in the same latitude a little further west. They were offered Russian citizenship and exemption from taxes and military service. By 1867 175 such colonists had been attracted. Next year further exemptions were granted in the hope of attracting Russians,

[1] Hakluyt (1809), vol. 1, pp. 308–10. [2] Belov (1956), p. 344.
[3] Belov (1956), p. 350.

Finns and Karelians. These measures had some success, and in 1884 a government commission sat to recommend further measures to increase the flow of colonists. The result was that by the turn of the century there were 2185 settlers in 40 settlements distributed along the Murman coast. Over half the settlers were Finns or Karelians.[1] Kola was again the district centre, with 610 Russians living there in 1897, but shortly afterwards it was replaced by Yekaterinskaya Gavan', a new settlement further down the inlet. There was some more growth of the settlements in the period up to 1917, and they had every appearance of flourishing.[2] Pl. VII shows Teriberka, a typical small one.

The foregoing refers to the Murman coast. The southern and eastern coasts were also settled from early times, while the interior was populated only by Lapps until after 1917. The coastal settlements formed part of the true Pomor'ye region, and grew up from the fifteenth century onwards, in the same way as such places as Kem' or Mezen' further south.[3] Kovda, Kandalaksha, Umba and Varzuga are known to have existed in the sixteenth century. Varzuga had 167 inhabitants, by implication all Russian, in 1563, and a church was built at Kandalaksha in 1526.[4] The census of 1897 recorded the following Russian populations: Kuzomen' 1480, Tetrino 1150, Umba 980, Ponoy 220. At that time the Russian population for the whole peninsula was 6020.[5]

The importance of the peninsula as a fisheries centre was thus early established. The realisation, induced by the First World War, of its potentiality as a port brought about a dramatic change in its settlement. The tremendous importance of the never-frozen south-western portion of the Barents Sea, which washes the Murman coast, was underlined when both the Baltic and the Black Sea approaches were blockaded. In 1915–16, therefore, the railway to the Kola inlet was built, making possible not only the construction of the port of Murmansk, but also, as a later and equally important result, the exploitation of enormous mineral resources. These two developments, as will be shown later, fundamentally changed the settlement position of the whole peninsula.

[1] Trudy vysochayshe (1885), pp. 17–38; Romanov (1904), pp. 1–29.
[2] Volens (1926).   [3] Shaskol'skiy (1962), pp. 278–9.
[4] Tikhomirov (1962), pp. 273–5.   [5] Engelhardt (1899), p. 83.

The Numbers of Settlers

This region was also, by extension, a part of the Pomor'ye. The first appearance here of Russian settlers is as difficult to pin down as in the case of Kol'skiy Poluostrov. There is no record of any Novgorod settlements. A military force of Ivan III of Moscow reached the Pechora river in 1498,[1] and at a 'desolate place' (*pustoye mesto*) at its mouth they built the fortress of Pustozersk, apparently the first Russian settlement in the area. It was followed by other, predominantly peasant, settlements, all south of the Arctic Circle, however—Ust'-Tsil'mskaya Sloboda and Izhemskaya Sloboda on the Pechora, and Okladnikova Sloboda (which later became Mezen') on the White Sea coast.[2] A surviving administrative document mentions 282 Russian inhabitants of the Pustozersk region in 1575–76, their occupation being fishing and sea mammal hunting.[3] The military character of the settlement remained, however, and it was often called *ostrog*. The *voyevoda* of Pustozersk played an important part in preventing foreign voyages to Siberia and to Arkhangel'sk in the seventeenth century—an indication that the settlement was significant as a port. It became also a place of exile. Its importance in all these connections was maintained throughout the eighteenth century, and the number of settlers presumably grew, although the place probably never exceeded a large village in size. Then followed a decline, and by the end of the nineteenth century it had become 'little more than a wretched-looking village', in the opinion of the Governor of Arkhangel'skaya Guberniya, with 25 houses and a population of 180. The administrative centre was now Ust'-Tsil'ma, which had grown to 4000 (or, according to another source, 6000). The Russian population of the Pechora region was mostly concentrated along the river Pechora, and numbered 9296 in 1897.[4] There was, however, a very small settlement of a church and four houses at Khabarovo on Yugorskiy Shar in the north-east corner of the region. This was a trading post where Russian merchants met the Nentsy (Samoyed). Unlike the Kola district, where the population was predominantly Russian, in the Pechora Russians were now in a minority of one to three.

[1] Belov (1956), p. 36.   [2] Belov (1956), p. 63.
[3] Belov (1956), p. 51; Tikhomirov (1962), p. 256.
[4] Engelhardt (1899), p. 253; Novosiltsov (1902), p. 378.

To point the contrast with the adjacent area to the south-west, the Mezen' district, it may be noted that the Russian population there at the same time (1897) was 24,144 out of a total of 25,619.[1] This large jump, both in density and proportion of Russians, shows clearly that conditions for peasant settlement were considerably easier there.

ISLANDS OF THE EUROPEAN NORTH

The islands to the north were never settled. Kolguyev, Vaygach and Novaya Zemlya were known to the Russians from the sixteenth century and probably well before, but their bleak terrain had little to attract settlers. Russian whalers and sealers may perhaps have used them as temporary bases from time to time, but that was all.[2] The idea of settlement was discussed more than once, however. As early as 1787, Count A. R. Vorontsov, the President of the College of Commerce, urged the establishment of a permanent settlement to exploit silver deposits at Guba Serebryanka in Novaya Zemlya. This proposal was brought up again several times in the nineteenth century, but in vain.[3] In 1880 the suggestion was made by the Governor of Arkhangel'skaya Guberniya that a fishing settlement in Novaya Zemlya would be helpful to the industry. There was by now the possible added incentive of countering a likely Swedish–Norwegian claim to Svalbard, which had been pressed on the Swedish government in 1870 by private citizens, and had been dropped because of Russian objections. But the suggestion got nowhere.[4] So, apart from a weather station at Malyye Karmakuly on the south island of Novaya Zemlya, which was one of the first such stations in the Russian north, starting regular observations in 1896, there were no permanent inhabitants of the islands except the Nentsy hunters, and there were very few of them.

THE OB' VALLEY

The earliest Russian settlement in Siberia is nearly a century later. The early Novgorod and Muscovite forces and expeditions which had entered the lower Ob' valley left no permanent settlements. These

---

[1] Engelhardt (1899), p. 226.   [2] Trofimov (1961), p. 180.
[3] Belov (1956), p. 348.
[4] Trudy vysochayshe (1885), pp. 177–84; Mathisen (1951), pp. 19–36.

were founded only after the general advance which followed Yermak. Two of the earliest of them—Tyumen' (1586) and Tobol'sk (1587)— formed the centre of what quite quickly became the main area of Russian settlement in Siberia, the region of the Tobol–Irtysh confluence. The road eastwards passed through it, and Tobol'sk remained the administrative capital, first of Siberia as a whole and then of western Siberia, until 1838. But this area is rather too far south to fall within the scope of this book, which is concerned essentially with regions north of the main east–west trunk road.

Of direct concern are the settlements further downstream.[1] Obskiy Gorodok, although the earliest of all, was abandoned shortly afterwards. The others survived, however. The fact that Berezov and Obdorsk were both on the sites of existing native settlements was useful, because it facilitated contact with the natives for collection of fur tribute. Certain other Russian settlements were founded soon afterwards: Nadym on Obskaya Guba, a trading post which was busy for a period but later declined to the point of disappearance; the Kondinskiy monastery, upstream from Berezov, a sixteenth-century foundation, and Surgut, of the same period; and, most important, Mangazeya (1601), the story of which has already been told. These were the principal settlements, and it was in them, almost exclusively, that the early Russian settlers concentrated— a result of pre-occupation with the fur trade and the need to be on the defensive against natives. Only in the eighteenth century did settlers spread out along the rivers. The early Russian population of the towns had a high proportion of service men, including cossacks. Obdorsk had a garrison of cossacks which disappeared at the end of the eighteenth century, while that at Berezov lasted into the nineteenth.

Tracing the history and population changes of these small towns is beset with the usual difficulty of scant data. Of the three main ones, Obdorsk, Berezov (the administrative centre), and Surgut, none was ever quite abandoned, like Mangazeya or Nadym. But there was certainly not a history of steady growth. When Dmitriy Ovtsyn of the Great Northern Expedition went to Obdorsk in 1734 in search of a guide to the waters of the estuary, he found the town depleted, and no one in it who knew enough to act as guide. At Berezov, on the

---

[1] For this section, extensive use has been made of Kabo (1949).

other hand, he was provided with a bodyguard of 74 cossacks to accompany him to Obdorsk.[1] The population of the town and district of Berezov in 1710 was 1900, and of the town and district of Surgut 1100. It is not worth while giving details of the correct Russian name and the dimensions of these districts, as both were frequently changing, and the object of this chapter is not to give the most accurate details but simply the general idea. Although not explicitly stated, these figures presumably refer to Russians, or Russians and people of mixed blood. If natives were included, the totals would be much bigger.

The next set of population figures relates to the nineteenth century, but cannot be directly compared. Karnilov, a provincial governor making a visit of inspection in 1807, was unimpressed by both Berezov and Obdorsk, thinking them memorable only because of their age, and grudging Berezov its 170 cossacks, whom he considered to be of no value to the country, but a mere survival from more turbulent times.[2] In about 1820 the town and district of Berezov had 1100 Russian inhabitants.[3] In 1850 the town numbered 1186, while the district, Berezovskiy Kray, had a further 2500 Russians, out of a total population of over 25,000, but it now included the towns of Obdorsk and Surgut. These two accounted for 1018 (Surgut) and perhaps a few hundred (Obdorsk). The remainder were spread, in small groups, among the 20 or so Russian villages along the waterways.[4] There was little change at the end of the century. Obdorsk had 378 Russians out of a total population of 876 in 1891.[5] Berezov had 1071 inhabitants at the 1897 census and Surgut 1110, presumably about half of these also being Russians. The total population of the region, now divided into two *okrugi* of Berezov and Surgut, was 28,400.[6] In 1911 the two towns had risen somewhat, to 1280 and 1383.[7]

[1] Belov (1956), p. 290.   [2] Karnilov (1828), p. 71.
[3] Zamechaniya (1824), p. 277.
[4] Abramov (1857), pp. 363, 381–3. Erman (1848), p. 33, reports about 60 Russians in Obdorsk in 1828–29.
[5] Bartenev (1896), p. 9.
[6] Naseleniye Imperii (1897), p. 24.   [7] Glinka (1914), p. 348.

PLATE VII

(*a*) Teriberka, one of the fishing settlements on the Murman coast, about 1900 (Romanov, 1904).

(*b*) Obdorsk about 1910 (Glinka, 1914, opp. p. 301).

PLATE VIII

(*a*) Olekminsk on the Lena, about 1850 (Boulitchoff, 1856).

(*b*) Olekminsk about 1910 (Glinka, 1914, opp. p. 317).

The Numbers of Settlers

The lower Yenisey was reached early in the seventeenth century, and Turukhanskoye Zimov'ye (1607) was the first settlement there. This place was known for a period as Novaya Mangazeya, but later reverted to Turukhansk, by which name it is known today. The site was changed, however, to a point on the opposite bank of the river and about 20 km. away. It was for long the only settlement of any size, and became the district centre. In 1676 480 Russian men swore allegiance to Tsar Fedor Alekseyevich at Turukhansk. They were no doubt mainly from that town, but settlements up and down stream were already in being, such as Dubchasskaya Sloboda (1637) and Zavorokhinskoye (1652). Tax returns for 1702, though incomplete, show 130 Russian households on the lower Yenisey.[1] In 1710 the population of the town and district was said to be 1360,[2] and in 1719 that of the town alone was said to be 522. In each case these figures presumably refer to Russians, but this is not explicitly stated. It was from the lower Yenisey that hunters reached over to Taymyr and the valleys of the Pyasina, Kheta and Khatanga. The tax returns of 1702 mentioned above indicate 57 Russian households on those three rivers.

Members of the Great Northern Expedition record the presence in 1738 of Russian hunters and cossacks at many places on the lower river, including Golchikha and Glubokiye Magaziny on the Yenisey estuary, and at Zimov'ye Volgina further towards the Pyasina—this last being the most northerly inhabited place at that time. As a result, in 1797 the district of Turukhansk, which included every-where north of Turukhansk town, contained 474 Russians.[3] Turu-khansk at this time was still quite a flourishing centre, with a population of 500, there being an annual fair of forest and river products—chiefly fur—which attracted merchants from far away.[4] But early in the nineteenth century there was very bad famine several years in succession and many died. The fur bearers and the natives were disappearing also, so that by about 1868 there was a population of only 196 in Turukhansk town (which was now wholly Russian).[5] The district meanwhile counted 811 Russian peasants

---

[1] Aleksandrov (1960), pp. 22–3.   [2] Klochkov (1911), pp. 61–9.
[3] Latkin (1892), pp. 106–7.
[4] Statisticheskoye obozreniye (1810), p. 295; Latkin (1892), p. 434.
[5] Tret'yakov (1869), p. 322.

about 1830,[1] and in about 1868 they had increased to 1663 and were scattered among 58 inhabited points along the Yenisey;[2] Dudinskoye, the modern Dudinka, may be mentioned in particular with 40 inhabitants, and Tolstyy Nos with 50. There were also *zimov'ya*, usually empty most of the year, scattered throughout the region; there were even 35 along the base of the Taymyr peninsula between Dudinskoye and the Anabar.[3] Throughout, the Russians were a minority of the total population—probably between a quarter and a fifth. The census of 1897 shows the population of Turukhansk as 219, presumably all Russian, and that of the district as 11,117,[4] of whom 3282 were Russian.[5] In 1911 the town of Turukhansk had dropped to 162, with a municipal budget of 190 roubles a year.[6]

THE LENA VALLEY

The first *ostrog* established on the Lena was Yakutsk (1632), and this remained the most important centre of Russian settlement in the whole vast region of the Lena basin. The Russian population consisted of the military garrison, largely cossacks, and traders in fur. The former remained fairly stable in numbers in the short term, but grew gradually in the long term. The traders fluctuated sharply from year to year, and dropped, in the last quarter of the seventeenth century, to a very low level as a result of the growing scarcity of fur bearers. Thus the Yakutsk garrison was 531 in 1676, 920 at the end of the century, and 1431 in 1737.[7] But it was the fur seekers who really occupied the country, going out into the forests in search of the natives who had the fur. In the early years after the foundation of Yakutsk, about 1000 came or went each year. Some of them settled at Yakutsk, forming the *posad*, or suburb, outside the walls of the *ostrog* where the garrison lived, and this *posad* was the true ancestor of the town of today. Both *posad* and *ostrog* are clearly visible on Pl. II (*a*) and (*b*). But by the end of the century there were only 46 inhabitants of the *posad*. The number of visiting fur seekers dropped: there

---

[1] Pestov (1831), pp. 106–7. From Dolgikh (1960 b), p. 25, it appears that half of these lived in the settlements round the Yenisey estuary.

[2] Tret'yakov (1869), pp. 322, 361.   [3] Tarasenkov (1930), pp. 26–7.

[4] Naseleniye Imperii (1897), p. 23.

[5] Tarasenkov (1930), p. 26. This writer's population figures for the earlier part of the century are about 15 per cent higher than the sources quoted.

[6] Glinka (1914), pp. 342–4.   [7] Bakhrushin (1955 b), p. 28.

50

were 205 in 1696–97, and none the following year. At this time the adult male Russian population of the whole Yakut province,[1] which at that time meant the Lena basin and everything east of it, was 1222. About 20 per cent were peasants.[2]

The eighteenth century saw slow growth. Peter the Great's suppressed census of 1710 counted 4161 inhabitants of both sexes in town and district—presumably mostly Russians.[3] In 1775 the Russian population was 2413 adult males, or perhaps 5000 in all. The Russian population of Yakutsk was then 1932.[4] Other settlements, though very much smaller, were beginning to arise. Zashiversk, Podshiversk and Verkhoyansk on the overland trail to the Kolyma; Ust'-Yanskoye, Russkoye Ust'ye and Siktyakh on the lower reaches of the Yana, Indigirka and Lena respectively; Olekminsk on the upper Lena and the artery to the rest of Russia; and Amginsk on the Aldan. Some of these date from the seventeenth century, some from the eighteenth. None is likely to have had a Russian population exceeding two figures, for they were not really much more than *zimov'ya*, which some had originally been. The most northerly *zimov'ye* in the second half of the eighteenth century, surpassing the Zimov'ye Volgina near the Yenisey estuary, was that of the Russian Skordin of Khatanga, who lived on the east coast of Taymyr at Petrovskaya Guba (latitude 76° 37′ N.). Semen Chelyuskin of the Great Northern Expedition came upon it—empty when he was there—in 1742.[5] The rest of the peninsula, beyond the Pyasina and Khatanga, was, and remained, uninhabited.

Growth was maintained in the nineteenth century. The Yakut province—still a vast area, as indeed it remained—had a total Russian population of 4610 in 1818 and 17,158 in the 1890's. Yakutsk itself meanwhile rose from 2485 in 1824 to 6499 in 1889.[6] It may be assumed that Russians constituted the majority in Yakutsk.

---

[1] The Russian term for the administrative area changed frequently (*voyevodstvo, uyezd, okrug, oblast', guberniya*), so it is simpler to keep an English word.
[2] Bakhrushin (1955*b*), pp. 30, 35–6.   [3] Klochkov (1911), pp. 61–9.
[4] Bakhrushin (1955*b*), pp. 30, 35–6.   [5] Belov (1956), p. 312.
[6] Bakhrushin (1955*b*), pp. 30, 35–6. The figures for Yakutsk itself are contradicted by Gagemeyster (1854), table 8, which gives 4204 for 1823, and by Cochrane (1824), who gives 7000 for 1820. This is a fairly typical situation, and it is difficult to choose between Bakhrushin, the careful historian of a century later, Gagemeyster, the compiler of a statistical handbook, and Cochrane, an Englishman who was there at the time. Bakhrushin is preferred because he is likeliest to have weighed the evidence the most carefully.

They were said to be 64 per cent of the total in 1862, and 54 per cent at the end of the century, when they numbered 3525.[1] Three of the outlying settlements were by now dignified by the name of town: Olekminsk (247 in 1829, 626 in 1887), Vilyuysk (220 in 1829, 454 in 1887), and Verkhoyansk (81 in 1829, 236 in 1887).[2] The populations of these three were largely Russian. Some of the other settlements were in decline. Uyandinskoye disappears from the map about this time, and so does Podshiversk. Zashiversk was reported to have only three Russian families in 1820, one of them the 87-year-old priest Mikhail and his brother.[3] But newer settlements like Nyurba, upstream from Vilyuysk, and Suntar, were growing,[4] and the post stations down the Lena to Yakutsk were another important concentration of Russian population. The census of 1897 shows in general slight increases: Olekminsk 1157, Vilyuysk 627, Verkhoyansk 353, but Yakutsk itself remained roughly stationary at 6382.[5] The proportion of Russian speakers in the towns was about half, while in the Yakut province as a whole it was only 11·4 per cent (30,807).[6] The last figure, however, does not apparently mean that there were that many Russians in the province, but reflects rather the growing tendency for Yakut to speak Russian.[7] Pl. VIII shows Olekminsk about this time.

The final figures before the Revolution relate to 1911. Bakhrushin[8] states that the administrative area contained 18,035 Russians, and Yakutsk itself 8200 inhabitants, of whom the majority were Russian. The other towns had also increased in the aggregate (Olekminsk 1050, Vilyuysk 1000, Verkhoyansk 450). Over the whole period the Russians had been in a small minority, because the Yakut were numerically the strongest of the peoples of northern Siberia.

THE KOLYMA VALLEY AND CHUKOTKA

Settlement on the Kolyma followed a somewhat similar pattern to that on the Lena, by way of which the Kolyma was, of course, reached. Within the first few years, by 1647, there were nearly 400

---

[1] Tokarev (1957), p. 202; Maynov (1927), p. 372.
[2] Gagemeyster (1854), vol. 2, p. 193; Priklonskiy (1890), p. 69.
[3] Vrangel' (1840), p. 36.   [4] Meinshausen (1871), pp. 30–1.
[5] Naseleniye Imperii (1897), p. 24.   [6] Troynitskiy (1905), vol. 2, pp. viii, 38, 74.
[7] Pamyatnaya knizhka (1895), p. 113.
[8] Bakhrushin (1955*b*), pp. 30, 35–6, quoting Glinka (1914), pp. 86, 350.

Russians on the Kolyma in search of fur. But they were by no means all permanent residents, and by the end of the century they were in any case fewer. Nizhnekolymsk, meaning the town on the lower Kolyma, was the first permanently inhabited place (1644), and it was quickly followed by Srednekolymsk and Verkhnekolymsk, on the middle and upper river respectively. All three have survived. A fourth, although not as enduring, should be bracketed with them: Alazeysk, on the neighbouring Alazeya, which was founded two years before Nizhnekolymsk.

Population figures for the villages and for the district as a whole are lacking for the first century and a half of their existence. Dmitriy Laptev of the Great Northern Expedition found Nizhnekolymsk very dilapidated and almost empty in 1740.[1] Krasheninnikov of the same expedition notes the presence of 20 cossacks there, at Srednekolymsk and at Alazeysk.[2] The reason for this was that these places were stations on the road from Yakutsk to the mouth of the Kolyma. Towards the end of the century members of Billings's expedition passed through the region and, according to the report of a member,[3] in 1786 Nizhnekolymsk was the biggest, with perhaps at a guess 250 Russians, while the other three places consisted of only a few houses each.

During this period there was only one Russian settlement east of the Kolyma, in the peninsula of Chukotka (Chukotskiy Poluostrov). This was Anadyrsk, which grew out of Dezhnev's original *zimov'ye*. It was on the middle reaches of the Anadyr', near the modern Markovo, and is not to be confused with the modern settlement of Anadyr' at the mouth. It became an *ostrog* in 1666, and for a century was the strong point from which the Russians attempted to control the Chukchi, and at the same time it secured the road to Kamchatka, which at that time was reached by an immense detour round the Sea of Okhotsk by way of Nizhnekolymsk. But when the sea route to Kamchatka was first used at the beginning of the eighteenth century, and then officially replaced the Chukotka road in 1716, Anadyrsk lost much of its usefulness as a strong point on the lines of communication. Although the campaign of the 1730's against the Chukchi was largely inconclusive, the government

[1] Belov (1956), p. 321.   [2] Krasheninnikov (1949), pp. 518–19.
[3] Sarychev (1952), pp. 65–87.

became disturbed at the cost of maintaining a garrison there. Anadyrsk was therefore destroyed and abandoned in 1766.[1]

In the nineteenth century the explorer F. P. Vrangel' noted the male Russian population of the Kolyma district in 1820 as 325, implying a total of between 600 and 700, or about 8 per cent of the Russian and native total combined.[2] In the 1860's the Russians numbered about 1000 altogether, of whom half were cossacks and their families. This proportion was rather high, because of the frontier nature of the area, but in fact few still functioned in an active military capacity. 700 Russians lived in Nizhnekolymsk and Srednekolymsk. Verkhnekolymsk had declined, but there were a number of small new settlements on the lower reaches of the river.[3] The 1897 census records the population of Srednekolymsk as 538 and omits the others, which indicates that Srednekolymsk had replaced Nizhnekolymsk as administrative centre and probably exceeded it in size. In 1911 it had a population of 650.[4]

In Chukotka, meanwhile, merchants were beginning to be active among the now somewhat less hostile Chukchi, and the settlement of Markovo, 10 km. from Anadyrsk, had grown up in the latter's place. This had some 20 houses in the 1860's, and a Russian population of perhaps 50–100.[5] By 1892 it had a population of 380 Russians, including russianised natives. There were 150 more Russians in half a dozen other settlements on or near the Anadyr'.[6]

THE OKHOTSK SEA LITTORAL AND KAMCHATKA

The point at which Moskvitin reached the Pacific Ocean in 1641 became the major Russian settlement in the region: Okhotsk, at the mouth of the Okhota, which gave its name to both town and sea. It was first the site of an *ostrog*, built by some of the earliest cossack travellers and subordinated to the *voyevoda* of Yakutsk. For the rest of the century it remained a local outpost of Russian power, and as such, under attack from time to time by the local Tungus (Evenki) tribesmen. It was only when the sea route to Kamchatka came into

---

[1] Maydel' (1893–96), vol. 1, p. 90; vol. 2, pp. 503–5.
[2] Vrangel' (1840), p. 54.   [3] Maydel' (1893–96), vol. 1, pp. 75–94.
[4] Naseleniye gorodov (1897), p. 31; Glinka (1914), p. 350.
[5] Maydel' (1893), p. 230.   [6] Olsuf'yev (1896), pp. 29–30.

use, and more particularly when Bering found it necessary to use Okhotsk as a main base for his two expeditions (1725–42), that Okhotsk started to grow. There was at this time (late seventeenth and early eighteenth centuries) a shift in interest from the northern regions of the Lena and Kolyma valleys to more southerly regions, including the newly discovered Kamchatka, and the importance of Okhotsk became greater in 1732, when Kamchatka ceased to be under the direct authority of Yakutsk but became subject to Okhotsk. In 1776 the officials in Okhotsk, together with naval and military forces, numbered about 600.[1]

The first *ostrogi* in Kamchatka itself were established at Atlasov's orders, in the first decade of the eighteenth century. They were Nizhnekamchatsk, at the mouth of the Kamchatka river, which became the administrative headquarters, Verkhnekamchatsk some 400 km. upstream, and Bol'sheretsk on the west coast.[2] There was a rising of the native Kamchadal in 1731, as a result of which Nizhnekamchatsk was destroyed, but it was rebuilt the following year. In 1760 Bol'sheretsk became the 'capital', but 23 years later Nizhnekamchatsk was again chosen. Russian population increased here considerably quicker than in more northerly areas, mainly because the climate, although sub-Arctic, was a good deal less extreme. A member of Billings's expedition[3] reported 1687 Russians in Kamchatka in 1792, the majority in Nizhnekamchatsk (population 548) and the other two old centres, but some in newer settlements such as Tigil' or Tigil'sk, founded in 1752 (population 338), and Petropavlovsk, first used by Bering as a port in 1740 (population 85). The Russians would have been more numerous but for a catastrophic smallpox epidemic in 1768 which killed two-thirds of the inhabitants of the peninsula. In Kamchatka, unlike all the other regions except Kola, Russians were by this time a majority of the population (62 per cent).

One other place should be mentioned here, although not properly part of Kamchatka. This is Gizhiga, also called Gizhiginsk or Ishiginsk, on the mainland to the west of the neck of the peninsula. It was founded in 1753 by the cossack Avram Ignat'yev, and it was to it that the Anadyrsk garrison was withdrawn thirteen years later.

---

[1] Sgibnev (1869), no. 11, p. 53.   [2] Krasheninnikov (1949), p. 476.
[3] Sauer (1802), pp. 291–307.

Its importance was as a town on the winter line of communication to Kamchatka (when the Sea of Okhotsk was frozen).

In the nineteenth century, however, there was an apparent decline in Kamchatka. In 1813 the administrative centre was moved to Petropavlovsk, where it remained, this having become the principal port (see Pl. IX). Cochrane, the English traveller, reports[1] that the Russian population in 1821 was 1260, or about a quarter of the total. No disaster comparable to the smallpox epidemic is mentioned to explain this fall. A possible explanation is that Cochrane is speaking only of pure Russians and excluding those of mixed blood, who, by all accounts, were numerous. Ditmar,[2] travelling through the country in the 1850's, gives no total for the Russian population, but mentions some eight further settlements in addition to the five listed above. In 1854 Petropavlovsk was attacked by a Franco-British naval force in one of the remotest actions of the Crimean War, and as a result the settlement was evacuated the following year to Nikolayevsk on the Amur. It was later re-occupied, but lost some of its importance with the sale of Alaska in 1867. Its population in 1897 was 394, and by 1911 was said to have increased, it is not clear why, to 1100.[3] About the same time the Russian population of the whole peninsula was given as 1850, which was still about a quarter of the total.[4]

Meanwhile on the mainland Gizhiga was apparently declining. Having had a population of 700 in about 1820, it was reported to have only 475 in 1853 and 435 in 1897. But a figure of 700 is recorded for 1911, the reason for the increase being again not clear.[5] The population was at all times largely, but not entirely, Russian. Okhotsk, on the contrary, flourished initially and then declined dramatically. Cochrane, probably somewhat exaggerating, reports[6] a population of 1500–1600 in 1821, and this must have been almost all Russian because the main importance of the town was as a port and naval base. There were, he said, over 600 naval personnel there

---

[1] Cochrane (1824), vol. 2, p. 45. He may be more accurate in reporting facts about Kamchatka than elsewhere, since he married a native girl from here and took her back with him to England.

[2] Ditmar (1890).

[3] Naseleniye gorodov (1897), p. 30; Glinka (1914), p. 350.

[4] Infant'yev (1912), p. 74.

[5] Shakhovskoy (1822), p. 296; Ditmar (1890), pp. 489–90; Naseleniye gorodov (1897), p. 30; Glinka (1914), p. 350.

[6] Cochrane (1824), vol. 2, p. 404.

then, and the governor was a naval captain. The hinterland, however, was hardly settled at all. Eastwards along the coast there was no place of any significance until Gizhiga, 1200 km. away, and westwards the road to Yakutsk was reported by Erman[1] to be very scantily populated by Russians in 1829, in spite of its being the main post road. In 1845 the Russian American Company moved its base from Okhotsk to Ayan, 300 km. to the south-west, and the Government followed suit in 1850.[2] Just before the move there were 884 people in Okhotsk, presumably mostly Russians.[3] The census of 1897 records only 304, but in 1911 there were alleged to be 600 inhabitants (see Pl. XII*b*).[4] Ayan did not flourish either, as a result not only of the dissolution of the Russian-American Company, but also of the Russian occupation of the Vladivostok area, which became the base for all Pacific operations and for transport to Kamchatka.

RUSSIAN AMERICA

During the existence of the Russian-American Company (1799–1867), there was never a great movement of Russians into the American colonies. The number of settlements at no time exceeded twenty, of which the biggest was always Novo-Arkhangel'sk, the administrative centre. The number of Russians living in the company's territory was 354 in 1818, 652 in 1833 and 730 in 1836.[5] It is unlikely that there was much growth after 1836. In all probability, therefore, there were never more than 1000 Russians living there. People of mixed blood, however, with Russian fathers and native mothers, were rather more numerous than the true Russians. But the two groups together did not exceed 20 per cent of the population.

The general impression derived from the scanty and patchy evidence available may be summarised in this way. Conquest brought a small but significant influx of Russians, chiefly of adventurers interested in furs, but also, particularly in the regions most

[1] Erman (1848), vol. 2, pp. 450–536.
[2] Sgibnev (1869), no. 12, p. 42; Priklonskiy (1896), p. 158.
[3] Sgibnev (1869), no. 12, pp. 47–8.
[4] Troynitskiy (1899), no. 76, p. 1; Glinka (1914), p. 350; Naseleniye gorodov (1897), p. 30, gives 197 for 1897.
[5] Materialy dlya istorii (1861), opp. p. 238; Vrangel' (1839), pp. 11 and 326.

remote from Moscow, of men in the service of the government. Settlements were established, but the small Russian population was not stable. It seems to have dropped notably in many areas a generation after conquest, no doubt a result of the scarcity of fur bearers after the initial onslaught upon them, and it remained low for perhaps a century. But no region, once reached, was ever totally abandoned. Numbers crept up, particularly in the nineteenth century, and were now measured in thousands rather than hundreds. By the end of that century there were probably between 40,000 and 50,000 Russians living in the north as defined for this book. Everywhere, except in the peninsula of Kola, and at times in Kamchatka, they were in the minority, often a minority of less than 10 per cent.

Detailed deductions from the population figures would be out of place, because not only are some figures probably inaccurate and certainly imprecisely defined, but also the numbers, in absolute terms, are too small for it to be advisable to interpret their fluctuations as trends. They are quoted only in order to give a general idea of the scale of the whole settlement process. For information about its character, it is necessary to examine more closely these small groups of Russians and see how they were made up.

4

CONSOLIDATION: THE CHARACTER
OF THE SETTLEMENT

The Russians who went to live in northern lands did so for a number
of different reasons. There were the hunters and traders in fur, who
led the advance into many regions of the north. There were the
agents of the Moscow government, who followed them, or in some
remote areas preceded them: the fighting men—cossacks or *strel'tsy*,
the administrators, the collectors of fur tribute; all these were
collectively known as 'service people' (*sluzhilyye lyudi*). Peasants, who
were pouring into southern Siberia, also formed a significant group
in the north. Then there were the exiles and the convicts, from whose
unwilling presence the settlement at once suffered and benefited.
Religious groups, both monastic and sectarian, played a greater part
than might at first be supposed. And finally, in the nineteenth
century there arose a need for labour in the newly founded industrial
undertakings of the north, principally mines; this force, although
largely recruited from the other groups already there, does constitute
a separate entity. Although there is overlapping, each of these
groups had different motives, and made a different sort of impact on
the region.

HUNTERS AND TRADERS

That the search for furs was the driving force which took the men of
Novgorod, and later of Moscow, into the north, and, more particularly, the north-east, has already been made clear.[1] In Europe of
the sixteenth and seventeenth centuries, it should be remembered,
fur was a normal and widely used commodity. The fur worn by most
people was of local origin—rabbit, dog, cat, sheep—but fine furs
which indicated rank and wealth came largely from Russia, because
there could be found the more luxurious pelts induced by a sub-
Arctic habitat.[2] It was the desire to keep this market that prompted
the Novgorod merchants to send out their men. Moreover, it may be

[1] An excellent and detailed exposition of all aspects of the Russian fur trade at this
time is found in Fisher (1943).　　　[2] Rich (1958), vol. 1, pp. 1, 47.

noted in passing, the market has never been lost, for even today the annual fur auction at Leningrad is the central event in the fur trade of the world. Giles Fletcher, Queen Elizabeth's ambassador to Russia in 1588, noted 'The natiue commodities of the Countrey are many and substantiall. First, furres of all sorts. Wherein the prouidence of God is to be noted, that prouideth a naturall remedie for them, to helpe the naturall inconuenience of their Countrey by the cold of the Climat.'[1]

By the seventeenth century fur had become for the Moscow state the main item of foreign trade and thus the main source of foreign currency.[2] It has been calculated that in 1605 about 11 per cent of the total income of the state was derived from fur; not, as some have averred, a third, but nevertheless a considerable fraction.[3] As far as the use made of the fur is concerned, there is a parallel, as Pokshishevskiy mentions,[4] to the way in which Spain and Portugal a century earlier used the precious metals they found in their overseas territories. Not only was it sold abroad, but it was used extensively as gifts and bribes by the rulers of Moscow. It played a significant part in diplomatic exchanges, for it could sometimes attain ends which money could not. The gift of furs from Tsar Fedor Ivanovich to the Holy Roman Emperor in 1595, over 400,000 pelts including 120 sables so rare as to be priceless, is only one example of attainment of a political purpose which would not have been attained without this resource.[5] And this took place, it may be noted, before Siberia was contributing on anything like as large a scale as became the case later.

Because so much was at stake, the state always played a very large part in the trade. Fur tribute was the source of supply. The state did not ever acquire a complete monopoly, either in obtaining the furs or marketing them. But, in addition to framing the regulations under which the whole trade functioned, it was itself, in the person of the ruler, much the biggest operator, and in the traffic with Asiatic countries, virtually the only operator.[6] Both a parallel and a contrast may be noted here with the fur trade in Canada in the sixteenth and seventeenth centuries. There also it assumed great economic significance, and the pursuit of furs attracted the French and later English

---

[1] Hakluyt (1809), vol. 1, p. 538.
[2] Fisher (1943), p. 232.
[3] Fisher (1943), pp. 119, 122.
[4] Pokshishevskiy (1951), p. 57.
[5] Fisher (1943), pp. 137–8.
[6] Fisher (1943), pp. 83, 204–6, 210–14.

traders into the interior. But the state itself was not engaged. Fur was never the motive for the annexation of the territory, and there was no French or English equivalent to fur tribute. Fur was the convenient commodity which enabled settlers to trade with their mother country, and natives with settlers, as the historian of the Canadian fur trade makes clear.[1]

The main way in which the furs were obtained by Russians was by inducing the native population to part with them. It was not so common for a Russian to hunt and trap the animals. He hunted the natives. After all, in most places where there were fur-bearing animals, there were also natives who had hunted them for many generations; partly for their own use, and partly for the Central Asian and Chinese markets, whose influence had been felt in these regions long before the arrival of the Russians. This method could, of course, be the most profitable by a wide margin, if the abuses to which it so obviously lay open were practised, as they frequently were. The acquisition of furs by traders was often closely connected with the payment of fur tribute; a native, in making his annual contribution, would also have other pelts available, and these would be obtained by the cossack or other official whose job was to collect the tribute. This will be referred to later in the section on 'Servants of the State'.

Seekers after fur were called *promyshlenniki*, or *promyshlennyye lyudi*, words meaning at that time people who practise a craft for their living.[2] But there were Russians who did actually hunt. The phrase *okhochiy chelovek*, meaning hunter, was used, although it was not so common as the other. And it is quite clear from regulations about Russians not encroaching on native hunting grounds that they did kill a number of animals. Their success, which was disproportionate to their numbers, was due in large part to the introduction of new methods: trapping, rather than shooting with bow and arrow.

In most districts into which the Russians moved, the fur bearers were hunted so intensively in the early years that their numbers dropped dramatically in quite a short time. Thus the Lena valley, in which fur bearers were first exploited in the 1630's, was losing interest for traders by the 1660's because returns were dropping.[3]

---

[1] Innis (1956), pp. 382–92.
[2] Müller (1750), vol. 1, p. 309. [3] Belov (1956), p. 181.

Indeed, the very speed of the advance across Siberia can be attributed in part to the need to move on to new hunting grounds after the depletion of the local animal population. The number of *promysh-lenniki* fluctuated similarly. It was generally at its highest soon after a region had been reached, and then it gradually fell off. After an interval, the species would generally build up its numbers again, leading to a return of the fur seekers. It is not likely that any species was quite exterminated, because the territory was so vast, but local scarcities were certainly produced. Falling returns were reported again and again in this or that district, but the evidence is that the same fur bearers are still there today (although in some cases they might not have been if protective legislation had not been introduced in this century). Those most frequently taken were the sable (*Martes zibellina*), the ermine (*Mustela erminea*), various squirrels (*Sciurus vulgaris fuscombens* and others), and the Arctic fox (*Alopex lagopus lagopus*).

It was in the first great harvest of furs, in the seventeenth century, that the proportion of *promyshlenniki* in the total Russian population was at its highest, reaching over 75 per cent in some areas. That was the real period of the 'fur rush'. The later restoration of animal population probably did not attract so many in absolute figures, and certainly the proportion was lower because by then other groups were arriving.

Another reason for the reduction in the number of *promyshlenniki* towards the end of the seventeenth century was attributable to political causes. In 1689 Russia and China signed the Treaty of Nerchinsk, which regulated relations between the two countries, and in particular established the frontier. This was the signal for trade with China to start, and the trans-Siberian road which passed through Yakutsk lost importance to a more southerly route, which led to the Chinese frontier beyond Baykal. The attention of some merchants and traders was thus diverted from the fur-producing regions of the north to the exciting new openings further south.[1] But the effect of this was partly offset by the fact that fur later became an important article of trade between the two countries.

It has been pointed out that the fur seeker was normally a trader rather than a hunter. As time went on, the trader became concerned

[1] Bakhrushin (1955*b*), p. 30.

less exclusively with fur and dealt increasingly in other commodities. He found it profitable to bring into the region the manufactured products which the natives began to want—bread, tobacco, iron-ware, and (illegally) alcohol—and he took out not only fur, but ivory. This was either from walrus and obtained in coastal areas, or more surprisingly from mammoth tusks. The mammoth had been common in northern Siberia during the Pleistocene, and remains were found so frequently that hunting for them became a recognised pursuit among the natives, once they understood the value of the ivory to the outside world. In the latter half of the nineteenth century some twenty tons of mammoth ivory reached the market at Yakutsk annually. In thus broadening his activity, the Russian trader started to find—again this is moving forward to the nineteenth century— that among such advanced native peoples as the Yakut he had rivals. The Yakut, according to a general handbook[1] on Siberia, were the equal of the Russians in intelligence, cunning and effectiveness, and there were by mid-century more Yakut than Russians practising trade in the Lena valley. But it is unlikely that this sort of situation existed elsewhere in the north, for the Yakut were significantly more sophisticated than the other native peoples.

In the eighteenth and nineteenth centuries some of the richer and more adventurous traders played a leading part in the exploration of the north. One such was Nikita Shalaurov, who financed and led two notable sea-going expeditions along the coast eastwards from the mouth of the Lena, the first in 1759–62 and the second, on which he perished, in 1764. Ivan Lyakhov, a decade later, made important discoveries in the Novosibirskiye Ostrova while in search of mammoth ivory, as did his successor Ivan Sannikov between 1800 and 1812. The names of these three are now prominent on the maps of the region, but there were a number of others who were also active in this mixture of trading and exploration.

While the dealer in fur started to merge into the general Russian commercial population, there remained small groups of Russians who continued actually to hunt the fur bearers. Such were the inhabi-tants of some of the isolated settlements where Russians had come for some other purpose (as cossacks, perhaps) but had remained, forgotten, long after that purpose had ceased to have any validity.

[1] Gagemeyster (1854), tom 2, p. 192.

Russkoye Ust'ye at the mouth of the Indigirka was an example of this in the eighteenth and nineteenth centuries—even down to 1912, when a political exile spent a year there and recorded the extraordinary preservation of ancient Russian speech and customs.[1] But there are not many cases of this sort, and the numbers of Russians involved can never have exceeded a few hundreds. Their depressed condition struck a nineteenth-century observer[2] so strongly that he developed the argument that no more settlement should take place, and he considered that even the natural increase of such poor wretches was to be deplored.

As the nineteenth century passed, the number of traders in the north did not increase. By its close there were only 139, or 262 with their womenfolk, in the whole of the Yakut province. This refers, it must be admitted, to the Russian social group of 'merchantry' (*kupechestvo*). Members of the lower middle class (*meshchanstvo*) also engaged in trade, but although the number is not known, it cannot have been large because the whole of that class in the province comprised under 2000 people at that time.[3] Fur was still a prominent, perhaps in places the most prominent, commodity involved, but the manner in which it was obtained from the natives had become somewhat more organised. There were annual fairs at particular centres, such as Berezov, Obdorsk, Turukhansk, Yakutsk, Zhigansk and Nizhnekolymsk, and to these came the merchants and the natives. Such fairs had long existed,[4] and nineteenth-century reports of them give the impression that from the Russian point of view they were a useful and quite well-organised institution, and provided the most economic way of acquiring pelts. But it is true that the prices obtained by the natives were often outrageously low. Gmelin reports[5] that in the early days many natives in the Turukhansk area preferred the old method of selling to individual Russians in the forest, because they feared that they would be forced to sell too cheaply if they got into close contact with the main buyers at the fair.

All this time the natives had been continuing to pay fur tribute to the Government. But an important change in the system was intro-

---

[1] Vrangel' (1840), pp. 23–34; Zenzinov (1913); Zenzinov & Levine (1932). The settlement was still in existence in 1952 and numbered 65 families (Gurvich, 1953, pp. 33–7).

[2] Argentov (1876), p. 394. [3] Maynov (1927), pp. 378–9.

[4] See Drew (1961), p. 426. [5] Gmelin (1767), vol. 2, p. 58.

duced on the recommendation of the first *Yasak* Commission, set up in 1763: fur tribute might in certain cases be paid in money and not in fur. This change was confirmed and enlarged by the second *Yasak* Commission 65 years later.[1] The result was that many fewer pelts reached the market, because the native, no longer obliged to bring some, was able to appear at a Russian centre without any at all, provided he could find the money in some other way.

Thus that element in the Russian immigrant population which had been the most important at the outset gradually receded into the background, in very much the same way as occurred in Canada, until it was no longer distinguishable as a group. The fur seekers either merged with the traders, or lived on as a residual curiosity in a few of the most distant settlements.

SERVANTS OF THE STATE ('SLUZHILYYE LYUDI')

The first agents of government to play an important part in Siberian settlement were the cossacks. 'Cossack' in this connection is a translation of the Russian work *kazak*. Their origins, somewhat obscure and undoubtedly mixed, have been briefly discussed already.[2] They were a part of the *sluhzhilyye lyudi*, but there were others in that group (considered below) who were not cossacks, although sometimes so called. Baddeley[3] calls attention to this confusion, but prefers to keep the name cossack for all *sluzhilyye lyudi*, admitting that 'the term is a loose one and covers many who were not Cossacks'. Here, however, it seems preferable to restrict 'cossack' to *kazak*.

The cossacks' period of glory was the first century of the Russian advance into Siberia, when many cossacks, such as Yermak, Stadukhin and Dezhnev, performed stirring feats, and it was the toughness and tenacity of the cossacks as much as anything else which secured the country for Moscow. They were primarily warriors, and most of such fighting as there was took place in the early stages. The *ostrogi* that were set up generally had a small cossack force based in them in case of any trouble with the natives, and trouble was not uncommon at first. The town of Tomsk, for instance, was attacked in 1609, 1614, 1624, 1630, 1654, 1674, 1680 and 1682,[4] but Tomsk admittedly stood near the exposed southern flank of the

[1] Tokarev (1957), pp. 134– , 180– .   [2] Pp. 21–2.
[3] Baddeley (1919), p. lxxxiii.   [4] Kabo (1949), p. 49.

advance. The cossacks, at that time always irregular forces, were not highly disciplined. Many deserted, and their frequent drunkenness appalled even Siberians.[1] They were very loosely organised. Each group took the name of the town where it was based, and there was little cohesion between groups. The *voyevoda* was the local com- mander, and each *voyevoda* was independently responsible to the *Sibirskiy Prikaz*, the government office concerned with Siberia. Besides the town garrisons, there were cossacks at *zimov'ye* level, supervising the collection of fur tribute and on the look-out for natives who had not yet been forced into paying. These cossacks also had the job of guarding the native hostages, the taking of whom was the standard way of securing regular fur-tribute payments. Thus in the Yakut *voyevodstvo* in 1676, there were *sluzhilyye lyudi*, in this case cossacks, at Yakutsk, three smaller *ostrogi*, and 21 *zimov'ya*.[2] Yet the total number of cossacks deployed in the north about this time, when cossack activity was probably at its zenith, is unlikely to have ex- ceeded a few thousand. Garrisons of over 200 cossacks were to be found only in certain key places.

The essential part of cossack service was always that it was for a long period. This varied between 19 and 25 years, but it amounted in effect to a lifetime. The precise nature of the agreement between a cossack and his sovereign changed from time to time, but it was always based on the principle that the cossack obtained certain privileges, and in return stood ready to serve whenever he might be needed. Thus when resistance collapsed, and the natives became sufficiently docile not to require a military force to control them, the cossacks were not necessarily drafted away to other regions, as regular forces would have been. In the eighteenth century, when Kamchatka and Chukotka were finally subdued, all was quiet in northern Siberia. But the cossacks were not only still there, but were more numerous than before, due to their natural increase; the service was not exclusively a hereditary one, but most cossacks' sons became cossacks too.

It is true that a much greater number of cossacks were by this time stationed in southern Siberia, where there was still a line to hold against hostile tribesmen, such as the Kirgiz or the Dzhungarians. This led, in Peter the Great's time, to a division of the Siberian

[1] Bakhrushin (1959), p. 95.   [2] Tokarev (1957), p. 45.

cossacks into two sorts: line cossacks, such as those in the south, who were true frontiersmen, and town cossacks, such as those in the north, whose role became more static and less military. The differences between the two became marked, and the Yakutsk and Kamchatka cossacks, who numbered 1500 in 1733—their peak—were in effect a separate body.[1] From now on the cossacks in the north shared less and less the attributes commonly ascribed to cossacks in general, and missed the further evolution of the line detachments—the re-organisation of cossack forces which took place in the nineteenth century, especially under Alexander I.

The nominal duties of the town cossacks were those of a police force, with the addition of certain responsibilities for communications. But in far northern areas there was little police work to be done, and cossacks became an increasingly obvious anachronism. Numbers dropped somewhat, and attempts were made to bolster them by drafting soldiers under sentence in European Russia and their families. This was done, for instance, in the Turukhansk region in 1858.[2] In the Yakut province in 1862 there were 618 cossacks, a sharp drop partly explained by the redrawing of administrative boundaries. It is clear that lack of activity was making them into a depressed class. Perhaps their most useful function was in acting as guides and interpreters for visitors, but not all visitors appreciated this. Martin Sauer of Billings's expedition to north-east Siberia saw something of them in 1786–88, and found 'these hardly animated lumps of clay' lazy, faithless and sly.[3] Cochrane, the English naval officer travelling in Siberia in 1820–23, thought much the same of them, but because it was impossible to get shelter, food or assistance without their help, considered them 'a necessary evil'.[4] In the late nineteenth century Maynov, a careful and thorough investigator, considered that 'their conditions of service, and a certain semi-security, to such an extent paralysed their energy and prevented any economic activity, that their material position was somewhat precarious, and cossacks constituted an intermediate layer between low-ranking service people and the semi-proletarian middle class'.[5] One of the few laudatory references to them comes from the

---

[1] Andriyevich (1889), p. 152.
[2] Smirnov (1928), p. 6.   [3] Sauer (1802), p. 66.
[4] Cochrane (1824), vol. 1, pp. 221–2.   [5] Maynov (1927), p. 380.

official 'Statistical Survey of Siberia' of 1810, which is obviously concerned to put the official view.[1] But at least the cossacks continued to constitute a group, even if not a very admirable one. The Yakutsk cossack regiment existed until the First World War.

During this period of decline, which started about the middle of the eighteenth century, cossacks did, however, play a positive role sometimes. In particular, they farmed. Already in the seventeenth century the senior cossacks started to acquire land. In the eighteenth, the Government sometimes chose to pay cossacks in land rather than food, and in the nineteenth this practice became common. In the first third of the nineteenth century cossacks in the Yakut province received 5456 *desyatin* (one *desyatina* was about one hectare, or 2·7 acres) of land from the administration—not much less than that allotted to Russian peasants in the same region.[2] But they were seldom efficient farmers, preferring to rent out their land to natives or peasants. The flourishing farming villages of cossacks in southern Siberia, known as *stanitsy*, were not found in the north. In the early twentieth century there were still 315 cossack households in the Yakut province, containing 1052 people, and in addition there were a smaller number of retired cossacks.[3]

Most of the examples given above refer to the Yakut province which, although very large, was not the whole of the Siberian north. This is because there is more information about it than about the remaining areas. However, it is clear in this case that it was the most important, and that the situation elsewhere must have been similar but on a smaller scale. Thus there was a cossack *sotnya* (a unit originally of 100 men) for at least 150 years at Turukhansk, where it constituted a particular element in the population; but it was disbanded in 1870 when the Yeniseysk cossack regiment, to which it belonged, was abolished.[4] Similarly a force of 170 cossacks was vegetating at Berezov in the early nineteenth century, and was disbanded only in 1881.[5]

The general picture, then, of the cossacks in northern Siberia, is of a series of small groups of tough warriors, who played a key part in the early stages, but who went to seed after the conflicts were

[1] Statisticheskoye obozreniye (1810), pp. 76–83.
[2] Basharin (1956), p. 261.　　　　　　　[3] Maynov (1927), p. 380.
[4] Smirnov (1928), pp. 28–9.
[5] Bartenev (1896), p. 25. See also p. 48 above.

over. The constitution of the cossack units lent itself to this. Did the government leave them behind as a deliberate act of policy, to act as a nucleus for settlers? On the face of it, of course, the action was entirely deliberate. The authorities were always aware of the numbers and locations of the cossack units, and therefore cannot be accused of forgetting about them. But Siberia was notorious for the corruption and inefficiency of its administration. This was almost as true after Speranskiy's reforms as Governor-General in 1819–22 as it was before. So the fact that nothing was done about the deteriorating situation of the town cossacks could perhaps have been due simply to administrative inertia. On the other hand, if the government wanted to retain any sort of hold over its northern territory, the cossacks provided a good, and certainly the cheapest, way of doing this. The yearly pay of a rank and file cossack in northern Siberia in the eighteenth century was 1 rouble 80 kopecks, supplemented by 6 roubles 58 kopecks ammunition allowance, 12 roubles grain allowance, and 24 poods (= 864 lb.) of grain. In addition he received 40 acres of grazing land.[1] After 1812, according to Vrangel',[2] the pay and the food were both stopped, at least in certain remote areas like the lower Kolyma, but the cossack paid no tax. It could be argued, then, that any government which could persuade settlers to stay in northern Siberia on those terms, and was able to call on their services whenever necessary in addition, was doing very well. Moreover, Speranskiy, when he re-organised the cossack force as part of his reforms, appeared to have such considerations in mind.[3] This, and the fact that the Yakutsk cossack regiment was the last to be disbanded, may be taken as evidence of deliberate government action. So it may be not unreasonable to suppose that there was at least some awareness in St Petersburg of a purpose being served by the continuing presence of cossacks in the north.

But if that awareness existed, it must have been accompanied by the realisation that, as settlers, the cossacks had only the smallest value; they were better than nothing, and that was all. For their influence both on the society and the environment in which they lived was negligible, once the period of decline had started. As Maynov summarises it, 'the cultural significance of the cossacks for

---

[1] Maydel' (1893–96), vol. 2, p. 768.   [2] Vrangel' (1840), p. 54.
[3] Raeff (1956), pp. 63–7.

the population of the Yakut territory was almost as slight as the economic'.[1]

While the cossacks were the first agents of state power to operate in Siberia, and remained for long both the most numerous and the most prominent, they were not, of course, the only ones. There were other military personnel, and there were administrative officials. As far as the military are concerned, the *strel'tsy* have already been mentioned as forming the garrison of Mangazeya in the early seventeenth century. There were also regular forces at certain other places, notably the town of Okhotsk in the eighteenth and early nineteenth centuries, when it was Russia's base on the Pacific. But there were never more than a few hundred men involved.

The administrative officials were always a very small group, but naturally the most important one. It was their duty to supervise collection of fur tribute, operate the hostage system, control the natives, administer the law and keep the peace. At first, as might be expected from this list, the administration was in effect military government. In 1642, when there were hundreds of Russians coming into the Lena and Kolyma valleys, the administration of the newly created Yakutsk *voyevodstvo* numbered ten: two *voyevodas*, a *d'yak* (secretary or clerk), two *pis'mennyye golovy* (office heads), and five *deti boyarskiye* (esquires), with perhaps some clerks.[2] Later the names were changed, and the administrative services broadened to include medical care, education, police and law courts. But even in 1905 they numbered only 318 for the whole of the Yakut region.[3]

The quality of these officials was never high, except possibly in the earliest stages. But even then it was the attraction of quick riches which brought to Siberia such high-ranking *voyevodas* as Prince Gagarin, Prince Volkonskiy, and Prince Baryatinskiy. Distance from Moscow was the controlling factor. How could an official, whom the fastest messenger from the Tsar could not reach in a year, be expected to avoid the temptation of arbitrary and corrupt practices? 'God is high and the Tsar far away' was the saying. So from the first there are reports of barbaric cruelty of governor towards governed. Petr Golovin, the first *voyevoda* of Yakutsk, cut off the nose and ears of Yakut, put out their eyes, hanged them from their ribs and buried

[1] Maynov (1927), p. 380.
[2] Maynov (1927), p. 373.   [3] Maynov (1927), p. 374.

70

them alive. At the same time he imprisoned for two years his second in command and his secretary, together with 100 other Russians, on charges of inciting natives against him.[1] At Yesseyskoye Zimov'ye, Tungus who did not bring sables because hunting was bad were beaten to death with cudgels; and here, in 1680, Panteleyev, the man in charge, beat to death a Tungus who had brought in his fur tribute, but did not bring with it sufficient extra furs for the officials.[2] Posts in the Siberian administration came quickly to be regarded as a good way of making quick money during a three-year tour of duty, if the life could be endured, and that chiefly is what controlled the quality of the men who went.

The decline in the fur trade, however, removed this incentive. It had not, in fact, been able to ensure enough recruits; the Siberian administration, at least in northern regions, was always below establishment in the seventeenth century.[3] But very soon the use of Siberia as a penal colony started to grow, and it was natural that the administrative posts should also come to be regarded as punitive. In this way the minor positions at least could be filled without too much difficulty; but the quality of those filling them was likely to continue to be low. A governor of Kamchatka or Yakutsk in the eighteenth or nineteenth century was probably a serving or recently retired officer (in Kamchatka, normally naval) who had blotted his copybook in some way. Some, like Admiral Zavoyko in Kamchatka in 1849–54, did make real efforts to develop their territory,[4] but most were time-servers. Sauer[5] reports of Kamchatka that the officials' pay in the 1780's was so low that other sources of income had to be found to make a living wage, and the most obvious one, of course, was by exploiting the natives.

Only right at the top were really outstanding men to be found, such as the Governor-General Speranskiy (1819–22) and Murav'yev-Amurskiy (1847–61). These had greater problems on their hands than the administration of remote northern regions, nevertheless each left his mark in the north. Speranskiy was a law-giver rather than an administrator, but his laws endured. Those dealing with the native population, for instance, were still in force in 1917. Moreover,

---

[1] Krasovskiy (1895), pp. 172–4.
[2] Ogorodnikov (1920), quoted by Tarasenkov (1930), p. 8.
[3] Tokarev (1957), p. 63.   [4] Gapanovich (1933), vol. 1, p. 67.
[5] Sauer (1802), p. 311.

he had some personal interest in the north, for he tried to organise a trading company in the Yakut province with his friend the Irkutsk merchant Basnin. Murav'yev, on the other hand, was a first-class practical administrator (Amurskiy was added to his name after his successful acquisition for Russia of the lower Amur region), and he was remembered in the north for his protection of the ordinary citizen from exploitation by merchants and arbitrary behaviour by officials. He was particularly concerned to improve the quality of the officials by bringing in the right sort of man from European Russia—a process much resented by Siberians, who failed to appreciate that it was for their own good.[1] Unlike many Governor-Generals, he travelled himself in the north country, making the journey to Okhotsk via Yakutsk in 1849.[2]

Unpromising though nineteenth-century Siberian officialdom generally was, its officers, teachers, lawyers and doctors constituted the only permanent body of educated people. This intelligentsia, if it can be so called, often received powerful reinforcement from the ranks of the political prisoners resident at the time, frequently men of first-class intellect. Many accounts of social life in nineteenth-century Yakutsk or Petropavlovsk emphasise the part played by exiles. But this was transitory, and although potentially a greater influence than that of the officials, in the long run it was the latter which prevailed.

PEASANTS

The Russian colonisation of Siberia as a whole was fundamentally a movement of peasants. This is certainly true of the eighteenth and nineteenth centuries, but even in the late seventeenth peasants probably constituted the largest single group. For all the hunters, the exiles and the miners about whom one hears, Russian Siberia was primarily an agricultural country. The exiles in many cases were, or perforce became, peasants. This being so, there is no difficulty in finding information about the Siberian peasant.[3] What is difficult, however, and often impossible, is to distinguish in such sources the parts which refer to the north.

[1] Maydel' (1893–96), vol. 2, pp. 668– .
[2] Sgibnev (1869), no. 12, p. 51.
[3] The half-century of greatest flow (1861–1914), for instance, is well covered by Treadgold (1957).

The peasants followed the fur seekers and the cossacks as they went into Siberia. This was to be expected, for the government paid its servants in grain as well as money. Scales were laid down according to rank, and they called for large quantities: from half a ton to nearly five tons per head per year, in the Tomsk area in 1699.[1] This posed a big supply problem, which would clearly be best solved by local farming.

There is some argument about the interval at which the peasants followed. On the one hand, it is asserted that it was not until about 1650 that Siberian settlements started to obtain Siberian-grown grain.[2] The source of the grain was the fertile plains of the Irtysh around Tyumen' in the south of Russian-occupied western Siberia (still today a major grain-growing region), but agriculture was practised in the seventeenth century in this area almost as far north as latitude 60° N.—for instance, at Pelym on the Tavda and Narym on the Ob'. On the other hand V. I. Shunkov, who has made a very detailed study of Siberian agriculture in the seventeenth century, maintains that the first peasants arrived almost at the same time as the first Russians, and even claims that the movement into Siberia should not be described as one of fur hunters and cossacks, because peasants in fact accompanied them.[3] Possibly these statements are not mutually incompatible; agriculture may have taken time to reach a useful level of production. But further east, certainly, the time lag was less, possibly because the vastly increasing distance from established producing regions made local agriculture the more essential. While Tyumen' is 1000 km. from Kazan', Yeniseysk is 2600 and Yakutsk 4800. The number of peasant households in the seventeenth century got notably fewer as the distance to the east increased, but they did penetrate further to the north: in the Yenisey valley, to the junction with the Podkamennaya Tunguska, and in the Lena valley to Yakutsk—or to about latitude 62° N. in each case. The first attempts were made in both regions in the 1640's. In the Lena valley, it is true, not very much progress was made for the rest of the century; the local belief in the 1890's was that agriculture had started only in the early nineteenth century.[4] But riverside meadows and natural clearings in the forest were ploughed, and

---

[1] Shunkov (1956), p. 303.
[2] Pokshishevskiy (1951), pp. 62–3.
[3] Shunkov (1956), pp. 38, 94.
[4] Maydel' (1893–96), vol. 2, pp. 619–20.

there was even some clearance of standing timber. Grants of animals and tools were made to early agricultural settlers here as an incentive. Later, a money subsidy (*podmoga*) became commoner. Rye was found to be the most successful crop, but wheat, barley, oats, peas and hemp were also tried. By 1700 there were 500 peasant households on the Lena, representing a third of the Russian population; but most of these were on the upper reaches, south of the area with which this book is concerned.[1]

These beginnings of northern crop-growing did represent a considerable advance on what the Siberian natives had been doing, in that new crops were introduced, and also new techniques—for instance, the plough replacing the hoe. Furthermore, the Russians tilled the soil in more northerly regions than did the natives; but this was because the line of advance happened to be a northerly one, due both to the pressure of hostile natives in the south and to the search for fur.

The peasants who worked these farms were not, of course, a homogeneous group. Peasants in Siberia as a whole at this time were mostly so-called 'government peasants', serfs who owed allegiance not to a private owner but to the state. They came from European Russia singly or in small groups, the rate depending upon conditions at home; it increased in times of political unrest or famine, and at the Great Schism of the 1670's. Some also came illegally, and therefore clandestinely. They mostly ended up living in villages in which some fields belonged to the government and some to individuals. All had to work in the government fields for part of the time, the government taking the produce, but they supported themselves from their own plots. A *prikazchik*, or head man of the village, saw that this was done.[2] But the northern peasant outposts were atypical of this situation. In their case, many peasants were either former fur seekers, who wanted to support themselves locally, or exiles.[3] It was rare for peasants to be directed by the government to the northern areas, because there was a shortage of them in the south also. And the remotest areas, such as the Lena valley, were seldom reached by peasants who were free to move where they wanted. Cossacks became peasants of a sort as their military functions dropped away, but in the seventeenth

[1] Shunkov (1956), pp. 165, 175; Tokarev (1957), p. 49.
[2] Shunkov (1956), pp. 397, 411.   [3] Shunkov (1956), pp. 172–4.

century this process was only just beginning. Thus there tended to be few real peasants in the north at first, and for that reason, as well as through the harsh conditions, the lack of capital, and even local attacks by nomads, agriculture did not particularly thrive.[1] Moreover, it became less effective as the distance from European Russia increased.

One point should be made here, in considering the status of the Siberian peasant. The reason for the flow, later to become a torrent, of peasants into Siberia is justly ascribed to the desire of the peasants to escape from serfdom. But it is not true to assert, as many have, that serfdom never existed in Siberia. The villages of government peasants mentioned above were clearly based on the serf system, but the grossest manifestation of serfdom, the buying and selling of serfs, was absent. Later, work in the government fields was replaced by a tax (*obrok*). Serfs were in fact owned by a few individuals, and by religious houses until the time of Catherine the Great, when church serfs were transferred to the state. This last is a relevant matter, because monasteries played a significant part in the north. There were two employers of serf labour in the Yakut region in the seventeenth century, and they were the Spasskiy and Pokrovskiy monasteries.[2]

By 1700, then, peasants, or at least tillers of the soil, were established, if somewhat precariously, roughly along the line of the 60th parallel, but with northward extensions in the Yenisey and Lena valleys. There they remained, without any significant advance northwards, for over two centuries. Numbers, meanwhile, gradually increased.

The Lena valley is in many ways the most interesting of the areas of peasant settlement. It is both the most northerly and the most remote from European Russia, and became probably the most flourishing. Certainly it is the area about which there is most information. At the beginning of the eighteenth century it contained 164 peasant households, sowing between them 370 acres with grain.[3] They were distributed in the Ilim, Vitim, Aldan and Kirenga regions. In 1731, 50 peasant families were settled on the Amga, 180 km. south-east of Yakutsk, which thus became the most northerly

[1] Bakhrushin (1959), pp. 81–2.   [2] Bakhrushin (1955*b*), p. 32.
[3] Tokarev (1957), pp. 47–9.

farming community. In fact this was the second time the region had been settled, the first attempt having been unsuccessful.[1] From the middle of the century the government started to take a serious interest in farming on the Lena. It was viewed no longer just as a way of feeding employees, by providing the cossacks' grain allowance, but as a colonising factor which could improve the lot of all immigrants. There were thus a number of projects for improving agriculture, but none of these was an outstanding success.

In the time of Catherine the Great a road was constructed to Yakutsk, which up to that time had been reached normally by water and therefore in the summer. Essential equipment of the road was a series of stations where post horses were available. Thus by 1798 there were 23 such stations between the Vitim and Yakutsk, manned by some 200 'coachmen', the *yamshchiki* who appear so frequently in Russian literature. These became the nucleus of important peasant settlement, but not at once, because the *yamshchiki* had no land to begin with. They were granted it later, and by the 1840's there was significant farming at and near the post stations. The further growth of river traffic took some of the burden off the post stations in the summer, and so made more opportunity for farming. The gold mines which started operating in the vicinity created a new market for output, and as a result there were 2465 peasants in 1893. Some of them were originally, and indeed remained, *yamshchiki*. Others were exiles, of whom more will be said later. The extent of their cultivation, along the line of the post road to Yakutsk, was 3000 acres of arable land and 7200 acres of pastureland—an average per head which was, however, only a tenth of the permitted amount for Siberia as a whole.[2] At the turn of the century, free migrants (that is, those who migrated of their own free will and avoided all the legal controls) started to reach the Lena in considerable numbers; they were flooding over the Ural mountains at that time, and the government were certainly unable, and perhaps unwilling, to control them. As a result of this, the peasant population for the whole of the Yakut province was 10,646 in 1917.[3]

Meanwhile, there was settlement of a similar sort along the

[1] Maynov (1912), p. 2.
[2] Tokarev (1957), pp. 269–71. Maynov (1927), p. 381, mentions 5000 peasants for about the same period.
[3] Maynov (1927), p. 382.

Yakutsk–Ayan road, Ayan having succeeded Okhotsk as the Pacific terminus of the Siberian road. There had been post stations and *yamshchiki* here since the road was first used, but not many: Yakut largely did the job. In 1851 Murav'yev decided to settle the region more effectively, and sent 102 Russian families there, a total of 589 people. But sixteen years later Alaska was sold, Ayan lost its significance, and most of the families moved southwards, with official encouragement, to the Amur.[1] The remainder concentrated into three settlements, of which the most flourishing was Pavlovskoye, 30 km. from Yakutsk.

All the peasants in the Lena region were notably influenced by the Yakut. The two races were always in close contact, the Yakut being very much the stronger numerically, and both were trying to extract the means of life from the same environment. The type of farming practised was not dissimilar from that further south. It was mixed, some land being ploughed for grain crops, but more being kept for grazing and for hay. The importance of cattle becomes clear when the low expectation of a good harvest is realised. Records are available for 35 years between 1837 and 1892, and they show 19 bad harvests, 10 medium and only 6 good ones.[2] Farming methods were primitive, and no fertiliser was used. Some fishing was also done at most settlements, but this was not a major activity. All this food production, while undoubtedly helping with the supply problem, did not of course come anywhere near solving it. Grain still had to be imported into the area.

North of Yakutsk, in the regions of Zashiversk, Zhigansk, Srednekolymsk and the mouth of the Olenek, there were a few Russians in the early nineteenth century who might be described as peasants. They did not exceed a few hundred.[3] They lived, however, by hunting and fishing, and did not practise agriculture.

In the lower Ob' valley, below the confluence with the Irtysh, there was no cultivation of the soil, beyond the growing of a few vegetables in places. Russian peasants in the area were not very numerous (probably about 3000 in 1850),[4] but those there were also lived in a manner that owed something to the natives. They fished

---

[1] Maynov (1912), pp. 6–7.   [2] Maynov (1912), p. 263.
[3] 154 'census souls' (males able to work), according to Tokarev (1957), p. 199.
[4] Abramov (1857), pp. 381–3.

and hunted, and collected forest products—nuts and berries—for which there was some market. They also kept cows, horses, some sheep and a few pigs. Very few kept reindeer, which were the mainstay of the native population.

The situation was essentially the same in the Yenisey valley. Peasants in the Turukhansk region lived largely on fishing, for fish were exceedingly abundant. It was for long difficult to market them, but the advent of large river craft in the mid-nineteenth century gave a fillip to the industry. Here, as for peasants in other remote areas of northern Siberia, it was true that the richness of nature was such that life even for the poorest was not necessarily bad. Food, clothing and shelter were never short, as was noted by a writer in 1835.[1] But a certain measure of skill and aptitude was needed to obtain them, and this was not always present. The lower Yenisey was so sparsely settled in the early nineteenth century that it was difficult to maintain communications down the river. So on two occasions a boatload of families, with cows and horses, was sent downstream and three or four families deposited at selected points. But this plan did not succeed, apparently because most of the families were urban workers rather than peasants, and they could not look after cattle properly, nor even in some cases build houses.[2] The region was never at all thickly settled, but towards the end of the century there is evidence that some grain was being grown on the middle Yenisey, for the Government was able to do away with the grain stores it had established on the lower river after the famines of the early years of the century.[3]

Peasant settlement occurred in other districts besides the main river valleys of the Siberian north. In the European Arctic, the White Sea had been reached in the thirteenth century, and the more southerly parts of the Pechora basin, subject to Vologda, were settled by peasants in the sixteenth century, when the advance into Siberia was only just beginning. But there was presumably no incentive to a peasant to move further north when there was a great and fertile space waiting to be filled to the east. Significant peasant movement up to the coastal regions of the Barents Sea started only in the second half of the nineteenth century. From about 1860 the government

[1] Stepanov (1835), vol. 1, p. 268.
[2] Tarasenkov (1930), pp. 25–6.   [3] Tarasenkov (1930), p. 33.

made efforts to populate the Murman coast, encouraging in particular Norwegians and Finns to come and live there, because they
were believed to know the agricultural techniques for that latitude.
In fact, the settlements were primarily concerned with fishing,
although pressure was continually put on the inhabitants to till the
soil also. Thus the 2000 and more settlers who were living there at
the turn of the century were peasants, but mostly peasant-fishermen.
Some were concerned with sea-mammal hunting, for which Kola
had been a centre from time to time. There was also, both in Kol'skiy
Poluostrov and further east, some development of the timber
industry. By the second half of the nineteenth century, the timber
industry of Arkhangel'skaya Guberniya, to the south, had acquired
considerable importance, and started to reach out northwards. Trees
were scarcer, but there was easy access to the sea. By 1914 there were
mills at Kandalaksha, Kola and Umba in Kol'skiy Poluostrov, and
Pustozersk at the mouth of the Pechora. Much foreign capital was
invested in the industry and many of the firms operating in the White
Sea area—particularly on the lower Pechora—were Scandinavian or
British, and interested primarily in the export trade.[1] The number of
workers employed by each of these mills is not known, but they
might have averaged 100 each.

There is one remaining area where peasant settlement was
encouraged from an early date, and that is Kamchatka. It was clear
from the first reports that there were areas of Kamchatka which
might make good agricultural land. The first attempt to act on this
was made in the reign of the Empress Anna, who signed a decree
in 1733 by which agricultural settlers were to be sent there. As
a result, in 1740, or perhaps later, 20 peasant families arrived at
Verkhnekamchatsk and Nizhnekamchatsk, and outside these two
centres of Russian settlement they set up the farming villages of
Mil'kovo and Klyuchi. These may have been reasonably successful,
in so far as descendants of the original settlers were reported still in
the region a hundred years later;[2] but on the other hand a visitor to
Kamchatka half a century after the settlement had been started
observed that the peasants had found it more profitable to engage
in trading furs for imported goods, and practised agriculture only
enough to feed themselves. They could pervert the government's

[1] Trofimov (1961), pp. 110–42.   [2] Ditmar (1890), p. 419.

purpose in this way, he said, because they were under no supervision of any kind.[1] Agriculture was, however, encouraged by certain governors of Kamchatka, and was never permitted to die out.

More attempts were made to settle Russians on the land in Kamchatka. A report by the Governor-General of Siberia, Pestel', to the Tsar in 1810[2] mentions an unsuccessful importation of 104 peasant families and some retired soldiers from the Siberian mainland at a date not given, but probably towards the end of the eighteenth century. He dwells at greater length on an attempt at military settlement undertaken in 1803–10, when a regiment of cossacks under Colonel Somov were designated as 'settlers'. This new method also was a failure, because the soldiers did not know how to farm in this area, and were not interested in learning to become peasants. Many were reported as returning to the mainland after a few years.

Nevertheless, there were some Russian peasants who got a living from the soil in Kamchatka, most of them of cossack or exile origins. They grew few crops, preferring to fish and keep cattle. The growing of vegetables was introduced in 1846, and its success was attributed to the fact that they were grown round the houses, where the snow melted early. Another helpful factor were the fairly frequent falls of volcanic ash, darkening the snow and thus hastening melting.

Finally, it is relevant to mention the situation in Alaska. Here, there were to all intents and purposes no peasants at all. The distance was much too great for runaway peasants to get there; and the government never permitted their free exodus. The Russian-American Company, which amounted to the government of the colony, was constantly troubled by the lack of labour, but was nevertheless not permitted to take across large numbers of peasants. All they could recruit was the riff-raff of Siberia, and the treatment accorded to these was not likely to tempt others to go if they could help it.

It is interesting that Belov, pronouncing judgement as a historian, states his opinion that it was the failure of Russia to organise any large-scale peasant settlement in Alaska that in fact decided in advance the question of whether the country would remain Russian.[3] This is surely true. There were many other factors, which Belov

[1] Sauer (1802), p. 291.   [2] Pestel' (1926), pp. 179– .
[3] Belov (1956), p. 455.

PLATE IX

(a) Petropavlovsk-na-Kamchatke about 1850 (Boulitchoff, 1856).

(b) Petropavlovsk-na-Kamchatke about 1910 (Glinka, 1914, opp. p. 317).

PLATE X

(*a*)

(*b*)

The two most distinguished administrators of Siberia: (*a*) Count M. M. Speranskiy (1772–183
(*b*) Count N. N. Murav'yev-Amurskiy (1809–81).

mentions, but this was the fundamental one. Can one go further, and maintain the converse, that it was the establishment of peasant settlers in northern Siberia that ensured its retention by Russia? Here again, it was certainly not the only factor. Peasant settlement was extremely sparse, and very large areas between the major rivers, and in the far north-east beyond the Kolyma, were quite untouched by it. Nonetheless it is true that such peasant settlement as there was gave body and continuity to a Russian occupation which was otherwise both superficial and sporadic.

EXILES AND CONVICTS

In any Russian context, Siberia and exile have become almost interchangeable terms. In the public imagination, Siberia has always been the land of exile. Although it is also the land of many other things, there is every justification for the popular image. It was used as a penal colony from the very earliest years of Russian possession—already in the 1590's there are reports of prisoners being sent to the Tobol'sk region—and it has probably never ceased to be so used from then until now. Successive Russian governments have always had two problems on their hands: what to do with troublesome subjects, and how to populate empty expanses. Siberian exile has always seemed a neat way of solving both at once. Evidence of how early the Russian government saw the importance of exiles as settlers is provided by the fact that exiles were permitted to take wives and families with them from the 1640's.[1] But the flow of exiles into northern areas has been only a part of this picture, and the factors controlling it have not always been the same as those controlling the exile movement into Siberia as a whole. In general it is true to say that exile to the north has been reserved for those for whom especially severe punishment was desired.

It should be understood that there was a considerable range in the various degrees of exile which could be awarded by law, extending on the one hand from freedom to order one's life in whatever way one liked, subject only to the obligation not to return to European Russia, to what on the other hand amounted to a prison existence. In the early days most exiles tended to be treated rather more as

[1] Aleksandrov (1961), p. 12.

prisoners—many, in fact, were prisoners of war, Swedes and Poles. But they were not actually confined in a prison, because nature provided a quite sufficient barrier. An early reference to prisoners is in a report by Vasiliy Pushkin, *voyevoda* of Yakutsk in 1644–45, in which he objects that they ought not to be sent from Yeniseysk into his charge at Yakutsk because food for them would have to be sent too.[1] Whether they went or not is not known, but some certainly reached the Yakut province not long after, for the *voyevoda* Frants-bekov received orders on how to deal with exiles in his charge in 1649. There soon came political exiles, supporters of Dem'yan Mnogogreshniy, a cossack who was himself exiled to Irkutsk in 1672, and they were followed by Old Believers (of whom more will be said in the next section). Criminals started to come too, but the worst were generally put in prison rather than exiled. The number of exiles in the region in the seventeenth century has been estimated as many hundreds, and a part of the town of Yakutsk is known to have been set aside for them.[2]

Exiles constituted the largest group of involuntary settlers in the north. From the eighteenth century there was also the category of those condemned to forced labour (*katorga*) in Siberia—a more severe punishment—and for them the word convict is more appropriate. But the main centres for forced labour were in southern Siberia—Nerchinsk, Chita, and later Sakhalin—so few convicts in this sense appeared in the north.

The eighteenth century saw little change in the system. Possibly more exiles went to the Berezov and Turukhansk areas and fewer to the Yakut province. Also, since by now the Russian advance had overrun significant parts of southern Siberia, there were new and somewhat less harsh regions for exiles to populate, with the result that the north became more especially reserved for hard cases. Leading politicians, and men who had been disgraced at court, appeared in Arctic settlements: General G. G. Skornyakov-Pisarev, one of Peter the Great's lieutenants, was exiled by the all-powerful Prince A. D. Menshikov to Zhigansk shortly after Peter's death; and within a year Menshikov himself was sent to Berezov, where he died. The palace revolutions of the next few years saw more leading figures sent to these remote areas. The uttermost place of exile, then

[1] Al'kor & Grekov (1936), pp. 156, 196. [2] Tokarev (1957), p. 228.

and until 1917, was the lower Kolyma, over 7000 km. and normally two years' travel from the capital. Here Count M. G. Golovkin, a leading diplomat under Peter and Anna, languished for 14 years, and also Baron Mengdon—both exiled by Elizabeth.[1] Kamchatka, too, came to be used as a place of exile; no closer to the capital than the Kolyma, but obviously a good deal pleasanter. It was from here that one of the few wholly successful escapes took place. Count M. A. de Benyowsky, exiled for his part in a Polish uprising, arrived at Bol'sheretsk in 1770, won the favour of the Governor of Kamchatka, Nilov, became engaged to his daughter, led a revolt of exiles, killed Nilov, and sailed to freedom with a shipload of fellow-conspirators.[2]

In the first half of the nineteenth century there was some increase in numbers, and at this time the number of exiles entering Siberia as a whole was rising sharply.[3] They were used to populate the route down the Yenisey from Yeniseysk to Turukhansk, to man post stations on the Lena, and beyond to the Pacific coast. There was an important, although numerically very small, influx of political exiles after the uprising of December 1825—the so-called Decembrists, who included in their number leading social and intellectual figures. Among the 14 who were sent to the Yakut province were A. A. Bestuzhev, a writer who later produced tales of Siberian life which were very popular, and M. I. Murav'yev-Apostol, the brother of one of the ringleaders. P. F. Vygodovskiy, another Decembrist, spent 25 years in the Ob' north, after which he was transferred to Yakutsk and then to Vilyuysk, where he was still living as an exile at least until 1866, 41 years after the uprising.[4] But it was in the second half of the century that the wave of exiles to the north increased notably in volume. In the Yakut province in 1889 exiles numbered 6090 (with their dependants, 7284), and this was apparently two-thirds of the Russian population. Political exiles represented only a very small proportion of these—something less than five per cent.[5] In the

---

[1] Tokarev (1957), p. 229.
[2] Oliver (1893). As the editor makes clear in his introduction, Benyowsky by no means always told the truth. But the substance of the story is corroborated by Ditmar (1900), p. 202.　　　　[3] Treadgold (1957), p. 33.　　　　[4] Tokarev (1957), pp. 231–4.
[5] Bakhrushin (1955*b*), pp. 33–5. Bakhrushin supports his high proportion of two-thirds exiles with figures from the *Pamyatnaya knizhka* for 1891. It has not been possible to check this, but the *Pamyatnaya knizhka* for 1896 quotes a somewhat larger number of exiles and their dependants (7968), but shows that they were under half the total population.

Turukhansk region the pattern was evidently similar. An increase in population was noted between 1861 and 1888, and this was thought to be due almost entirely to an increase in the number of exiles.[1] The high-water mark was reached in about 1890, and labour in the gold mines accounted for a substantial part of the increase.[2] It is quite clear that at this time the proportion of exiles to local inhabitants rose in certain places well above the legal maximum of 1 : 5.[3] At the turn of the century, however, numbers were already dropping considerably.

It was in this period—the second half of the nineteenth century—that exiles probably exercised the greatest influence in the north. Apart from the sheer weight of numbers, some reached positions of importance. There are records of exiles owning mines, trading, practising law, and becoming contractors. Their impact on the cultural life of the region was great. N. G. Chernyshevskiy, the political theorist and writer, spent eleven years at Vilyuysk (1872–83), where, being held a prisoner rather than being permitted free movement locally, he was fed and housed and thus able to spend his time reading. E. K. Pekarskiy, V. G. Bogoraz, V. I. Iochel'son and I. I. Maynov all pursued ethnographic and linguistic studies of the greatest value.[4] The Polish rising of 1863 caused an influx of Poles. The Polish geologists A. L. Czekanowski and I. D. Czerski made very extensive surveys of northern Siberia, where the names of each are now attached to mountain ranges. Waclaw Sieroszewski, another Pole, spent twelve years in exile in the Yakut province and made important studies of the people.

Apart from reinforcing the intelligentsia of the region, however, the exiles were not good settlers. They did not fit into the economy of their place of exile at all easily, since the native language was unknown to them and many were quite ineffective as farmers. It was estimated that the number of exiles in the Yakut province in the 1890's who had settled down to useful work on the land in the region where they were supposed to be was only six per cent.[5] The local

---

[1] Latkin (1892), p. 116. [2] See pp. 93–4.
[3] Pokshishevskiy (1951), p. 124.
[4] Pekarskiy produced a monumental Yakut dictionary. Maynov's work has been a major source for this chapter. Bogoraz and Iochel'son (known outside Russia as Waldemar Bogoras and Waldemar Jochelson) became leading authorities on the peoples of northeast Siberia, where they worked on after the end of their periods of exile.
[5] Maynov (1927), p. 384. See also Maynov (1912), p. 340.

authorities tried in two cases to turn exile groups into farming communities, at Nikol'skaya Sloboda and Dobroye, but in neither case was it successful. Other factors which contributed to the ineffectiveness of exiles as settlers were the scarcity of women, the high wastage rate, whether by death or escape, and the low quality of the criminal element. As a result, the exiles tended to drift into the gold mines, to which they were also in the main unsuited, and frequently ended as vagrants.

Perhaps as a result of these experiences, exiles were not subsequently used much as settlers in the north. There were plans to use them in Kamchatka in the early years of this century, in order to increase the Russian strength in an important frontier region, but they came to nothing.[1] An Imperial Decree of 1900 in fact terminated the sending to Siberia of any but political or religious offenders. Although this does not seem to have been very closely adhered to, and there were in any case many political offenders, it nevertheless had some effect.

There is plenty of evidence of the bad conditions in which many lived. George Kennan, a kinsman of the United States diplomat of the mid-twentieth century, made a deep impression with his detailed work *Siberia and the Exile System*, published in New York and London in 1891. The Soviet history of Yakutiya claims that 'the archives contain an abundance of documents, which clearly illustrate the dreadful material conditions of life deliberately created by Tsarism for exiles in Yakutiya'.[2] This is undoubtedly true, although by no means all the unpleasantnesses were deliberately contrived. It is not necessary to quote chapter and verse to show that some exiles were maltreated by the Tsarist authorities and that others died of hunger. Perhaps the most surprising feature of the system was the comparative freedom enjoyed by at least a few exiles who were nominally under close supervision.[3]

One cannot speak of prisoners in the north without mentioning the famous case of the construction of the Murmansk railway in 1915–16. This was a strategic objective of the first importance, and the Tsarist

[1] Okun' (1935), pp. 132–4.
[2] Tokarev (1957), p. 300.
[3] For instance, Zenzinov in northern Yakutiya in 1910–14. See Zenzinov & Levine (1932).

Government employed at least 70,000 men on it, a large proportion of them prisoners of war. Conditions were terrible, and there is no doubt that casualties were extremely heavy.[1]

The years preceding the 1917 revolution brought a number of Bolshevik leaders into northern exile. Lenin was in eastern Siberia, but the southern part of it. Stalin, however, was at Kureyka on the lower Yenisey, and Sverdlov was sent to the same region after being held earlier in the Narym region on the Ob'. At Narym Kuybyshev also spent a period of exile. The 1905 revolution and the period of repression following it caused another surge of political exiles into Yakutiya, where there were said to be 500 on the eve of the First World War. As a result, the revolutionary movement was, of course, closely followed by many exiles.

The exile as settler in the north, then, was not a marked success. For most of the three centuries under review he and his kind were not very numerous and played an almost entirely negative role. Only in the last half century did numbers become large enough for any marked influence to be felt. Of this period, much the most important effect was the cultural one, stemming from the superior ability of some of the political exiles. Scientific study of the north owes much to these people, whether they were Czerskis carrying out large-scale expeditions, or more modest figures quietly recording weather information at their remote place of exile. Russia's knowledge of her own territory would have been much poorer without them. It is also interesting to consider the possible effect of north Siberian exile on those who subsequently became political leaders; whether, for instance, Stalin's very important decisions on Arctic development in the 1930's were influenced by his years at Kureyka. There is no solid evidence that they were, but it is hard to believe that his first-hand knowledge did not play some part. Apart from this, the presence of even large numbers of exiles had the effect only of providing an inefficient and unskilled labour force, whose usefulness as settlers extended barely beyond the fact that they helped to occupy the territory for the sovereign power. From the point of view

[1] Griner (1949), pp. 184–5, a Soviet historian, gives 33,000 prisoners of war out of a total labour force of 70,000, admits casualties but does not give a number. But Elsa Brändström (1929), pp. 137–42, the daughter of the Swedish ambassador in Petrograd, claims that there were 70,000 prisoners of war out of an unnamed higher total, and that casualties included 25,000 dead.

of both the local administration and the native population, they were in the main a nuisance and a burden.

Other territories, notably Australia, have a history of settlement in which penal colonies played an important part. It is worth examining the parallel. In Australia, the prime purpose of establishing the colony was to find a place to settle convicts, and for some fifty years (1788 to the 1830's) convicts were the dominant social group. But from the 1830's this gradually ceased to be true, as the number of colonial-born and of free migrants from Britain increased, and over the next three decades the convicts themselves ceased to be sent out to Australia. During the whole period of 1788 to 1868, 155,000 convicts came to the country.[1] In northern Siberia, on the other hand, penal colonisation was not the original purpose, but was practised for more than three centuries. It was more important in the south, where a closer parallel with Australia is to be found, but nevertheless was significant in the north in spite of the much smaller numbers involved. It is from the length of time during which the system operated that the main differences between the Australian and the Siberian experience spring. In Australia, the convict period lasted for 50–80 years at the beginning of settlement, and then disappeared for ever. In Siberia, it continued much longer, increasing in importance with the passage of time. There is much literature in both cases drawing attention to the poor quality and small usefulness of the convicts as colonists. No doubt the human material was not greatly dissimilar in the two places. There were fewer political prisoners in Australia, but in both cases these were such a small proportion of the whole as to make little difference. But it was written of Australia in 1836 by as impartial an observer as Charles Darwin, that the penal system, although unsatisfactory in various ways, 'as a means of making men outwardly honest—of converting vagabonds, most useless in one hemisphere, into active citizens of another, and thus giving birth to a new and splendid country—a grand centre of civilisation—has succeeded to a degree perhaps unparalleled in history'.[2] This was said at a time when convict influence was waning, but by no means negligible (1840 was in fact the peak year for convict numbers, with 56,000 serving sentences).[3] One

[1] Greenwood (1955), pp. 4, 12–13.
[2] Darwin (1890), p. 324. [3] Greenwood (1955), p. 85.

searches in vain for such a statement about northern Siberia. An American observer, more sympathetic than most democrats to the Tsarist autocracy, wrote of Siberia in 1903 that 'an even longer experience than that of England has demonstrated the inherent and ineradicable viciousness of the [exile] system'.[1] Seen in perspective, there does seem to be an essential difference between a society which had a strong convict element in its early development, and one which was continually reinforced by convict settlers over centuries.

RELIGIOUS GROUPS

To settle in the remote parts of the north for religious motives is something which, while not peculiarly Russian, does accord with the Russian character more naturally than with that of most other peoples. The Russians who were activated by such motives exerted an influence out of proportion to their numbers, and they merit consideration as a group. It is necessary at the outset, however, to distinguish two kinds of religious community. The first kind is the ecclesiastical foundation, often monastic, set up in a remote northern area for any or all of several reasons: because remoteness is desirable for its own sake in a life of contemplation, for the pastoral care of the few Russians in the vicinity, or for missionary work among the northern peoples. The other kind were exiled dissenters, who were compelled to live in remote areas but were able to retain community feeling in exile. Both were present in the north for their religious convictions, and both stood out as examples of successful settlement.

Mention has already been made of the monasteries on Kol'skiy Poluostrov. The best known was that on the Pechenga, dedicated to the Trinity (Troitskiy), and founded in 1553 by the monk Trifon, who came from the monastery on the Solovetskiye Ostrova in the White Sea, and who had been active in the peninsula for some time before this. At the same period, another monk from the same monastery, Feodorit, was also preaching to the Lapps, whose language he had learnt at Solovetskiye. He founded another Trinity monastery at Kola in 1542, but left the region soon afterwards, and the monastery appears to have functioned for only a few years. He became known as Feodorit Kol'skiy, just as Trifon became Trifon Pecheng-

[1] Wright (1903), p. 322.

skiy, and both acquired the title *Prosvetitel' Loparey*, or Enlightener of the Lapps. These were examples of the missionary activity of Russian monasticism, strongly tinged with the spirit of asceticism.[1] The Pechenga monastery was sacked by the Swedes in 1590, and only re-established on the original site three centuries later, in 1886. It had meanwhile been replaced, however, by a monastery in Kola, a safer place, built in the seventeenth century—perhaps a revival of Feodorit's original foundation. Both monasteries were important outposts of Russian settlement in the north-west.[2]

While these monasteries were much the earliest, other regions acquired religious institutions very shortly after the arrival of the first Russians, who were in any case often accompanied by priests. By 1710 there was the Voskresenskiy monastery and four churches on the lower Ob' (Surgut and Berezov regions), the Troitskiy monastery (1660) and three churches on the lower Yenisey (Turukhansk region), and the Spasskiy monastery (1664) and four churches on the Lena (Yakutsk region).[3] Shortly afterwards another monastery, the Pokrovskiy, was founded near Yakutsk. The monasteries were the most important as colonising influences, for they were centres for activity of the most diverse kinds: not only religion and education, but agriculture, animal husbandry, ship-building, fisheries, mining, trade, and even defence. Property was owned and undertakings operated over a very considerable radius from the monastery itself— the Troitskiy monastery at Turukhansk ran a mill, farms, and fur-hunting centres up to nearly 1600 km. away. Among the property were serfs, until the Church was forbidden to own them towards the end of the eighteenth century. Monasteries tended, therefore, to be focal points in the settlement process. This was no accident, for the settlement function was emphasised in the sixteenth and seventeenth centuries, and largely replaced asceticism as the reason why remote monasteries were founded.[4] In Siberia, their heyday was the first century of Russian occupation. Thereafter, some decline is noticeable. The Troitskiy monastery, for instance, was found to house only a few old monks in 1735—a change mainly attributable to the finding of the Bishop of Tobol'sk in 1720 that the sainthood of Vasiliy of Turukhansk, whose shrine brought many pilgrims there, was

[1] Makariy (1887), pp. 330–5. [2] Korol'kov (1908).
[3] Klochkov (1911), pp. 61–9. [4] Smolitsch (1953), pp. 181–2, 192–3.

inadequately proven, and to the consequent direction that the relics be removed.[1]

The churches were much less rich and powerful. Missionary work, which might be imagined to be the main task, was at first slight. Some natives offered themselves for baptism because there were certain practical advantages in so doing: in this way they could avoid payment of fur tribute, marry Russians, or work for the Russian administration. But it was to the advantage of the authorities, interested in fur-tribute returns, not to encourage proselytising, and this factor no doubt played a part. Later, however, missionary activity was encouraged, and by the mid-nineteenth century all Yakut (to take the largest native group) were said to be Christian. But it was perhaps no accident that by then fur tribute had lost most of its importance. The nature of the conversion, too, was open to question. There is plenty of evidence of the unspiritual attitude of some priests to these conversions, and of the very shallow roots the new faith struck in some natives. There is no doubt that sometimes the baptising of the natives into the Orthodox Church was a purely formal, not to say farcical, proceeding. But it should not be supposed that all missionaries were drunken good-for-nothings. A shining exception was Ioann Veniaminov, who was active in northern Siberia for 47 years (1821–68). He did remarkable work in the Aleutians, including scholarly studies on linguistic problems. Later, when Bishop of Kamchatka, the Kurils and the Aleutians, he chose to make his centre at Yakutsk, and this led to his translating the gospels and prayers into Yakut. In 1859, thanks to him, the liturgy was available in Yakut. After 28 years as Archbishop of Eastern Siberia, Veniaminov became Metropolitan of Moscow in 1868, taking the name Innokentiy. His career not only shows the high quality of at least one Siberian missionary, but was of great practical help to church affairs in the north.[2] The Orthodox Church certainly cannot be said to have ignored the north in later years. In 1900 there were 370 priests and monks in Yakutiya, serving over 100 churches—a not insignificant figure.[3] By this time there were some Yakut in the priesthood, but not many. Of those 370, only eight were monks. It is not likely that either the Berezov or the Turukhansk monasteries

[1] Gmelin (1767), vol. 2, p. 63.
[2] Glinka (1914), p. 222.　　　　　　　[3] Maynov (1927), p. 397.

were in a much livelier state. Only the reconstituted Pechenga monastery seems to have been really flourishing, with a population of about 150 in the settlement.[1]

The presence of dissenters in the north also dates from early times. The Great Schism, or *Raskol*, of 1658, gave rise to the Old Believers, or *Raskol'niki*, who objected with astonishing fanaticism to the revision of the liturgical books. Their leading propagandist was the Archpriest Avvakum, and he was exiled for his beliefs to Pusto-zersk on the lower Pechora, and was in 1681 burned at the stake. Thereafter the Old Believers were persecuted in all sorts of ways, and many either fled, or were sent, to remote parts, where they practised their observances undisturbed. They reached Yakutsk in the 1670's, for Prince Yakov Volkonskiy, who was the *voyevoda* from 1671 to 1675, was reproached on his return to Moscow for dealing too leniently with them.[2] In the Ob' region there are records, for the period 1679–1757, of the practice of a most extraordinary mani-festation of religious dissent: self-immolation by burning, as being the only escape from fire eternal. In the Tobol'sk area in 1679 no fewer than 2700 people are said to have killed themselves in this way.[3] Old Believers continued to settle in Siberia throughout the eighteenth century, but the number reaching northern areas was never more than a trickle. Certain settlements, however, such as Pavlovskoye near Yakutsk, were still known as Old Believer settle-ments in the late nineteenth century.[4]

In the nineteenth century, members of two further dissenting groups appeared in the north: the *Skoptsy* (Castrates) and the *Dukhobory*. Of these, the *Skoptsy* were the more important. The sect, as its name implies, practised castration as a necessary aid to sal-vation. This belief was held by individuals within the Orthodox Church as early as the eleventh century, but an organised sect did not appear until the eighteenth. Catherine the Great declared the sect illegal in 1772, and punished its adherents with exile to Siberia. This law was later modified, but Nicholas I re-introduced Siberian exile as the punishment. Thus from 1847 a group of exiled *Skoptsy* appeared in the Turukhansk region. Before long they sought per-

[1] Opisaniye Murmanskogo poberezh'ya (1909), pp. 50–62.
[2] Maydel' (1893–96), vol. 2, p. 506.
[3] Baddeley (1919), vol. 1, p. lxxxvii; Glinka (1914), p. 204.
[4] Maynov (1912), p. 15.

mission to move to a more favourable farming area, and in 1859 Murav'yev, who knew their reputation as farmers, arranged for them to be transferred to the Yakut province. In 1860, therefore, 223 exiled *Skoptsy* arrived in the Aldan–Maya region, south-east of Yakutsk. They were joined by others, so that in the 1890's there were nine flourishing settlements (see Pl. XI*b*), of which the largest was Markhinskoye, just outside Yakutsk, counting 375 inhabitants. During the last quarter of the century there were between 1100 and 1200 *Skoptsy* in the Yakut province, the numbers being kept up not, of course, through natural increase, but through new exiles arriving. Throughout, they were notably successful as farmers; partly because they were more intelligent than most peasants in the region, and partly because they retained strong community feeling. They were almost the only farmers with produce to sell, while most of the others scraped a bare subsistence, and this led the local authorities to permit them to live near towns such as Yakutsk, despite orders to the contrary from St Petersburg. In the Yakut province in 1894 the sown area at *Skoptsy* settlements was 22 per cent of the total for the province; and the amount of grain harvested per unit of land was at least 50 per cent greater with the *Skoptsy* than elsewhere. Their influence on agriculture in the north was out of proportion to their numbers, for not only were they disproportionately effective, but by their example they showed both other peasants and the authorities what could be done. Yet there was nothing basically new in their techniques; the manner in which they were applied was simply more efficient. The *Skoptsy* were, as might be expected, unpopular among local peasants.[1] In 1904 they were permitted to leave their place of exile, with the result that their numbers dropped sharply, and this, as Bakhrushin writes,[2] adversely affected the economy of the region.

Less numerous, and also less effective as settlers, were the *Dukhobory*. This sect also originated in the eighteenth century. The position of the *Dukhobory* at its most extreme was to deny all authority but God's—essentially the position of the Christian anarchist. They were proscribed as a sect, and their members were exiled originally to the Caucasus. But in 1897 a group arrived in the Yakut province, where three settlements grew up in the neighbourhood of Yakutsk,

[1] See Maynov (1912), pp. 297–338, for the fullest account.
[2] Bakhrushin (1955*b*), p. 34.

numbering 162 people by 1905. P. V. Verigin, their leader, had been exiled to the Berezov region on the Ob' shortly before. The same ordinance which permitted the *Skoptsy* to leave applied also to the *Dukhobory*, who went off to join some of their fellows in a newly established settlement in Canada. There, it may be added, they have also come into conflict with the authorities, and there has even been mention of the possibility of their returning to the Soviet Union. They were therefore present in the north as an organised group for only about a decade, and their influence on local affairs was accordingly much less than that of the *Skoptsy*. Nevertheless, they were better farmers than most of their neighbours.[1] For the purpose of population statistics, the dissenters were included either as peasants or as exiles, so the numbers given in the preceding paragraphs are not an addition to, but a subdivision of, those given earlier.

The impact of religious groups in the north, then, may be summarised in this way. In the earlier years, the monasteries were important centres of settlement, while later on dissenters, although under sentence of exile, were effective agricultural settlers. In both cases these groups totalled only a small proportion of the Russian population of the region.

MINERS

The expectation of finding minerals played a part in attracting the Russians into certain areas of Siberia—for instance, silver prospects in the Baykal area attracted the first Russians in 1629. And indeed from the time of Peter the Great, rather less than a century later, mining became the main stimulus of government activity in Siberia, the most important centres (apart from the Urals) being the Altay and Nerchinsk, in the south. The first northern deposit to be worked was silver near Kandalaksha, exploited in 1733 by two Arkhangel'sk merchants.[2] At about the same time salt started to be mined at Kempendyay, a tributary of the Vilyuy in the Lena basin. From 1737 some tens of tons a year found their way to Yakutsk, but this was not more than a purely local industry, operated on local resources. Not until the nineteenth century did large-scale mineral exploitation reach the north. Gold was discovered in 1838–39 in the Yenisey basin, on the river Uderey, a tributary of the Verkhnyaya

---

[1] Maynov (1912), p. 17.   [2] Trofimov (1961), p. 104.

Tunguska. This led to a gold rush in the 1840's, and in 1851 there were estimated to be 20,000 miners working in the 106 gold mines of the district. Up to 1876 this was the biggest goldfield in Russia, and produced over 20 per cent of the country's gold. The number of miners fell to 7000 by 1882, although more mines were operating— an indication of the exhaustion of the richest deposits.[1] By 1917 this area had lost some of its importance. The Yenisey goldfield is just south of the southern limit of the north as defined for this book, and the numbers of miners quoted above are for that reason not included in the chapter on numbers of settlers (p. 50). But it would be misleading to omit mention of it here, in view of the subsequent importance of gold mining in the north.

Meanwhile other mining centres were opening up. The most significant of these was another auriferous region in the Lena basin, on the rivers Olekma and Vitim. Mining started here in 1846, and the greatest development took place on the Vitim, the settlement of Bodaybo becoming the main focus. The Lena goldfields employed 5000 men in 1870, and 12,000 men and 1100 women in 1889.[2] The biggest company operating at this time was the Lenzoto (short for Lenskoye Zolotopromyshlennoye Tovarishchestvo, or Lena Goldmining Company), and control of this, and of many other undertakings in the area, was acquired in 1908 by the British firm Lena Goldfields Ltd. By now 25,000–30,000 employees worked at the mines. It was here, in April 1912, that a famous strike took place, leading to police action in which 250 miners were killed. This had political repercussions throughout the country, but mining continued.[3] At the turn of the century these two goldmining areas, on the Lena and the Yenisey, accounted for about 70 per cent of Russian production (see Pl. XIIa).

Another and much smaller undertaking was the mining of graphite at Fat'yanikha and Kureyka on the Nizhnyaya Tunguska. This was started in 1862 and continued until after the 1917 revolution, but production was sporadic and averaged less than 100 tons a year. The size of the labour force is not stated, but it cannot have been great.[4]

The miners, who were almost all Russians, form a distinct group

[1] Chudnovskiy (1885), pp. 98– ; Danilevskiy (1959), pp. 250–6.
[2] Tokarev (1957), p. 268.   [3] Tokarev (1957), pp. 394–5.
[4] Tarasenkov (1930), pp. 355–6.

of settlers, and an important one, because it was the beginning of an industrial population which was later to expand enormously. Apart from a few engineers, they were unskilled, for this was alluvial gold and the method of recovering it was primitive. Some miners were convicts, but more were exiles who could find no better employment. The northern mines, unlike many in southern Siberia, were not state-run with forced labour, but were private undertakings which obtained labour however they could. A Soviet writer on Siberian settlement makes the point that the mines did not attract great numbers of Russians into Siberia, since most miners were transient Siberians.[1] As in the case of the dissenters, the miners were numbered among the other groups discussed earlier, so the figures quoted in this section are not to be taken as being additional to figures mentioned earlier.

GENERAL CHARACTER OF RUSSIANS IN NORTHERN SIBERIA

At no stage did northern settlement attract the highest quality of human material. Very few, if any, settlers went north out of a conviction that there lay their life's work. Most went because they had to, or because they could derive from it some profit, such as fur, or some less tangible advantage, such as distance from other people. It was from among the exiles that the most intelligent Russians in the north came, but they seldom stayed there longer than they could help—which was often, admittedly, many years. The bulk of the settlers probably represented a fair cross-section of the Russian peasantry, whose salient characteristics they exhibited: above all tough and strong; knowing hardship in some of its most acute forms, for instance famine; patient and enduring; self-reliant, not intelligent, but ingenious with a certain slyness. Furthermore, they loved gossip—a result, no doubt, of the sparseness of human habitation. 'From Tyumen' to Yakutsk, what is done, and even what is not done, is known.'[2] A significant proportion of them came from the northern parts of European Russia: from towns of the Pomor'ye, such as Mezen', Pinega, and Kholmogory, and towns further inland, such as Ust'yug.

[1] Pokshishevskiy (1951), p. 162.
[2] Tarasenkov (1930), p. 42, quoting Stepanov (1835), vol. 2, p. 102.

The occupations which Siberia offered in the early years were not such as to make it likely that wives and children would frequently be brought along too. And without wives and children there could be no permanent settlement. Clearly this problem was solved, but there has been little comprehension of how this was done. Large-scale intermarriage with the native peoples certainly took place, and from them came children of mixed blood who formed quite significant groups; in Kamchatka, for instance, the term Kamchadal has been used by some ethnographers to mean the descendants of unions between Russians and the native Itel'men.[1] But an investigator studying the Yenisey region has been at pains to show[2] that this was by no means the only method of creating settlers. After an initial period when almost all Russians were without families, by about the middle of the seventeenth century many cossacks had successfully petitioned for permission for their families to join them. Exiles were allowed to take their families from the 1640's. Thus Russian women came to Siberia, and by the 1680's it appears that peasant families on the Yenisey were comparable in size and structure with those in European Russia. Something of the same sort may have happened on the lower Ob' also. A late nineteenth-century writer comments on the rarity of mixed marriages there.[3]

In the north, the Russian was facing the same conditions as the native. Thus, in the words of a nineteenth-century ethnographer and historian, 'for the struggle with a stern nature, and for hunting, he came to use the primitive expedients of the natives and gradually acquired the natives' way of life and customs'.[4] This was noticed by Castren at Obdorsk in the 1840's, where it had clearly been going on for some time.[5] It was also noticed by many in the Yakut province, where Yakut culture proved notably stronger, in its local context, than Russian, and 'Yakutisation' of Russians, especially in the matter of language, became the rule rather than the exception.[6] As early as the 1730's Gmelin noted that Russians had learnt Yakut and even adopted Yakut religious beliefs.[7] Probably nowhere else in the

---

[1] Arsen'yev & Titov (1928), pp. 72–80.   [2] Aleksandrov (1961).
[3] Bartenev (1896), p. 24.   [4] Pypin (1892), p. 431.
[5] Castren (1853), p. 280.
[6] For instance, Pypin (1892), p. 431; Erman (1848), pp. 341, 357, 373; Ditmar (1890), p. 33.
[7] Gmelin (1751–52), vol. 2, pp. 370, 492.

PLATE XI

(*a*) Russian peasant 'old settlers' (*starozhily*) of the Yenisey region about 1910 (Glinka, 1914, opp. p. 181).

(*b*) *Skoptsy* settlement of Spasskoye, near Olekminsk, in the late nineteenth century (Maynov, 1912, opp. p. 288).

PLATE XII

(*a*) Gold mine in the Lena basin, late nineteenth century (Maynov, 1912, opp. p. 320).

(*b*) Okhotsk about 1850 (Boulitchoff, 1856).

Russian dominions was Russian culture so strongly influenced by, often indeed submerged by, that of another ethnic group. In the settlement on the Amga in 1895, for instance, out of 86 heads of Russian peasant households, 54 did not understand Russian, 19 expressed themselves in it with difficulty, and only 13 spoke their 'native language' reasonably well.[1] Similarly, there is evidence of 'Tungusisation'.[2] Some interesting customs were introduced in this way. 'The Russians here', wrote Vrangel' when at Nizhnekolymsk in 1820,[3] 'smoke in the manner common to all the people of northern Asia; they draw in the tobacco smoke, swallow it and allow it to escape again by the nose and ears. They speak much of the pleasurable sensation of the sort of intoxication thus produced, and maintain that this manner of smoking affords much warmth in intensely cold weather.' Is inhaling one of the results of Yakutisation?

This tendency to adopt native methods has led some to castigate the Russian settlers for taking the line of least resistance. Shvetsov[4] concludes from his study of the Surgut area on the Ob' that in three centuries the Russian settlers not only did not raise the natives to their level, but dropped quite significantly towards the native level. They had forgotten, he says, many crafts which their ancestors knew, such as wood carving, cart making, and road making, and learnt nothing new apart from borrowing techniques from the natives. This charge no doubt contains much truth, but at the same time does not make sufficient allowance for the fact that copying the natives was probably a wise course, as well as an easy one. Shvetsov makes the further point that the Russian peasant, fisherman or fur trader living outside the towns was a more admirable person than his townsman opposite number, because in the country one had to work, while the towns only kept going through state support, as centres of administration, garrisons, or control of exiles, and the inhabitants therefore became lazy. Such settlement, he says, gave nothing to the region or to the native inhabitants.

Yet the settlement must be accounted a success, at least in the sense that the Russian state has never lost its hold on the region. In the long perspective, it was the peasants (including the fishermen) who provided the backbone of the settlement. Few and scattered

---

[1] Maynov (1927), p. 383.
[2] Arsen'yev & Titov (1928), p. 75.
[3] Vrangel' (1840), pp. 58–9.
[4] Shevtsov (1888), pp. 59– .

though they were, without them there would have been no continuing and effective occupation of the region by Russians. Baddeley writes of the earliest stage of the Russian conquest of Siberia: 'Russia's success as a colonising power was due in the first place, indubitably, to the qualities of her people.'[1] With that view there can be no quarrel; and in so far as the later stages can be considered successful, those qualities were still the most important factor.

LIFE IN NORTHERN SIBERIA IN THE NINETEENTH CENTURY

Accounts of day-to-day life in northern Siberia after the initial period of conquest and exploration come mainly from two sources: from travellers, whether Russian or foreign, and from exiles. The voluntary Russian residents either wrote nothing (few could write), or if they did, their writings seldom found their way into print. Of the two classes of author whose works are available, the exiles are likely to give the truer picture. Their stay was long enough for them to be more than just visitors, and many were well educated and good observers. Their accounts can be informative, therefore, if due allowance is made for the authors' circumstances.

M. I. Murav'yev-Apostol was a Decembrist who spent 30 years in Siberian exile for his complicity in the uprising of 1825, and then lived another 30 years after his release, to die in 1886 at the age of 96. Near the beginning of his exile, in 1828, he spent a year at the little settlement of Vilyuysk, to the north-west of Yakutsk. Long afterwards he wrote of his life there:

When the spring sun started to appear, having been absent all winter, and under its rays the snow started to melt with astonishing speed, at the end of May, I became unspeakably happy at the imminent return of warm days; although I had been warned that in summer the midges vanquish everything, I had known them before and was in no way distressed at this. In the end the summer came, and it convinced me that this was a real plague, only to be compared with the Egyptians' boils in the time of Pharaoh. My passion for bathing in the river compelled me to neglect all sound precautions; I embarked on a desperate campaign, and in my battle with the insects acknowledged myself beaten; not only could I not think of bathing, but I could not even poke my nose outside my yourt [Russian

---

[1] Baddeley (1919), vol. 1, p. lxxxvii.

yurta]. Whole clouds of midges of great size stick to you cruelly. The Yakut wear masks against them, woven from hairs from horses' manes. In the yourt they protect themselves by means of smoke from a dung fire. There is a large pot containing coal, and they put into it pieces of dried dung paste, and this they also use in autumn to smear on the outside of the yourt. This fumigation, far from fragrant, continues day and night, and the chimney acts as a ventilator, without which one would suffocate with the smoke. The abundance of insects is easily explained by the position of Vilyuysk.

A few yards from the river on a low hill, out of the reach of the spring floods, rises the church, in the middle of a few dozen yourts, with four modest houses in addition; round about there is nothing but forest with coniferous trees only and boggy soil. On the other side of the river there is again impassable forest. You see no fields, no grain is sown, no vegetables are grown, for the simple reason that summer, although intolerably sultry, lasts no more than six weeks. The only abundant things to ripen are berries in the forest: raspberries, currants, cloudberries which Yakut labourers brought me, and grass, which grows in clearings and provides a store of hay for the whole winter for the few cows. I had my own cow, which Zhirkov [a cossack living in the village] kept in his yourt. I ventured to plant potatoes, and my attempt was fully successful. I wanted to sow millet, and its quick growth delighted me, but the frost did not let it ripen. The absence of any vegetables is a real hardship, and is insufficiently compensated for by the abundance of game and fish. The regional police chief Myagkov was good enough to send me, as a kindness, a large round box of birch bark containing frozen cabbage soup. The sight of a long-forgotten cabbage reminded me of my native part of the country and of times past.

I have mentioned the unattractive features of the place, which is at 63° 45′ north latitude, and they compel me to conclude that Vilyuysk exists simply for collecting fur tribute and for merchants to obtain furs from the Yakut. When this branch of industry is exhausted, Vilyuysk is likely to empty, as being little suited to settled life. Many years later I read in the newspapers that gold mines had opened near Vilyuysk, as a result of which it must have changed much, and the arrival there of exile labour will undoubtedly have had a harmful influence on the natives. The building of the church bears witness to the good intention of converting the natives to Christianity. But, as far as I could see, the plan had little success, although there were three priests at the church. The Yakut observe some rituals, but keep to the superstition of their ancestors. The church was built in the reign of the Empress Catherine. The three priests attached to it cared little for their missionary duty. They went off on horseback round their far-flung flock, and returned with valuable furs collected from the Yakut, the furs being their whole income and only means of subsistence.

I awaited with impatience the end of the summer, and was heartily glad when the cold mornings started, heralding the return of the longed-for winter. People call Siberia the frozen icy region, because of its severe frosts, but anyone who has lived in the far north blesses this saving frost which brings him a long rest after the tormenting summer.

Besides my constant occupations—reading, learning English, and writing to relatives and friends—I wanted, as a distraction which might help others, to teach children. Two boys started coming to me: the son of the local shopman and the grandson of one of the priests, and their parents were delighted at my suggestion of teaching their children.

There being no bell in this distant place, I had to find another way of announcing the start of lessons. I hoisted a flag over my yourt, and this was the sign that I awaited my pupils, and at this dumb summons they used quickly to appear with their books.[1]

Some fifty years later, another and more famous exile came to the same village of Vilyuysk. This was N. G. Chernyshevskiy, the radical social theorist and writer. During his eleven years there he wrote many letters to his wife and children. He was very much an intellectual, and more interested in ideas of social theory than in his immediate surroundings. Nevertheless, he mentions the latter quite often, but always in a favourable way, because he was anxious to reassure his family that all was well with him and that he was not suffering physically. In a letter of 1 March 1878 he wrote to his wife:

Here in this tiny town, of course, the shops have nothing but goods suited to the pocket of the common people. But people here are so used to travelling endless distances that Yakutsk, which is 700 versts away, seems to them a town you could reach out and touch. So, if anyone has the least little bit of money to spend, he buys everything in Yakutsk—a week and a half's journey away. People are constantly longing to go there.[2]

On 2 August 1882 he wrote to his wife:

My occupation, from which I have no respite from morning to night, has been for two weeks collecting mushrooms and drying them by a method developed by my experiments and deep cogitation. Don't think I am joking or exaggerating; no; literally, as soon as I wake, I start cleaning the mushrooms collected after supper the day before, and make little excursions for new collections. This lasts till three or five in the afternoon; I finish with yesterday's haul and the small new collections, and I go off on the main trip; I return with a burden of 50 lb.; and right up to the time when sleep overtakes me, I work away, cleaning the heap I've collected.[3]

[1] Murav'yev-Apostol (1922), pp. 62–3.
[2] Chernyshevskiy (1913), p. 68.
[3] Chernyshevskiy (1913), pp. 192–3.

The Character of the Settlement

And on 1 September the same year, also to his wife:

I have been spending much of the day in the open air, because the weather is keeping warm. Yesterday, for example, it was so warm that as I walked by the woods I took off my coat and put it under my arm, and went for a three hour walk in my shirt; and I do not like feeling cold. All summer the weather has been good for walkers. For cattle farmers it has not been quite so good: there were a few days of heavy rain, rivers and streams flooded at haymaking time and spoilt many meadows. And cattle are more important here than growing crops. However, the Yakut are beginning to get a taste for crop growing. Barley grows well here, in a normal year, and in a good year it is very abundant.[1]

[1] Chernyshevskiy (1913), p. 196.

5

GOVERNMENT POLICY

It is not easy to discern an official policy for Siberia as a whole over a period of time, and virtually impossible to discern one for northern Siberia. In the north, the government obviously had no conscious, consistent view of what it was trying to do. Its operations there were never more than a relatively unimportant sideline. But it does not necessarily follow that the whole process was entirely haphazard.

It is reasonable to suppose that the early phases were pioneered by fur seekers, with the government coming along afterwards and consolidating their gains. But as the distances increased, the position was reversed, the government taking the lead by sending forward cossack detachments, and the fur seekers operating under their protection. There can be no doubt that the government's main concern in the whole matter was economic, resulting from the great importance of the fur trade in the financial position of the state. Any thoughts of territorial aggrandisement for its own sake came a poor second. The search was primarily for *neyasachnyye zemlitsy*, areas where fur tribute was not yet levied. But, having occupied vast territory at comparatively little cost, and encountering no serious rival claimant (only the Manchu Empire could have played this part, and it was not interested), the Russian state naturally retained sovereignty. It would be wrong, however, to think of Moscow as exercising any close control over settlement questions. Once local administrators had been installed in office, it was they rather than their distant masters who organised activities and who planned further advance. Tobol'sk, Yeniseysk and Yakutsk were each in turn the effective centre for decisions on these matters. Moscow was consulted only when it was necessary to organise the administration of newly acquired territory.[1]

In the early stages of the Russian advance, in fact during most of the seventeenth century, there was certainly a greater official awareness of the north, and a higher priority accorded it in Moscow, than was the case later. This was both because the main lines of communi-

[1] Bakhrushin (1955a), p. 150.

cation ran closer to the north, even through it, and because the main interest was in fur bearers which inhabited the north. The government, in its encouragement of the fur trade, took certain measures which had a colonising effect. A typical one, which was repeated elsewhere, was the creation of a *sloboda*, or village, on the Yenisey in 1637, and again in 1668, in order to provide grain for Mangazeya. There is, in fact, some evidence of thought here, for these newly created settlements obtained the privilege of tax exemption for some years in order to encourage their development.[1] And then in about 1700 the route was changed, and the road no longer ran from Tobol'sk through Surgut, Narym and Yeniseysk, but from Kurgan through Omsk and Achinsk to Krasnoyarsk, some hundreds of kilometres further south. Now that the fertile lowlands of western Siberia were in the undisputed possession of Moscow, such interest as there had been in the north for its own sake obviously waned.

It was re-awakened, temporarily and in a somewhat different context, by one of the last actions of Peter the Great. This was his sponsorship of Bering's expedition to determine whether Siberia and America were joined or not, Dezhnev's report being still buried in the Yakutsk archives. That expedition itself neither solved the problem set it, nor bore witness to any special interest in northern Siberia, but it led straight on to the Great Northern Expedition. This, as already emphasised,[2] was a large and long undertaking, and its major product was a survey of almost the whole length of the north Siberian coast—a very remarkable achievement. There was even an 'academic branch' of the expedition, under three professors of the Academy of Sciences—G. F. Müller, a historian, Louis de Lisle de la Croyère, a mathematician, and I. Gmelin, a natural scientist—with a number of assistants. They did excellent descriptive work in an almost untouched field.[3] This was certainly testimony of government interest in the region. But it was mainly directed towards exploration, in satisfaction of a proper concern to know the extent and delineation of the realm, and the results were of little direct application to settlement.

The territory, meanwhile, had to be administered; and although

---

[1] Bakhrushin (1955a), pp. 212–17.   [2] See p. 26.
[3] Of the many accounts of this expedition, one of the best is in Grekov (1960), pp. 55–169.

the administration bore all the usual features of being a great distance from control—corruption, inefficiency, arbitrariness—it did exist, and was a reminder that sovereignty resided in the Russian government. It was also a reminder to the government that these regions existed, in so far as officials had to be relieved, and, more important, considerable expense incurred in keeping them fed. There was rarely any legislation which referred exclusively or particularly to the north, and the exercise of administrative functions was fundamentally the same as in other parts of Siberia.

But occasionally there was something which concerned the north specifically, and mention should be made of the two most important enactments. The first was the decision to set up fur-tribute commissions,[1] arising from the need to examine the position about payment of fur tribute after more than a century of operation of the original system. This decision was taken in 1763, when Catherine the Great created fur-tribute commissions for each province where the collection was made. The most important one was that for Yakutsk, sitting in 1766–67. It made a detailed investigation of the numbers paying, the manner, and the amount, and recommended changes in the method of payment, enlarging also the practice of accepting money in certain cases instead of fur. The recommendations were adopted. In 1827 a second fur-tribute commission was appointed to investigate various inequalities in collection which had become apparent. This was also split into sections, one for east and one for west Siberia, and included in its recommendations a further raising of the amount levied, with wider acceptance of money instead.[2] These commissions are mentioned here, not for critical evaluation of their work, but rather as evidence that the central government was capable of showing a deliberate interest in its northern domains—at least when revenue was at issue.

The other major piece of legislation which had special application in the north stemmed from Speranskiy's reforms of 1822. These have already been mentioned more than once, and there is no doubt that they were a turning point in the history of Siberia as a whole. Most were straightforward administrative reforms, badly needed but not of special interest to this inquiry. It has been argued[3] that they in fact

---

[1] The effect on the fur trade was referred to on p. 65.
[2] Tokarev (1957), pp. 134–48.   [3] Tokarev (1957), p. 166.

had very little effect in the Yakut province, and thus presumably no greater effect elsewhere in the north. The aspect of them which did apply particularly to the north was the well-known 'Statute for the administration of natives'. Speranskiy himself was especially anxious to see justice done to the natives, and to end their ruthless exploitation by Russian traders. He wished also to preserve what was best in their national culture. For the purposes of the Statute, which of course applied to the whole of Siberia, he classed native peoples as either 'settled', 'nomadic', or 'vagrant', with different procedures for each. The northern peoples were in the last two groups, and the principles underlying their treatment were that administration was to be based on their own customs, their internal autonomy was to be left untouched, their trade and industry protected, and their taxes made proportional to their abilities.[1] These were exemplary aims, and if their execution was less praiseworthy than their intention, that is not the point to be made now. Here it is necessary only to emphasise that the application of the Statute involved activity at the local level, and not just law-giving at St Petersburg or Irkutsk. A 'Steppe Duma' (a forum for nomads) was actually set up in 1825 at Yakutsk, and functioned for a decade. The second fur-tribute commission was closely concerned with implementation of the Statute, one of its jobs being to distinguish between 'nomads' and 'vagrants'. These two manifestations of government concern for the north were thus inter-related, and both were concerned with the native peoples. This last is no accident, for at all times the natives easily outnumbered the Russian population.

Nor, perhaps, is it an accident that the first fur-tribute commission was set up by Catherine the Great. For she was actively interested in promoting settlement, mainly in the fertile plains of south Russia as a bulwark against the Turks, but also in Siberia. Her difficulty was to find settlers without undermining the institution of serfdom by settling serfs in new areas in better conditions than they had had with their old masters, and this proved very restricting. But she was a monarch who, *par excellence*, had the imperial outlook, and she surely saw Siberia in that light. Her settlement schemes, however, were in the south or the Baykal region. But it was in her reign that

---

[1] The substance of Speranskiy's reform of native administration has been summarised in Raeff (1956), pp. 112–28.

settlement of the road to Yakutsk was undertaken as a link in imperial communications. So here again is evidence of conscious awareness of the north and of at least some of its potentialities.

Able and honest administrators were few. Food distribution often went wrong. Shortages were among the perennial difficulties in all parts of the north, and cases are on record of grain being available in government stores, but not being distributed to starving local inhabitants because authority to do so was lacking.[1] It is not hard to find examples of the inefficient performance of the other duties also, but the results were generally less disastrous.

Before the nineteenth century schooling and medical care were almost wholly neglected. Apart from the so-called garrison schools at Yakutsk and Okhotsk in the eighteenth century, the first school for natives in the Yakut province was a missionary school opened at the Spasskiy monastery at Yakutsk in 1801. In the next 25 years other non-Church schools opened, not only at Yakutsk, but at Olekminsk, Nizhnekolymsk, and Vilyuysk. By 1911 there were 114, with 3140 pupils, representing 11 pupils per 1000 population, but this was a quarter the proportion in, for instance, Irkutskaya Guberniya.[2] In 1911, the Yakut province was the poorest off for medical care in all Asiatic Russia, with one doctor per 25,000 inhabitants and per 350,000 square versts.[3] Administrative services were thus at the most primitive level.

Migration policy might give a yardstick by which to judge the government's intentions in the north of Siberia. Since Siberia was first overrun by the Russians, a gradually increasing stream of settlers went there from European Russia, and this stream the government was continually, and generally unsuccessfully, trying to control.[4] The government normally did pursue a policy in this struggle, and the changes in that policy might be a helpful indication. But here again, as in so many other contexts, the north is over-shadowed by the south, and government policy, while nominally concerned with the whole of Siberia, is dictated by the needs of the

[1] In a study of Speranskiy's work in Siberia, Vagin (1872) devotes the whole of his chapter 9 to food-supply problems.

[2] Glinka (1914), p. 260; Bakhrushin (1955 *b*), pp. 43–4. Maynov (1912), appendix 1, pp. 5–6, lists only 44 schools.

[3] Glinka (1914), p. 279.

[4] Glinka (1914), pp. 440–99. Treadgold (1957) deals with the period from 1860 to 1914.

much more important southern regions. The significance for the north of such events as, for instance, Speranskiy's measures permitting free immigration of state serfs into underpopulated regions, and making it easier for the ex-convict to settle, cannot be assessed.

The conclusion that may be drawn, then, is that the Russian government was always aware of its northern territory: at first clearly and purposefully, when there was economic advantage to be derived from it, later dimly, when the territory contributed much less. In this second period, say from 1700, the routine administration was carried on as much by the force of inertia as by any stimulus from above. But, at however primitive a level, carried on it was, and that, in face of the unremitting pressure of a most unpromising environment, must be reckoned an achievement.

FOREIGN INFLUENCES

It has been said or implied on more than one occasion in the preceding chapters that the ease with which the Russians occupied the north, and the looseness and inefficiency of their administration, are in part results of the virtual absence of any interference by foreign powers. Broadly speaking, this is true: there was never a direct threat by another country capable of taking and occupying large parts of the territory. But there were various lesser threats or pressures of an indirect nature, and these were not without their influence on the course of events.

The earliest foreign influences, which were also the most serious, were those affecting settlement on the White Sea littoral, and they extended in time up to the early seventeenth century, and in space up to the sea approaches to the Ob'. At many periods, but particularly in the twelfth and thirteenth centuries, the land to the west of the White Sea was in dispute. There was much fighting with the Swedes in the late sixteenth and early seventeenth centuries in the White Sea region. The Solovetskiy monastery was the main Russian defensive centre, a position it held right into the nineteenth century. There were more conflicts in the region in the time of Peter the Great, the enemy again being Sweden. And in the nineteenth century, there were two assaults by Britain on the White Sea approaches to Russia, and on each occasion Kola was attacked: one was during the

Napoleonic wars in 1808–10, and the other during the Crimean war in 1854–55.[1] But after 1701 these were incidental threats, the by-product of much more important ones aimed at the Russian state itself. Furthermore, these threats did not extend eastwards beyond the immediate vicinity of the White Sea.

It was only when the Russians reached right across Siberia that contact was again made with any potential rival. Rivalry with China may be ignored, for this, although real enough from the middle of the seventeenth century onwards, never affected the north. The first instance was a curious one, for the rival was no one more formidable than the natives of Alaska. According to Belov,[2] the Senate was genuinely worried in the middle of the eighteenth century about a possible threat to the far north-east from the combined forces of the Chukchi (still unsubdued) and the 'Alaskans'. It was this which prompted the establishment of a garrison at Anadyrsk after the sea route to Kamchatka had been opened, and from 1765 at Gizhiginsk. The cost of maintaining this garrison was out of all proportion to the revenue derived from the territory; from 1727 to 1751 it cost a million roubles, against income from furs of 22,000 roubles. This seems to argue a determination on the part of Moscow not to risk losing the Asiatic shore of Bering Strait. But this threat was replaced by another which was more serious.

Towards the end of the eighteenth century, after Bering's voyages had created Russian interest in the North Pacific and beyond, the attention of other European powers was directed there also—notably France and Britain. James Cook called at Petropavlovsk in 1779—his was the first foreign vessel to do so—and La Pérouse followed some years later. These voyages stimulated Catherine the Great into commissioning the elaborate and expensive North Eastern Expedition of 1785–93 under Joseph Billings. But there was no question of the expedition itself being prepared to defend north-east Siberia. On the contrary, Catherine's instructions emphasised that 'English, French, or other European ships' were to be met in friendly fashion, and there was to be 'not the least cause for quarrels and conflicts'.[3] Her object was presumably to show the flag, notice what others might be doing, and, as openly avowed, to find out more about that

[1] Trofimov (1961), pp. 52–9, 92–5.
[2] Belov (1956), pp. 408–9.　　　　　　　[3] Sarychev (1952), p. 35.

part of the Empire. On land, however, there were some defensive preparations, notably in Kamchatka after La Pérouse had called there in 1787.[1]

This manoeuvring in the North Pacific did not lead to any change, or even to any very energetic Russian measures, on the Asiatic mainland; although it is worth noting that Kamchatka in 1823 cost the government twice the income derived from it, the loss presumably being accepted for strategic reasons.[2] But it did lead to pressure on the Alaskan colonies, and finally to their abandonment. But Alaska is a special case, and such pressures were clearly inevitable there. It would be wrong to conclude from the Alaskan example that the Russian grip on northern territory was so weak that it gave way as soon as determined rivals were encountered. Other factors, such as the distance from the seat of Russian power, and the lack of sufficient strength at sea to maintain communications at such range, made any tenacious grip there unlikely in the first place.

During the nineteenth century American influence gradually replaced that of Britain and France. The growth of American whaling in the North Pacific was its first manifestation. Speranskiy was a little worried about the possible effects of the whalers and others establishing trading posts on the Siberian coast and by their commercial ability gaining influence and power.[3] He was far sighted, for this is what happened half a century later. Traders started calling regularly at Chukotka and Kamchatka. One commercial enterprise, although short-lived, was on a large scale. This was the Western Union Telegraph Company's project to lay a cable from New York to Paris by way of Bering Strait. The Company's agents were very active in north-east Siberia in 1865–67,[4] and satisfactory progress was being made in planning the route, when the trans-Atlantic cable was completed and the whole idea became quite uneconomic. There were no other large enterprises, but the volume of trading by a number of small firms, many of them one-man, was considerable. The activity increased after the Alaskan purchase, because the traders could then operate from much closer bases.[5] The Ostrova Komandorskiye (Commander Islands), off the east coast of Kamchatka, were leased

[1] Belov (1956), p. 358. [2] Okun' (1935), p. 117.
[3] Raeff (1956), p. 43. [4] Kennan (1910).
[5] D'yachkov (1893), p. 44.

to various American trading companies continuously from 1871 to 1917.[1]

By the beginning of the twentieth century the situation had reached a point at which the Russian government started to feel that its sovereignty was really being challenged. Several American trading concerns active in Chukotka had merged in 1902 to form the North East Siberia Company, which was registered in Russia but controlled from the U.S.A., and its proprietary behaviour was such that it was dissolved in 1912 by official direction.[2] Meanwhile a most ambitious scheme was put forward by the French railway engineer Loïcq de Lobel in 1900 for the construction of a railway line between New York and Paris, with a tunnel to carry it under Bering Strait. The idea had been mentioned in broad terms as early as 1870, and attracted the attention of a number of American businessmen. De Lobel, and, apparently, Edward Harriman, the American railway magnate, tried very hard to obtain a concession in the early years of this century, but it was finally refused by the Russian government in 1907.[3] In 1911 Russian ships for the first time made trading voyages to the Kolyma from the Pacific, and one of the reasons for initiating this unprofitable enterprise was to show the Russian flag in an area of increasing American influence and offer an alternative source of supplies to the local inhabitants. While it was the supposed challenge to sovereignty that motivated the government, Soviet historians are always anxious to point out that, in addition, the American traders exploited the native population most shamelessly. This may be true, but the intentions of Russian traders were surely just as dishonourable. The main difference was probably that the Americans were more effective. Governmental measures did not, however, put a stop to the activity, which continued until Soviet power was firmly established, some years after 1917.

The American influence was thus quite strong for half a century or so, along the Pacific seaboard as far south as Kamchatka. This influence was always a manifestation of private enterprise, and never of interest on the part of the United States government. But governments could find it useful to shelter behind the activities of

[1] Ye. P. Orlova (1962), p. 5.

[2] Slavin (1949*a*), pp. 136–42. This article is very anti-American in tone, but the main facts it quotes are likely to be correct. See also Okun' (1935), pp. 145–7.

[3] Slavin (1949*a*), pp. 142–53; Slavin (1949*b*); Stefánsson (1958), pp. 294–322.

private individuals, as no one knew better than the Russian government, which had used the Russian-American Company for precisely that purpose. So there was reasonable cause for suspicion on the part of the Russians.

There was even more cause for suspicion in the case of Japanese activities in Kamchatka, for this threat, although it lasted for a shorter time, was more closely linked with state power. There had been rivalry between Japan and Russia over Sakhalin and the Ostrova Kuril'skiye (Kurils) in the eighteenth and nineteenth centuries, and this had been temporarily resolved by the award of the former to Russia and the latter to Japan under the Treaty of St Petersburg in 1875.[1] But the resounding Japanese victory in the Russo-Japanese War altered the situation. Under the Treaty of Portsmouth (1905) Japan acquired the sole rights to fishing in Russian Far Eastern waters. A ten-year fisheries convention was signed in 1907, and this opened Kamchatka to the Japanese. Soon 20,000 Japanese fishery workers were going to Kamchatka each summer, organised by Kumiai, the Japanese association of fishing interests.[2] This constituted a threat about which Russia could do little, because it was within the terms of a signed agreement. Here again, it was not until some years after the Revolution that Soviet power was sufficiently strong in the region to end the threat.

Foreign influence affected government policy not only from without but from within. Non-Russians played a considerable part in exploration and exploitation of the Siberian north. Some were prisoners of war or exiles; Swedes and Poles have already been instanced. Others were private citizens, often distinguished, in the Russian service: scientists like Georg Steller and the half-brothers Louis de Lisle de la Croyère and Joseph Delisle, invited to work in Russia in pursuance of Peter the Great's plan of building up a Russian Academy of Sciences with foreign help; seamen like Vitus Bering, Sven Waxell and Joseph Billings. Later there were also business men, such as the British officials of Lena Goldfields Ltd., and Jonas Lied of Norway who pioneered trading into the river Yenisey. And there were travellers like Adolf Erman, the German geographer, or John Cochrane, the retired British naval officer, who spent a year or two in remote parts, and both by their presence there

[1] Harrison (1953), pp. 11–56.   [2] Gapanovich (1933), vol. 1, pp. 122–4.

as intelligent and observant people, and by their published accounts, were not without some small influence on the places they visited. There were, in fact, many foreigners in this category in the 300 years under review. It is true that through them information often leaked out of the country against the wishes of the always secretive government. They cannot really be described as serious security threats, however, for they made their contribution to Russia as individuals rather than as representatives of another nation. Their presence and activities, therefore, do not affect the main conclusion, which is that Russia's settlement of most of her northern territory was carried out in the absence of foreign pressures. Only in the extreme west and the extreme east was this not so. In the west the frontier, once defined in the thirteenth century, proved surprisingly stable, but the relatively close proximity of powerful neighbours caused later trouble. In the east Russia over-reached herself, and there was no stability until she fell back to the natural frontier of the Pacific Ocean. Thereafter, the indirect pressure of commercial penetration by both Americans and Japanese constituted a threat to much of the Pacific seaboard. Although counter-measures were taken by the Russian government, this threat was not extinguished until after the revolution of 1917.

PLATE XIII

(*a*) Yakut dwelling in winter (Boulitchoff, 1856).

(*b*) Kultuchnoye, a Koryak village in Kamchatka (Boulitchoff, 1856).

PLATE XIV

(*a*) A caravan of dog sledges in northern Kamchatka (Poulitchoff, 1856).

(*b*) A halting point on the trunk road to Okhotsk (Boulitchoff, 1856).

6

RELATIONS WITH THE NATIVES

When the Russians came into the north, the territory was not empty; the settlers were in a small minority until well after the Revolution. This was not as apparent as might be supposed, because the natives were spread so thinly over such a vast area that it was not difficult for the Russians to achieve local superiority. It is relevant to the history of settlement to know something of the relations which existed between the two groups. Certain facts have been mentioned already in other connections, but it is desirable to see if any general impression can be formed.

As might be expected, relations started by being bad, for the immediate purpose of the Russians was to obtain pelts, and this commonly meant forcing natives to hand them over. In addition there was the inevitable resentment at the intrusion of foreigners, but the impact of the intrusion was lessened by the abundance of space and the comparative ease with which the natives could withdraw out of reach. So there was initially hostility: from the Nentsy (or Samoyed), who attacked the party establishing Mangazeya in 1601, often harried the annual re-supply expeditions as they came from Tobol'sk (witness Cherkasov's report quoted on pp. 33–5), and worried Russians in the Pechora basin, at Pustozersk and elsewhere; from the Khanty (Ostyak) and Mansi (Vogul) of the lower Ob'; from the Ket of the Yenisey; from the Tungus (Evenki) on the Verkhnyaya Tunguska; and from the Yakut.[1] The first intrusion of the Russians was often bloody, and led to unrest and even risings. The Nentsy seem to have been the most pugnacious, but they were unable to rally a large enough force to be effective. One of the few significant revolts against Russian occupation was that of the Yakut in 1642, brought about largely by the repressive policy of the first *voyevoda*, P. P. Golovin.[2] There were others later, notably in 1681 when Yakutsk itself was burnt. But the *voyevoda*, Ivan Preklonskiy, wisely avoided taking bloodthirsty revenge. Having counter-attacked and

---

[1] Bakhrushin (1955a), pp. 80, 98, 220–5; (1955b), pp. 5–12, 37, 122–3.
[2] Tokarev (1957), pp. 68–70.

defeated them, he left them alone and they were quickly pacified.[1]
Indeed, the Russians by no means always took the obvious line of
repression in dealing with the natives whose lands they occupied.
From the time of Yermak, the Russians cultivated the friendship of
the Khanty chiefs of the Koda region on the lower Ob' near Berezov,
and were able to make use of their armed forces against other tribes.
The Koda chiefs had to recognise the Russians as overlords, but in
return the Russians were prepared to help them assert their own
authority over their Khanty subjects.[2] The standard way of holding
the natives in subjection, once their lands had been overrun, was by
the taking of hostages. The operation of this system continued well
into the eighteenth century; hostages are mentioned at Turukhansk
in 1735 and in the Yakut province in 1740.[3]

In most areas, after initial unrest, there was unbroken peace. But
this should not be taken as meaning that the spirit had gone out of
the natives, much less that they were too depleted numerically to
cause trouble. The reason is that apart from the payment of fur
tribute (and, admittedly, there were abuses in the collection of that
payment), the Russians were quite content to permit the natives to
do much as they liked. Bakhrushin, thinking mainly of the Yakut
province, wrote in 1927:[4] 'In contrast to the western European
colonisers of the seventeenth and eighteenth centuries, the Russians,
at least, did not exterminate the native peoples, did not enslave
them, and did not destroy their original qualities (*samobytnost'*)'. An
observant English traveller in Siberia in the 1840's noted with
approval, again in connection with the Yakut, that 'the terms of the
Russian contact with the wild man are free from the ferocity of that
of the Spaniards, and from the uncompromising character of that
of the English'.[5] The traditional 'protection' that the colonising
power generally claims it is affording to the inhabitants of its colonies
did mean something, in so far as inter-tribal conflicts were reduced,
and a real attempt was made to save the natives from the worst
exploitation. For instance, trade in alcohol was prohibited at an
early stage, because it was known that the natives would part with
their best furs in order to obtain it.[6] There were strict instructions

[1] Maydel' (1893–96), vol. 2, pp. 506–8.   [2] Bakhrushin (1955*b*), pp. 122–3.
[3] Gmelin (1767), vol. 2, p. 58; Krasheninnikov (1949), p. 519.
[4] Bakhrushin (1955*b*), p. 37.   [5] Hill (1854), vol. 2, p. 186.
[6] Krasovskiy (1895), pp. 168–9.

as to how fur-tribute collectors should behave, and Russians were forbidden to encroach on native hunting grounds.[1] Furthermore, Russians in the Yakut province were forbidden by an edict of 1685 to buy furs direct from natives in private deals, but obliged to make their purchases at the recognised fairs, where there was some sort of official supervision.[2] Later, and again in the Yakut province, there was apparently legislation forbidding the advancing of more than five roubles credit to natives, in order to prevent the latter becoming wholly dependent on unscrupulous money-lenders.[3] Soviet historians are quick to add that such measures were dictated by the desire to keep fur-tribute returns as high as possible. This may be so—indeed, in some cases it was explicitly stated. But a motive of self-interest does not alter the fact that the official attitude was a humane one. The real trouble was that these well-intentioned laws were widely disobeyed, and the administration was too corrupt to rectify the situation. More positively, however, the coming of the Russians did benefit the natives in certain practical ways. One of the earliest was by the introduction of agriculture, which was taken up, although in a very small way, by some of the northern peoples, in particular the Yakut.

By the eighteenth century, then, there was little trouble with the natives in the greater part of the north. The Yakut, Khanty and Tungus were quiet. Even the Nentsy were very helpful to Malygin of the Great Northern Expedition during his explorations of their shores in 1736–38. But in the more recently occupied Pacific seaboard all was by no means yet quiet. The turbulent Chukchi were actively and openly resisting until Pavlutskiy's campaigns of 1730–32 and 1744–47, and they remained hostile for many years after that, accepting subjection to Russia only in 1789. The Chukchi wars were small in scale, the forces under Pavlutskiy and his successors seldom numbering more than 200 men, but they were perhaps the bitterest conflicts since Yermak fought Kuchum. Afanasiy Shestakov, the leader of a cossack force, was killed in Koryak territory in 1729, and between 1745 and 1756 the Koryak also were in a more or less continuous state of revolt.[4] In Kamchatka there was a large-scale rising of the Kamchadal against the Russians in 1731. Some of these

---

[1] Fisher (1943), pp. 73–4.   [2] Voyevodskiy nakaz (1842), p. 204.
[3] Cottrell (1842), p. 110.   [4] Okun' (1935), pp. 50–86.

conflicts were due to the natural feelings of independence in a proud people, but in the case of the Kamchadal an irritant was the increased burden on the natives caused by Bering's first expedition of 1725–30, which made heavy demands on native labour and also caused an increase in fur tribute.[1] The Kamchadal chose a moment when most cossacks in Kamchatka had been summoned to reinforce Pavlutskiy's force fighting the Chukchi, and peace was restored only after some time and with difficulty; cossacks were still being murdered in 1740. But here again a surprisingly lenient view was taken once the revolt was put down. The Empress Elizabeth reduced the fur tribute to one pelt per head per year, and allowed the Kamchadal to be ruled by their own leaders. There was no more trouble after this.[2]

It remained true that the official attitude towards natives, once subjected, was liberal. Admittedly payment of fur tribute continued; and a new burden was imposed in the form of the obligation to maintain postal and transportation services. This weighed rather heavily along the road to Yakutsk and Okhotsk, especially when it was necessary to transport undertakings like Bering's expeditions— fortunately an infrequent occurrence. Later in the century Russian peasants were brought in as *yamshchiki*, and the obligation on the natives was thus somewhat reduced. It is quite clear that the natives were not enslaved. Their existing system of government, if it could be so called, was retained. This was not disadvantageous to the Russians, for it was following the pattern set in the case of the Khanty chiefs on the lower Ob'. But it brings down the wrath of Marxist historians, who see in it an alliance between ruling classes to continue exploitation of the masses.

The best example of this is found in the Yakut province, as the national home of the largest and most advanced northern people. There were cases of aristocratic natives attaining high positions in the administrative system. Trifonov, a Yakut, became *voyevoda* in 1724, and Starostin, another, became assistant *voyevoda* in 1769.[3] Indeed, the Yakut 'nobility' in the time of Catherine the Great thought it should have equivalent status to the Russian nobility, but this was not granted. A government official, travelling in the region in the early part of the nineteenth century, noted the mal-

[1] Belov (1956), p. 254.   [2] Ditmar (1900), p. 177.
[3] Maynov (1927), p. 375.

treatment of Yakut by their own chiefs.[1] Even if the Yakut or
Kamchadal chiefs, buttressed by Russia, did continue to oppress
their subjects, this was no worse than the behaviour of the Russian
oligarchy towards its own people. It might, of course, have been
considerably worse, had any ideas of racial superiority been given
currency. But this was not the case. The liberal trend continued,
and by an edict of the Governor of Irkutsk in 1808 Russians were
forbidden to live in Yakut regions. At the same time, individual
natives responded by rendering very considerable service to the
Russian cause. A case in point is N. I. Daurkin, a Chukchi who
accompanied Russian expeditions in the far north-east during the
period 1761–95 and was most useful, not only as interpreter and go-
between, but as a traveller and observer in his own right.[2]

A liberal official policy, however, did not preclude cruelty and
exploitation by individuals. As the number of Russians in native
territory increased, so did exploitation. Something has been said
already on the behaviour of Russian merchants in various parts of
the north. Grigoriy Shelikhov, the prime mover of the Russian-
American Company, was one of the worst.[3] His behaviour towards
the natives of the Aleutian Islands in the second half of the eighteenth
century was extremely cruel, and he even boasted of this. Another
example of oppression by individuals was the practice in Kamchatka
at this time whereby cossacks demanded *yasyr'*, a 'woman tribute'
parallel to *yasak*. This naturally aroused the strongest feelings.[4]
Vrangel', on his way from Yakutsk to the Kolyma in 1820, reported
that some Yakut he met complained bitterly of the oppression they
had suffered at the hands of the cossacks of Yakutsk. Native numbers
had dropped since the arrival of the Russians, he said, and 'some
numerous races have left only their names behind'.[5]

It was the continuing discrepancy between the liberal attitude of
the state and the extortionate practices of individuals which led to
Speranskiy's concern. His reforms as expressed in the statute of 1822
on the native peoples were directed at improving their lot and
reducing the opportunities for exploitation by Russians. His aim, in
Raeff's opinion,[6] was to achieve the organic amalgamation of the

[1] Dobell (1830), vol. 2, pp. 38–9.   [2] Alekseyev (1961).
[3] Pypin (1892), p. 253.   [4] Gapanovich (1933), vol. 1, p. 53.
[5] Vrangel' (1840), pp. 25, 186.   [6] Raeff (1956), p. 114.

natives into the Russian community. This was not to be a russianisation imposed from above, and no violence was to be used. Such points as prohibition of alcohol and of settlement by Russians in native territory were re-emphasised. Both the aim and the measures designed to achieve it were very laudable, and the statute remained in force for nearly a century. But in the north it does not really seem to have had as much effect as might have been expected. This was due partly to shortcomings in the statute itself, such as the absence of any provision for punishing offenders; and partly to the remoteness of some of the regions to which it applied—it is very unlikely that the Chukchi, for instance, were affected by it at all. The Soviet history of the Yakut province goes so far as to say that 'the harmonious system of rules of the statute turned out to be in many ways lifeless and unrealisable'.[1] Certainly the old practices continued.

In 1851, the normal trade rate with Tungus and Lamut was two leaves of Circassian tobacco for a squirrel pelt—the difference in value at Moscow being a factor of the order of several hundred. The Chukchi, it is noticeable, were able to demand the rather better price of up to three pounds of tobacco for a red fox pelt.[2] Later in the century, a Russian visiting the Surgut area on the Ob' writes of the natives' disease and poverty, the latter being largely due to exploitation by visiting dealers in fur and fish from Tobol'sk and Samara. The only cultural influence the Russians have had on the Khanty here, he says, was the introduction of drunkenness and syphilis.[3] Substantially the same was true of the Kamchadal, and they in fact became so debased as a national group that only a minority could still speak their own language.[4] Another damning account, the equal of anything written in the seventeenth century, refers to the Yenisey north in the 1880's:

The grasping nature of the Yenisey traders has reached its climax. The natives are quite enslaved by them and will never be able to free themselves from debt, and are therefore in a hopeless situation and completely dependent on the traders. The history of Siberia shows clearly the merciless

[1] Tokarev (1957), p. 171.
[2] Ditmar (1890), pp. 491–2.   [3] Shvetsov (1888), pp. 59, 72–3.
[4] Ditmar (1890), pp. 205, 489. If the term Kamchadal were used in the sense of a Russian-Itel'men mixture, this would not be surprising. But it was normally a synonym for Itel'men, and no doubt is so used here.

exploitation of natives by all who are in a position to do so, from the bread shop managers, rich peasants, cossacks, traders, and local clergy to the duly constituted authorities.[1]

This was written by a merchant and owner of gold mines. The Governor of Arkhangel'skaya Guberniya reported a similar situation among the Nentsy after he had visited them in 1912.[2]

And yet, despite all this, the numbers of many groups grew between the Russian conquest and the census of 1897. This is made clear by the painstaking work of the ethnographer, B. O. Dolgikh, who reconstructed from archive materials the numbers and distribution of the native groups in Siberia when the Russians first arrived.[3] The aggregate increase for the north as defined in Map 1 was from about 104,000 to 310,000, the most striking example of growth being the Yakut, who increased from 28,500 to 226,000. In general, Dolgikh ascribes growth to the introduction of Russian agricultural methods, and to the stopping of inter-tribal warfare. There were decreases too, but they were much smaller in absolute terms. They caused, however, deep concern among ethnographers in the late nineteenth and early twentieth centuries, who feared, with justification, that extinction threatened some of them.[4] In this connection Dolgikh brings evidence to show that groups whose names disappeared did not necessarily die out, but were often assimilated into other groups. In the same way, the decrease of the Asiatic Eskimo from 4000 to 1300 is largely explained by their assimilation into the Chukchi. This is not to deny, of course, that exploitation also took its toll, as did epidemic diseases introduced by the conquerors. Certain of the smaller groups, such as the Kamchadal, were particularly hard hit.

While the Russian authorities normally did not deport natives, there were some instances of natives being used as settlers. One was the settling of Yakut in Kamchatka in the nineteenth century. The Governor, Stanitskiy, arranged for some Yakut to settle in 1820 at a place which became known as Yakutskiye Klyuchi, on the south side of Avachinskaya Guba, the bay on which Petropavlovsk stands. Some other Yakut accompanied a group of Russian peasant settlers who were established on a small river flowing into the same bay in

---

[1] Latkin (1892), p. 182.
[2] Bibikov (1912), p. 117, quoted in Trofimov (1961), p. 238.
[3] Dolgikh (1960a), pp. 615–21. See Appendix I, table 2.
[4] For instance, Yadrintsev (1891), Patkanov (1911).

1825. But neither settlement appeared to be still functioning 30 years later.[1] A second example relates to the settling of Nentsy in Novaya Zemlya. Ten families were sent there in 1877, and constituted the first known permanent population of the islands, apart from one family which had come in 1869; and in 1894 eight more families volunteered to join them. Thus by 1898 there were 102 Nentsy in Novaya Zemlya, distributed between the three settlements of Malyye Karmakuly, Matochkin Shar and Belush'ya Guba on the south island.[2] A few Russians were with them, including a priest and a medical attendant. This experiment seems to have worked well, for there is still a native population there according to recent Soviet ethnographic maps (see Map 9, p. 185).

There is a remarkable consistency in the history of the relations between Russians and natives in the north. Over almost the whole period a mild and humane official attitude is stultified by the un-controlled, or unsuccessfully controlled, actions of individual exploiters. Corruption and greed were so prevalent among those responsible for executing the policy that it remained to a consider-able extent a dead letter. Alcohol, long prohibited for excellent reasons, was always to be found—at a greatly inflated price. And yet once Russian sovereignty had been firmly established, there was not often open conflict between Russian and native, in spite of the latter's superiority in numbers, and his causes for grievance. Most northern peoples were no doubt too unorganised, while the more advanced ones, like the Yakut, perhaps perceived that no lasting advantages would be likely to result from a conflict, or, more likely, preferred to express their resentment in other ways. In any case, it can never have been too difficult for any native who really wanted to have nothing to do with the Russians, to retire into the forest and lead his traditional life unmolested. To the Russian credit it must be said that there does not seem to be any evidence of the existence of racial prejudice at any time.

So the Russians were always the gainers, acquiring the territory and its riches and many new subjects. But perhaps one of the most important things they gained was the technique of living in this environment. Wherever they settled, there were always natives in the vicinity before them, demonstrating not only the possibility of

[1] Ditmar (1890), pp. 689, 695.   [2] Engelhardt (1899), pp. 172, 200.

existence, but probably also the most efficient way of supporting it. Not all native techniques were borrowed, by any means. If the traditional Russian peasant's hut (*izba*) could still be constructed from local materials, and if it would still function effectively, then its use would continue. But in certain matters of clothing, in most matters of food and its procurement, and in much concerned with transport, the Russian copied the native. There has apparently been little study of these influences, but they were clearly widespread.[1] The 'Yakutisation' already mentioned was an extreme form, where virtually the whole of the alien culture was accepted by the incoming Russians. At a less extreme level, Russians who could not be said to have 'gone native' borrowed such things as fur upper garments from tundra dwellers, and accepted the predominantly fish diet of the forest peoples. A taste for frozen fish and frozen reindeer meat, especially marrow, grew among the Russians on the lower Ob'. On the Yenisey, Russians took over various local types of household implements. The use of dogs and reindeer as draught animals was learnt from northern natives, and appropriate sledge types were most probably taken over too (see Pl. XIV). Native boats, which were chiefly lightweight dug-out canoes, were used, but only on local trips. For long-range transport with heavy loads, as noted earlier, the Russians had their own bigger boats of more advanced design. In the case of all these techniques, the native idea, once taken over, did not necessarily remain unmodified. The Russians could introduce improvements suggested by their own more advanced technology. But the important fact is that the Russians learnt from the natives. Moreover, this was facilitated by the fact that in almost all parts of the north, and at almost all periods, there was free intermarriage between the two.

[1] Some indications will be found in Shvetsov (1888), pp. 66–72; Yadrintsev (1891), pp. 167–201; Alekseyenko (1961), p. 97; Levin & Potapov (1961), pp. 62, 116; Dolgikh (1960*b*).

PART III

SETTLEMENT SINCE 1917

7

THE NUMBERS OF SETTLERS

Up to this point interest has centred upon the slow growth of tiny islands of Russian settlement over many centuries, and now, suddenly, in a period of less than half a century, the situation is entirely transformed. Soviet rule has led, in a variety of ways, to an astonishing increase in settlement, and, by comparison with this, the preceding period becomes no more than an introduction to the story. For this reason it is appropriate to deal with the Soviet period separately.

The last pre-revolutionary population figures quoted in chapter 3 were mostly from the census of 1897. There have been three Soviet censuses, in 1926, 1939, and 1959. The results of these are not easily comparable, chiefly because of changes in the boundaries of the administrative areas for which population figures are published. Moreover, the information required is of the national composition of particular outlying regions, and only the fullest results include it. The 1939 census is of no value in this connection, because only generalised results were published. The complete results of the 1959 census are not yet available, but enough has been published to give some useful indications. The full picture is not, therefore, obtainable, but the general impression that can be gained is not likely to be misleading.

The rough estimate was made earlier[1] that there were probably 40,000–50,000 Russians in the north as defined on Map 1 at the turn of the twentieth century. By 1926, there were about 100,000 in roughly the same area, and in 1959 there were about 1,600,000. This information emerges from a study of the results of the censuses of 1926 and 1959. An area approximating to that on Map 1 can be pieced together from the administrative areas for which results were declared in each case. These approximations are not an exact fit, territorially speaking, either with each other or with Map 1, but the error is under 10 per cent. On this reckoning, in round figures, the total population of the north was 460,000 in 1926 and 2,000,000 in

[1] See p. 58.

1959. The number of Russians in the area in 1926 was 100,000, most of the remaining 360,000 being northern peoples. The 1959 census results do not show the number of Russians in all parts of the area; but rough estimates can be made for those parts for which no figures are given, and the census results do show that the northern peoples have remained almost stationary in numbers. From these indications it may be deduced that the Russians in 1959 must have numbered about 1,600,000.[1] Between 1926 and 1959, therefore, the Russians increased by a factor of 15 or 16, from a position of a 1:3 minority to that of a 4:1 majority in relation to the natives— a remarkable change for the space of one generation.

The question of the reliability of Soviet census figures is one that requires comment. The 1926 census is generally accepted as having been an honest attempt to determine the true position in the country, although, in the case of the northern peoples, some small mistakes were made and later admitted. The 1939 census results, on the other hand, are suspect, for there can be little doubt that the reason the full results were never published was that they would have revealed many facts about the tremendous internal upheavals of the 1930's which the government wanted to hide. The 1959 census results, at least those relevant to this inquiry, seem plausible, for they are not particularly flattering to Soviet policy towards the native peoples. They will be used widely in this chapter. It is certain that one group of importance, and likely that another, has not been included in the figure of 1,600,000 mentioned above as the total number of Russians living in the north in 1959. These groups are members of the armed services and convicts. It is stated in the census results[2] that service men are listed as at their place of recruitment. It is possible that they were enumerated in the field, as the census instructions in fact required, but it seems likely that they, and also the convicts, may have been enumerated from records held centrally, as being administratively much more convenient. The reasons why the service men certainly, and the convicts probably, are not shown at their place of residence in the published results, appear to be two: first, the obvious advantages of security and, secondly, the principal users of the census results are the local authorities, who have to provide public services

---

[1] The basis for these figures is given in Appendix III. See also Armstrong (1962).
[2] Itogi (1963), p. 7.

for their regions, and they will not be interested in the population in service or detention camps.[1]

The distribution of the very rapidly growing immigrant population depends, of course, on its occupations, so the two things must clearly be considered together. The classification used in chapter 4 for the pre-revolutionary colonists cannot be closely adhered to. For instance, 'servants of the state' becomes a useless heading, and religious groups no longer played a part. But some of the other groups are still relevant. First, and most important, are the miners. It was the exploitation of vast newly discovered mineral deposits which brought in the greater part of the newcomers. Next in importance are those employed in transport and communications. A third group is composed of food producers and workers on the land, mainly farmers and fishermen (combining the hunters and peasants of chapter 4); and a fourth includes sundry categories not sufficiently prominent to be listed separately—the administrators being perhaps the most numerous of them. Finally, overlapping the miners and some of the other groups too, there is the convict labour, of great significance in this period. Although the Tsarist government sent many people to Siberia, comparatively few reached northern regions. But the Soviet government not only sent a great many people, but made a much more serious attempt to use them to economic advantage, and therefore directed many to the north.

It is not practical to try to trace the stages of growth during the Soviet period, for lack of data. It is possible and desirable, however, to try to gain some picture of the position in the late 1950's. This is a rough guide to the maximum growth attained up to the time of writing (1963); but it is no more than rough, for there is evidence that in some cases higher population levels had been reached earlier.

[1] Newth (1962).

8

THE CHARACTER OF
THE SETTLEMENT

Before 1917 there were two mining areas in the north, both for gold: in the Yenisey basin and the Lena basin. Both continued to exist, although the Yenisey goldfields had now become of minor importance, but they were quite overshadowed by a number of larger and more important mining developments which sprang up at widely separated points. Taken together, these developments unquestionably represent, for the greater part of the Soviet period, the most important activity going on in the north, and also that which has brought about the presence of most settlers.

In Murmanskaya Oblast' the foundations for a large extractive industry were laid in the 1920's by Academician A. Ye. Fersman, an economic geologist. The first mineral to be exploited was apatite (from which fertiliser is obtained), and the centre for this was the new town of Khibinogorsk, founded in 1929 and renamed Kirovsk in 1934. The apatite deposit is the richest in the world and supplies a large part of the Soviet demand. Kirovsk is therefore probably the most important of the Murmanskaya Oblast' mining centres, with a population of 39,000 in 1959.[1] In addition, and as part of the original Soviet development plan, the mining of nickel was started. For this, the town of Monchegorsk was created in 1935, and the first smelter went into operation in 1939. Copper and cobalt are also produced there. By 1959 the population was 45,500.[2] Another substantial nickel-mining centre in this area came into Russian hands in 1944, when Finland ceded the Pechenga (Petsamo) region, where the International Nickel Company had an important concession and had started operations. Here the mining centre of Nikel' has grown up.

Mention should also be made of a subsidiary product of the apatite

[1] A list of towns in northern U.S.S.R. with their 1959 population figures is given in Appendix II.
[2] Gladkov (1961).

PLATE XV

(*a*) Noril'sk in 1956: the town centre (*Soviet Weekly* photograph).

(*b*) Noril'sk in 1956: building in progress (*Soviet Weekly* photograph).

PLATE XVI

(*a*) Vorkuta in 1957 (*Soviet Union* photograph).

(*b*) Yakutsk in 1956: the Ministry of Finance (*Soviet Weekly* photograph).

mining, aluminium, which is obtained from the nepheline with which the apatite is associated. An aluminium refinery has been built at Kandalaksha, some 80 km. from Kirovsk, and partly accounts for the growth of Kandalaksha to 37,000 in 1959.[1] Murmanskaya Oblast' is, however, exceptional among northern mining areas in that there have been so many different developments that mining was not the chief cause of the increase in population (22,800 in 1926 to 567,700 in 1959, for an area which increased also, but by less than 10 per cent). The mining is likely, however, to have been responsible for about a third of the increase.

Moving eastwards, the next important mining area is the Pechora coalfield, of which the main centre is the Vorkuta region in the extreme north-east of Komi ASSR. The existence of coal here had been known for some time, and exploitation started on a small scale in 1933. During the Second World War the urgent need to replace output in over-run areas led to completion of a railway line to Vorkuta in 1942, and from then on expansion was rapid. Coal output is reported to have reached the level of 16,000,000 metric tons a year in 1957[2]—about $3\frac{1}{2}$ per cent of Soviet production for that year, and three-quarters of that of Scotland. The population of Vorkuta itself in 1959 was 55,000, but if its satellite mining settlements are added, the total population was 170,000.[3] Vorkuta had by now become a coal-producing centre of significance in the national economy, and replaced the Donbass for the supply of high grade coking coal to certain industrial regions, including Leningrad (see Pl. XVI*a*).

The lower Yenisey is the site of another large development of the Soviet period. A body of copper nickel sulphide ore was found near the mouth of the river at Noril'sk and was investigated geologically in 1925–26. The nickel was the principal attraction, for the Soviet Union was at that time without any source of her own, that at Monchegorsk having not yet been discovered. Exploitation started in 1940, after the site had been connected by railway with the river port of Dudinka. A refinery was constructed at Noril'sk. The copper was recovered as well as the nickel, for there was an acute shortage of copper in the country during the Second World War, and platinum was produced as a by-product of the nickel refining process. In 1939

[1] Dmitriyev (1959), pp. 53–100.
[2] Shishkin (1959), p. 84. [3] Korovitsin (1961), p. 55.

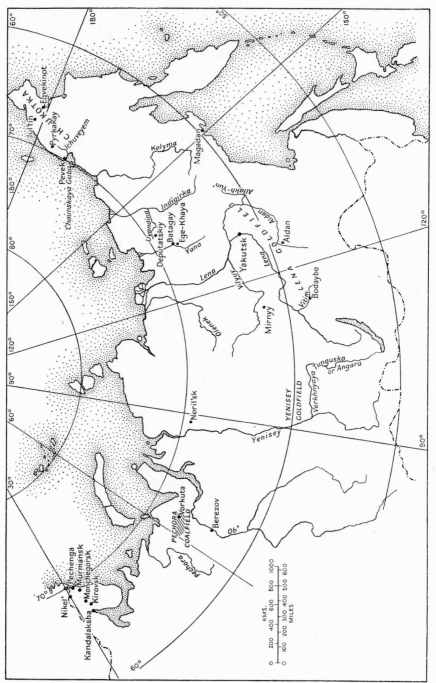

Map 4. Mining areas in the Soviet period.

the town of Noril'sk numbered 14,000, while in 1959 it was 109,000, or 122,000 with its satellites.[1] It entire *raison d'être* was mining, so that apart from administrative personnel and some local industry, the bulk of the population are directly concerned with the mines (see Pl. XV).

The goldfield in the upper Yenisey basin (Verkhnyaya Tunguska) is still worked, but it has become one of the smaller producing areas. Its output and labour force are not known, but the latter must be much smaller than that at Noril'sk.

Gold mining continues to be a major undertaking in Yakutskaya ASSR, and has expanded into new areas. The expansion is attributable to the increasing Soviet need for foreign currency. To the long-functioning placers on the Vitim (Bodaybo and environs) were added more on the Aldan around the town of Nezametnyy (renamed Aldan in 1939), where production started in 1923. The Aldan was one of the richest deposits of alluvial gold in the country when it was first worked, and it became the major mining area in Yakutskaya ASSR. Another new goldfield was found on the Allakh-Yun' River, further east, and work started there in 1939. Apparently even richer deposits were found further to the north-east on the upper Indigirka, and these also have been worked since 1945.[2] Output in Yakutskaya ASSR was said to be 20 per cent of the national total in the mid-1950's.[3] The town of Aldan had a population of 12,100 in 1959, the greater part of which must have been mine workers. But not all were necessarily gold miners, for another, lesser but vital, mining industry was also functioning in the neighbourhood—phlogopite mica. Production of this started in 1942, and the industry was said to employ in 1959, with its ancillaries, 10,000 people.[4] The figure of 12,100 refers only to the town itself and not to the group of mining settlements round it, so the true number must be bigger. Bodaybo in 1959 had 17,500 inhabitants, but this figure is for the same reason an understatement of the number of miners. Bodaybo has now ceased to be part of Yakutskaya ASSR, but is in Irkutskaya Oblast'. Much is made in one Soviet account[5] of the mechanisation introduced into mining methods, with consequent saving of man-power, but no

[1] Korovitsin (1961), p. 52; Itogi (1962), p. 32.
[2] Vasyutin (1958), pp. 17–18, 30–9; Mityushkin (1960), pp. 104–16.
[3] Pokshishevskiy (1957), p. 105.
[4] Vasyutin (1958), pp. 63–6; Pokshishevskiy (1962), pp. 22–3.
[5] Mityushkin (1960), pp. 104–16.

figures are given. The same account also mentions as a point of interest the employment of up to 1600 Yakut in the Aldan mines in 1931 and 1932—one of the few pieces of evidence, and quite precise at that, on the question of employment of native peoples in industrial undertakings. The fact that this figure, nearly 30 years old, is the only one quoted by the author of a book purporting to give a picture of the economy of Yakutskaya ASSR up to 1959 seems to indicate that he, too, knew of nothing more recent.

The gold mining of north-eastern Siberia has also extended beyond the confines of Yakutskaya ASSR eastwards, to the upper Kolyma basin. This was the area of operation of an organisation called Dal'-stroy, an abbreviation of Glavnoye Upravleniye Stroitel'stva Dal'-nego Severa, the Chief Administration for Construction in the Far North. Its predecessor, a state trust for industrial and road construction on the upper Kolyma, was created in 1931, and the name was changed to Dal'stroy in 1938. The prime purpose was getting gold. Dal'stroy remained in existence until 1957, when its functions were taken over by the regional economic soviet (Sovnarkhoz).[1] In the 26 years of its existence it developed a gold-mining industry which exceeded in size and significance that in neighbouring Yakutskaya ASSR. But Dal'stroy also acquired notoriety as an employer of convict labour, and this has meant that while little has been published in the Soviet Union on its operations, there has been quite a large literature by prisoners who escaped or were released, and were then able to leave the country. More will be said on this below, in the section on convicts, but here it is necessary to point out that it is this literature which provides most of the very scrappy evidence on which estimates of production are made outside the Soviet Union. These vary, but a common figure has been that Kolyma production is three-quarters of the total for the whole country.[2] Mining methods were for much of the time no better than primitive, as was to be expected if a cheap and expendable labour force was available. That Kolyma gold was the cheapest to mine in the Soviet Union is stated by a responsible Soviet source.[3] The reason given is the richness of the deposits, but it is impossible to suppose that the availability of

[1] Zhikharev (1959), pp. 13–47.
[2] Forced labour (1952), p. 25. Korol (1952), pp. 117–23, has a good critical discussion of estimates.
[3] Slavin (1961a), p. 11.

convict labour was not the most important factor. Further, the gold mining is stated by the same source to have paid for the whole development of the region—roads, towns, ports, agriculture—and to have subsidised the less profitable tin mining, to be mentioned shortly.

The size of the labour force has been the object of speculation, and at the most conservative estimate was of the order of hundreds of thousands at its peak.[1] The 1959 population of Magadanskaya Oblast' was 188,900, and Dal'stroy was said to employ 100,000 people in 1955,[2] so there has clearly been a falling off since a peak in perhaps 1940. This is likely to be true even if the figures are very considerably inaccurate. It would accord with the known closing of many camps after Stalin's death. But gold mining does undoubtedly continue, with increased emphasis on mechanisation.[3]

In the 1940's Dal'stroy was a great empire which in effect ran the whole of north-eastern Siberia east of the Lena. As a mining concern which exercised almost governmental authority, it has been aptly compared to the Union Minière du Haut Katanga in the Belgian Congo.[4] It spread beyond the Kolyma valley and its interests were not limited to gold. It operated mines not only in its original area, but to the north and east. Thus from 1938 it played a part in the other important mining industry of the far north-east—tin mining.

Tin, like nickel, was for long a metal in very short supply in the Soviet Union, and the economy had to depend on imports. Geologists were at work from the mid-1920's, in both the Yana basin in Yakutskaya ASSR and the Chaun region to the east, in Chukotka, where alluvial deposits were found. At Ege-Khaya on the Yana primitive refining plant was built in 1941, and at Batagay close by in 1942. A second tin-mining centre grew up at Deputatskiy on the Uyandina, a left tributary of the Indigirka, in the same general area, in 1951. Both sites were later improved and expanded.[5] The three settlements together had 10,800 inhabitants in 1959. Meanwhile in Chukotka the first mine to open was the Krasnoarmeyskiy near

---

[1] Barton (1959), pp. 52–3. The actual figures quoted in this source (350,000 in 1934, 500,000 in 1953, 3–5 million in 1940) are unsubstantiated, but may be regarded as a rough guide. Dallin & Nicolaevsky (1948), p. 71, give 300,000–1,000,000 in 1945–47.

[2] Dal'stroy (1956), pp. 225–6.

[3] Zhikharev (1959), pp. 49–63; Slavin (1961 *b*), p. 11.

[4] Kolarz (1954), p. 14.   [5] Mityushkin (1960), pp. 120–2.

Pevek, also during the Second World War. It was followed by another at Pyrkakay on the north coast, and most recently by the important Iul'tin mine, opened in 1959, in the centre of the peninsula. Before Iul'tin could function, a port had to be built at Egvekinot on the south coast.[1] As with gold production, there is no information as to the output of these tin mines, and therefore the number of workers is hard to guess. The Krasnoarmeyskiy, Pyrkakay and Iul'tin mines are, however, the major industrial undertaking in Chukotskiy Natsional'nyy Okrug, where the Russian population numbered 32,000 in 1959,[2] so clearly several thousand, perhaps over ten thousand are connected with the mines. Alluvial gold has also recently been found in Chukotka, and the first dredger started work at Ichuveyem in 1959. This is not yet a large undertaking, but in view of a call for more gold issued by the government in 1958, it may grow.[3]

There remains one other major mining development in the north—the diamond mining of Yakutskaya ASSR. After much searching, because diamonds were virtually unknown in the Soviet Union, alluvial diamonds were found in the Vilyuy basin in 1949, and finally a kimberlite pipe, the classic diamond-bearing rock formation, was discovered on a tributary of the Vilyuy in 1955. The pipe was called Mir, meaning peace, a settlement called Mirnyy grew up here, and production started in 1956.[4] Other kimberlite pipes were found in the same general area and to the north as far as the Olenek valley. The fact that an effective method of producing artificial diamonds was developed at about the same time does not seem to be altering the plan to work the Yakut diamond field as energetically as possible. Mirnyy remains the main centre, and had a population of nearly 6000 in 1959. The total number employed in the industry may well be two or three times as many.

These are the main mineral industries in the Soviet north. That they are large-scale undertakings is apparent, but the Soviet policy of not releasing any information on the output of non-ferrous metals makes it difficult to achieve any sort of accuracy in estimating the number of people these mines have caused to work in the north. Those enumerated are not in fact the only mines in the north. There

[1] Ryabov (1960), pp. 30–2.
[2] Armstrong (1962), p. 177; Slavin (1961 *b*), p. 14.
[3] Ryabov (1960), pp. 33–4; Zhikharev (1959), p. 51.
[4] Mityushkin (1960), pp. 116–20.

are a number which have only local significance. Most of these are for low-grade coal, which is worth mining, in spite of its poor quality, because of the high cost of bringing in coal of better grade. But the number of employees at these smaller mines cannot be more than a few thousands at most, and this is insignificant by comparison with the main labour force. Two natural gas deposits of importance were reported in the late 1950's: one on the lower Ob' near Berezov, the other on the Vilyuy in Yakutskaya ASSR. Still more recently, further very promising discoveries have been announced on the lower and middle Ob', and the northern part of the west Siberian plain seems likely to become a major gas-producing area.[1] In 1962, however, only the first two discoveries were said to be in process of exploitation, and here again there cannot be more than a relatively small number of workers involved.

The total for the whole mining industry is clearly hundreds of thousands of people, and may be between half a million and a million. This would include the dependants of the employees, but these would not be so numerous as in more southerly regions because many of the workers in the north are unmarried. It may be objected that perhaps a substantial part of this labour force was not immigrant at all, but was drawn from the native peoples of the region. In fact, this is not likely to have been the case, and the evidence against it is given below, in the chapter on relations with the natives.

TRANSPORT WORKERS

None of the mines, whose existence has to such an extent transformed the north, could have opened or could now function without an effective transport system. Transport has always been the key to northern development. Again, there are no details on the number of workers it employs, and the only course is to take stock of the various installations that the transport network has brought into being.

The biggest of these are the sea ports. The main western base of the Northern Sea Route (the shipping lane along the north coast of Siberia) is at Murmansk, which is in addition a port of the greatest national significance, as being the only major outlet to the sea which

[1] Armstrong (1963).

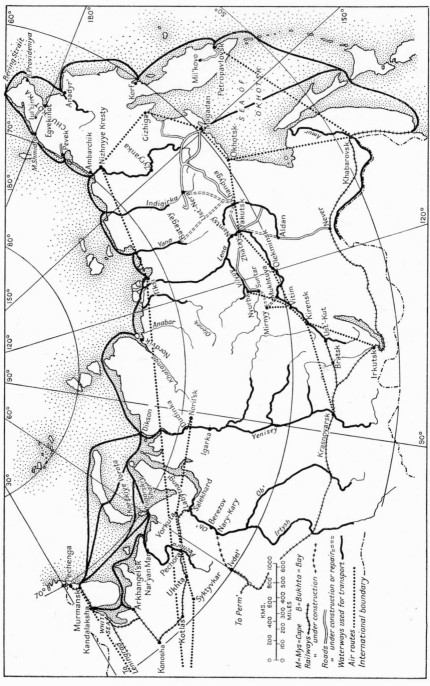

Map 5. Soviet transport network, 1962. The main land, water and air routes in the Soviet north are shown. Main sources: Slavin (1961a), Khachaturov (1960), Loginov (1962), Grigor'yev (1960–).

never freezes up. It therefore has reasons for growth which are un-related to the economy of its Arctic hinterland. That growth has been spectacular: from a population of 8800 in 1926 to 117,000 in 1939 to 222,000 in 1959.[1] It is much the largest town in the north as defined on Map 1, and indeed in the world at this latitude. Most of the inhabitants are directly concerned with the port. An important fishing and fish-processing industry has grown up, and the country's largest trawler fleet is based there. There are also well-equipped repair yards, but there is no shipbuilding industry. Kandalaksha, on the south shore of the peninsula, has already been mentioned in connection with its mineral industry. It is also a port, used mainly by White Sea fishing boats.

Further east, the ports are smaller communities, but a higher pro-portion of their inhabitants are concerned with running the port. Nar'yan-Mar, on the lower Pechora near Pustozersk, is a port for both river and sea-going ships and had 13,000 inhabitants in 1959, having been a very small fishing settlement in 1917. Amderma, on the shore of Yugorskiy Shar, the most southerly strait leading into the Kara Sea, is not a proper port but some ships stop there. It had a population of 2200 in 1959 (all population figures subsequently mentioned in this section relate to 1959 unless otherwise stated). Salekhard (formerly Obdorsk) is a river port at the mouth of the Ob' with nearly 17,000. Dudinka (16,400) is rather similarly placed on the lower Yenisey, but has special importance as a transport centre since it is the port for Noril'sk. Dikson, or Ostrov Diksona, is an island off the mouth of the Yenisey and has been used as an anchorage and refuelling point for ships on the Northern Sea Route since the nineteenth century. Its population was 2000. There are several other small anchorages and trans-shipment points, such as Nordvik, Ambarchik and Mys Shmidta. There are also three ports of some size. Tiksi (6000), at the mouth of the Lena, is the trans-shipment point for all goods coming by sea to central and northern Yakutskaya ASSR. Pevek (5800) is the port of the tin-mining region of western Chukotka, and Bukhta Provideniya (4800) is a fuelling point for the Northern Sea Route as well as the port for the Bering Strait shore of Chukotka. All three came into being about 1933, when the Northern Sea Route was being energetically pushed forward

[1] Lorimer (1946), p. 251; Itogi (1962), p. 31.

by O. Yu. Shmidt, the first head of the new government department set up the year before to run the route.

On the Pacific coast, there is Anadyr' (5600), Korf (2100), and a major Soviet fishing port Petropavlovsk-na-Kamchatke (86,000). And on the Sea of Okhotsk, Okhotsk itself (8500), and the port of Magadan (62,000), which is the main supply base serving the Kolyma mining area. Of these, Anadyr', Petropavlovsk and Magadan are administrative centres also, and the last two have considerable local industry in addition. The total number of sea-port workers (excluding fishermen) and their families must be of the order of tens of thousands; perhaps between 20,000 and 30,000 if Murmansk is excluded, or 100,000 if it is included.

Then there are the river transport workers. The rivers retain great importance as highways in a region which is still largely roadless and railless. Furthermore, there has been a tendency since the Second World War to prefer river to sea transport in supplying certain remote areas, mainly because of improvements in rail communication with the upper reaches of the Lena. Each of the three biggest rivers—Ob', Yenisey and Lena—has carried a river fleet since before 1917. The fleets operate down to the mouths, and each riverside settlement has its quay or jetty, but in the case of the Ob' and Yenisey the main bases are on the upper reaches, in the more populous belt round the Trans-Siberian railway. There are therefore no major centres of the river fleets of these rivers in the north, and the number of people they employ there cannot be large. This is partly true also of the Lena, but there are maintenance yards at Yakutsk, Namtsy and Zhatay on the middle river.[1] On the other hand, the Soviet period has seen the building up of fleets on the lesser rivers, such as the Yana, Indigirka and Kolyma, and these being wholly in the north, most of the employees are likely to be living permanently in the area. The Kolyma fleet has the largest job, in serving the mines on its upper reaches, and the town of Zyryanka (4200) is one of the bases for this fleet. Since the Second World War new ships have been added to all these river fleets by way of the Northern Sea Route. Almost every year there has been a convoy of river vessels, both powered and barges, sometimes numbering over a hundred, which has sailed from the White Sea to the rivers on which they were to

[1] Mityushkin (1960), p. 188.

work. The only recent freight turnover figures relate to rivers of Yakutskaya ASSR. In 1959 turnover on the Lena was 2,024,500 metric tons, and on the Kolyma 127,000 metric tons. In 1958 that on the Yana was 69,000, while the lesser rivers (Indigirka, Olenek and Anabar) carried under 6000 tons each.[1] There is no recent information on the sizes of the river fleets, but taken together, for the whole north they must be of the order of hundreds of vessels, with, therefore, thousands of employees.

By comparison with the water transport labour force, the numbers employed on the railways and roads are certainly less. The railways are quickly dismissed, because only three short lines exist in the north. The most important is the Murmansk line, running southwards from the port towards Leningrad. It is this line which has made possible the mineral exploitation in the centre of the peninsula, and no doubt its equipment (it was electrified before the Second World War) and rather numerous stations require quite a large labour force. An extension of this line to Pechenga was opened in 1960.[2] But the whole line runs for only 500 km. through the north. The other two lines are even shorter: the northern part of the Pechora railway to the Vorkuta coal mines, completed in 1942, and its extension to Labytnangi at the mouth of the Ob', completed in about 1950; and the short line from Dudinka to Noril'sk, completed in 1937 and with no connection to the national network. Operating conditions are admittedly difficult, and both these lines are in the permafrost zone, with the engineering and maintenance problems which that implies. But their combined length is less than another 400 km. Labytnangi, which exists because of the railway, but presumably is a river port also, had 5200 inhabitants in 1959.

It is worth mentioning that a long extension of the Pechora railway, beyond the mouth of the Ob' right through to the Yenisey at Igarka (about 1400 km.) was approved, and work started on it in the early 1950's. The idea was later dropped, however, on the grounds that the line was unnecessary, and all construction stopped.[3] This must have been a very expensive change of mind, for the terrain the line had started to cross is low-lying and swampy in summer, and must

[1] Granik (1962).
[2] *Komsomol'skaya Pravda*, 18 December 1960.
[3] *Izvestiya*, 14 July 1960. See also Slavin (1961a), pp. 203–9, for arguments for and against continuing the work.

have presented very serious difficulties. This particular line is only one of many northern spurs which have been proposed and argued about for a long time. Some will certainly never be built, but there is another now under construction which will in due course make an impact on the economy of the lower Ob' region. This is a line from the railhead at Ivdel' in northern Ural to Nary-Kary, close to Berezov, and it was expected to open in 1963 or 1964.[1]

There is a considerably larger network of roads than of railways, but this is not to say that roads are anything but extremely scarce by comparison with the rest of the country. The main road system in the north is in the Lena–Kolyma region. The Aldan mining area is linked to the Trans-Siberian railway by road, and so is the upper Kolyma and Indigirka mining area to the port of Magadan. There are some roads radiating out of Yakutsk, so that the networks almost, but not quite, link up to form a road from Never on the Trans-Siberian to Magadan. These roads have only a dirt surface, but can probably carry traffic for most of the year. The gaps are filled by *avtozimniki*, or winter roads, which have no proper surface but are negotiable when the ground is frozen. Such roads exist also in other parts of the north. Certain towns, such as Mukhtuya (7900) and Khandyga (4100), are mainly important as junctions of road and river traffic. The maintenance of the road network, whether permanent or seasonal, must demand at least as much labour as maintenance of railways in the north, while the labour force required to operate the fleet of vehicles must of course be much larger than that needed for trains. Comparative operating costs show that transport by road in the Kolyma–Lena area is more expensive by a factor of 30 than transport by rail in southern Siberia, and therefore presumably still many times more expensive than transport by rail in the north.[2] Furthermore, road mileage exceeds rail mileage by a factor of at least four (there are 2500 km. of road in Yakutskaya ASSR alone).[3] So it must be presumed that the roads employ many more workers than the railways.

Air transport, on the other hand, is likely to employ fewer than either. Although it has great importance as the medium of passenger transport, and every settlement of any size has its airstrip, the major

---

[1] *Gudok*, 2 February 1961. Later press reports imply that 1965 is a more likely date.
[2] Vasyutin (1958), p. 389. [3] Mityushkin (1960), p. 192; Vasyutin (1958), p. 377.

maintenance centres are in the south and the number of men required to keep a small airstrip serviceable is not large.

The total number of transport workers in the north can only be guessed at, but a figure in the region of 150,000–200,000 (including dependants) may not be too far from the truth. But it is likely that there are a number of natives in this total, perhaps about 10 per cent. Many accounts mention natives working, for instance, on river boats, and road maintenance seems another likely occupation.

FARMERS, FISHERS, AND LUMBERMEN

Working on the land or at sea, whether as hunter or fisherman or farmer, has remained the occupation of the great majority of the native peoples, so that in this activity Russians are not the only source of labour. Indeed, in certain branches they play almost no part at all. For instance, reindeer husbandry is an almost exclusively native concern, and natives predominate in hunting also. This may be true of cattle farming as well; and in certain important parts of the north, such as Yakutskaya ASSR and Tyumenskaya Oblast', cattle have outnumbered reindeer since at least 1940.[1]

Nevertheless, there are indications that quite a large number of Russians are involved. The seven National Districts (*Natsional'nyye Okrugi*) in the north (see Map 11, p. 191), which together make up about half the north as defined for this book, had in 1959 a rural population of 214,000, of whom 82,300 were natives.[2] There were thus up to 131,700 Russians living outside the towns in these regions, and therefore perhaps 250,000–300,000 in the whole of the north. Many of these must be engaged in agriculture. Of the 131,700 Russians in the National Districts, most were in the Khanty–Mansiyskiy Natsional'-nyy Okrug, which was the only one of the seven to have significant cereal crops and to be self-supporting in potatoes and vegetables.[3] This seems to indicate that Russians are mainly to be found in those areas where cultivation of the soil is practicable. This would be likely, for, as a result of Russian work in such fields as plant breeding, the limits of agriculture in the strict sense have moved substantially

---

[1] Narodnoye khozyaystvo RSFSR (1957), pp. 186, 198; Narodnoye khozyaystvo RSFSR (1961), pp. 262–3, 281.
[2] Konovalenko (1961), p. 22. [3] Konovalenko (1961), p. 30.

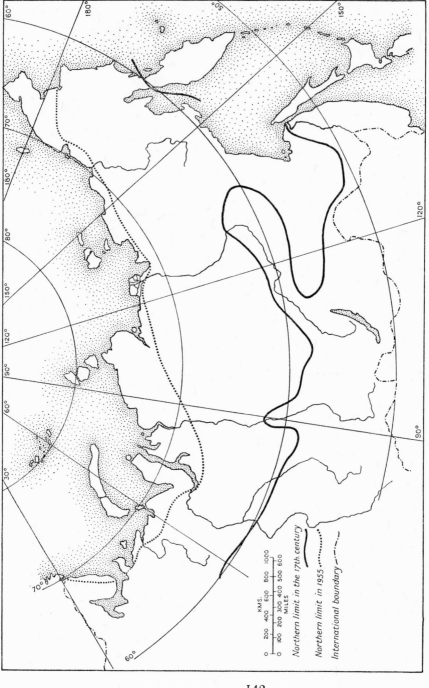

Map 6. Northern limit of crop growing (including hay) in open ground. The northward advance shown here was achieved mainly in the Soviet period. The 1955 line joins the most northerly points at which crops have been grown in the open (not necessarily regularly or in significant quantities). In fact, a distribution map of farming types in Yakutskaya ASSR in 1956–59 indicates that *pre-dominantly* crop-growing regions were still restricted to south of latitude 65° N., or not far beyond the seventeenth-century limit in

KMS.
0 200 400 600 800 1000
0 100 200 300 400 500 600
MILES

Northern limit in the 17th century ——
Northern limit in 1955 ·········
International boundary ———·———

142

northwards, even after allowance has been made for over-enthusiastic reporting (see Map 6), and Russians must certainly be active in the practical applications of this development. If this is true, then the Lena valley, which is not in one of the seven National Districts, is also likely to contain many Russian farm workers, for it is here that crop-growing is most highly developed.[1] Apart from crop-growing, Russians predominated in the quite primitive fishery on the lower Yenisey in the early years of Soviet power.[2] Where there is much mechanisation, as in the more advanced forms of fishing or lumbering, Russians may be expected to constitute a larger proportion of the labour force.

While many natives continue to catch fish, which are a staple food for them, Russians have established large commercial fisheries in the Arctic. Murmansk has already been mentioned in this connection, and it is much the largest. It has been, throughout the Soviet period, the base of a trawling fleet which takes cod not only in the Barents Sea, but latterly further afield in the North Atlantic also. It is the base of a herring fishery, which was at first restricted to the Murman coast but since 1949 has also moved further afield. These industries put it high among the country's sea fisheries. The landings there in 1957 were reported to be 500,000 metric tons, a quarter of the national total.[3] Sea fishery itself has grown greatly in importance in the last 20 years, and in 1950 for the first time catches in the open sea were said to exceed those in inland waters. Murmansk has also a fish-processing industry proportionate to the size of the fishing fleet.

The North Pacific is another important fishing ground for the Soviet Union, and recently this has been second in importance after that based on Murmansk. Some of its centres are at the southern end of the Pacific seaboard, but one is at Petropavlovsk-na-Kamchatke, already mentioned as a significant port. The fishery here is by no means so well equipped as the Murmansk fishery, lacking adequate vessels. Trawling is not yet widely practised, although there are good possibilities for this. The basis of the fishery has always been salmon, and the catch has been carried out by a number of small collectives rather than one central organisation. This, and the fact that fisheries

---

[1] Atlas SSSR (1962), pp. 114–15. [2] Tarasenkov (1930), p. 213.
[3] Slavin (1961a), p. 148; *Bol'shaya Sovetskaya Entsiklopediya*, tom 37 (1955), p. 497; Narodnoye khozyaystvo SSSR (1956), p. 89.

account for 80 per cent of the output value of Kamchatka's industry,[1] means that it is the population of the Oblast' as a whole (193,300 in 1959), rather than that of Petropavlovsk, which should be taken as the basis for the numbers engaged in the fishing industry. Besides the salmon fishery, which has been the cause of disagreement with Japan on many occasions, there is a flourishing crab fishery off the west coast. The total catch in 1957 was 255,000 metric tons, of which 92,000 metric tons were salmon.[2]

Outside the North Atlantic and the North Pacific, there are other, much smaller scale undertakings in which some Russians must be employed. The lower reaches of the major Siberian rivers are fished, mainly by seining, and in 1955 produced about 25,000 metric tons. Most of this came from the Ob' and Yenisey.[3] The main importance of this quite small fishery is the closeness of the catching areas to northern settlements, which always have a food problem.

Lumbering is a very important Soviet industry, since the Soviet Union has a bigger stand of timber than any other country. But there is plenty of more easily accessible forest in less northerly regions. Most timber felled in the north is therefore to meet local needs and is not concentrated in particular centres. There are, however, some exceptions to this. The most important is the timber export trade in the Yenisey valley, where timber of superior quality is found. It reaches its market by way of the Northern Sea Route across the Kara Sea to the North Atlantic, and the site of the sawmills, to which the timber is floated down the Yenisey and from which the sea-going ships fetch it, is Igarka. Igarka was originally a fishing settlement called Igarskoye, and it was selected as the timber centre in 1927, when the population was 49. By 1939 it was 20,000,[4] and it was thought to be bigger than that after the Second World War, but by 1959 it was down to 14,300. The export of timber has, however, continued to flourish, judging by the reports of ships calling each year at Igarka. In 1957 200,000 metric tons of timber left the port.[5] This traffic has apparently been the largest single freighting operation on the Northern Sea Route almost every year since 1947. Other

---

[1] Slavin (1961*a*), pp. 255–62.

[2] Slavin (1961*a*), p. 254; Slavin (1960), pp. 76–106.

[3] Mikhaylov (1958). Pirozhnikov (1962) gives larger figures for what is presumably a larger area.

[4] Papanin (1939), p. 92. [5] Kazanskiy (1960), p. 114.

exceptions are the growing timber industry on the Lena, which supplies the region to the north and east, and that on the Ob', where the railway at Labytnangi and the planned railway at Nary-Kary are primarily concerned with the transport of timber which has been floated down the Ob'. But the developments on the Lena and Ob' are of decidedly secondary importance.

An approximation to the numbers employed in the exploitation of renewable resources might be 100,000 in normal farm work, 250,000 in fisheries, and 50,000 in lumbering: the total, anyway, being of the order of hundreds of thousands.

OTHER WORKERS

There are several other categories of Russian settler which should be mentioned. Only one may constitute a large group, and that is the armed services. No information whatever on this subject is published in the Soviet Union, but it is certain that there are military installations in the far north. There are, for instance, military airfields in the Murmansk region and in Chukotka to cover the frontier, and no doubt there are others elsewhere in the north. Presumably there are rocket-launching sites as well, which may in some cases be replacing the airfields. It must be expected that there are Soviet equivalents to the radar defences in the North American Arctic—the Distant Early Warning (DEW) line, and the Ballistic Missile Early Warning System (BMEWS). The existence of the nuclear weapons testing area in the vicinity of the north island of Novaya Zemlya is well known. Naval shore stations must also exist, but probably as part of, or closely associated with, some of the ports already mentioned. The presence of any considerable contingents of ground forces on a permanent basis, however, may be doubted. Some remarks have been made above (p. 126) on how members of the services are fitted into regional census returns, and their absence from the total for the north. There is no means of ascertaining the number not included on this account. While it seems unlikely that it should be vast, a force of anything up to 50,000 men is not inconceivable. But it is reasonable to assume that at least some of those manning permanent installations such as airfields or naval shore stations, especially maintenance staff, are included under the administrative area in which they live. Of the total of 1,600,000 Russians, therefore, some thousands, even tens of thousands, may come into this category.

Of the other categories, none is likely to be so large. The chief of them is probably the administrators. The region contains eleven capitals of *oblasti* or *okrugi*, and the Soviet system is well known for its proliferous bureaucracy. The people running these must total thousands. Then there are a number of secondary industries—food and clothing factories, for instance. It has been part of the official policy to foster the creation of secondary industries in northern settlements of any size, as a way of attracting population and increasing stability.[1] And finally there are the 'cultural workers' of various sorts, from teachers in the numerous schools to the staff of Yakutsk University, of the ten scientific institutes in Yakutskaya ASSR, and of the Research Institute of Agriculture of the Far North (Nauchno-Issledovatel'skiy Institut Sel'skogo Khozyaystva Kraynego Severa) at Noril'sk. All these are urban dwellers and part of the permanent population.

CONVICTS AND EXILES

The extent to which northern Siberia continued to be a place of exile and confinement, after the downfall of the Tsars who had made it one, is a point of great importance to this inquiry as a whole. It is also, by its nature, a point on which the truth is hard to ascertain. In writing this book, scarcity of data has been the major problem, but there has been little reason hitherto to suppose that such evidence as can be found is deliberately falsified. The Tsarist governments never hid, or attempted to hide, the existence of convict and exile systems. They may have tried to conceal the bad conditions which those under punishment suffered, but many returned from the far corners of Siberia to record their experiences, and even foreigners like George Kennan were able to visit Siberia and publish what they had found out about the system. In any case, after 1917 the Soviet government did all it could to ensure that the world knew about the monstrosities, as indeed they were, of its predecessor's penal colonies. But the situation now is different. The government operating the system is still in power, and both its control over its citizens and its

[1] Vasyutin (1958), p. 293.

willingness to be ruthless in exercising that control are at least as great as those of its predecessor. It does not deny the existence of the system, but it tries very hard to conceal its true nature. It has more reason to do so than the Tsarist governments, because in the early years of the Soviet regime the official view was that crime, including political crime, would cease as soon as society was properly organised on socialist lines. The magnitude of the error in this attitude provides an incentive to keep as quiet about the whole matter as possible. But meanwhile another development took place which reinforced this incentive. The earlier attitude included belief in the efficacy of corrective labour for dealing with whatever criminals there might be. There were more than expected, so a labour force of considerable size was soon built up. It was then found—and this was the new development—that a force of very cheap labour which could be directed to work anywhere was of the greatest usefulness in implementing the industrialisation programme of the five-year plans, and its use was extended. So the fact that convict labour had played a significant part in the major achievements of the new social order was something that would be even more damaging to admit to the world. It is understandable, therefore, that there has been no possible opportunity for a George Kennan to gather material. But—and this is why it is possible to state with conviction that these things did happen—some individuals did get away from both labour camps and the country and have recorded what happened to them. Before the Second World War such reports circulated in the west, but were treated with some incredulity, both because of the difficulty of checking them, and because of the unbelievable conditions they described. But more recently better evidence has become available. One factor which brought this about was that, under pressure of the German onslaught, Stalin signed an agreement with General Sikorski in 1941 which permitted the release of thousands of Polish prisoners who had been in camps all over the country for up to two years. By now, many accounts have been published of life in forced labour settlements, and, however great an allowance the reader may feel he must make for the normal tendency to exaggerate in such circumstances, it is impossible to doubt the validity of the general impression they give.

It is difficult, however, to obtain from such accounts detailed information about the operating of the system beyond what the writers themselves saw. A prisoner is obviously not informed on these matters, and very few of those who are have yet fled. Probably the best idea of the scale of the forced labour contribution to the economic life of the country can be got from the entirely authentic economic plan for 1941, an official Soviet document captured in 1941 by the Germans and from them in 1945 by the Americans. This makes clear in general terms the planned share of the NKVD (the Peoples Commissariat for Internal Affairs, the ministry responsible) in particular activities for that year. The NKVD was to undertake, for instance, about 14 per cent of the construction work, including roads, to be financed through centralised capital investment—a larger share than any other ministry. A large contribution was to be made to lumbering and mining.[1] But this document does not specify where the NKVD was to conduct these operations. For any indication of that, or any other details, the only sources are the recollections of camp inmates, whose jobs or occupations did not provide them with any exact knowledge of these things beyond the evidence of their own eyes.

As in Tsarist times, there are several categories of directed or forced labour, varying with the severity of the punishment. All have not existed for the whole Soviet period, but the following have played an important part. At the bottom of the scale are the inmates of corrective labour camps, mostly political offenders but including some common criminals. Some of these camps were designated 'punitive', and they were, of course, the worst of all. Next above these come corrective labour colonies, where the regime is milder and the inmates work in local industrial enterprises. Prisoners in these categories may be appropriately called convicts. Then, less severe again, there are forms of punishment which may be loosely grouped together under the term 'exile'. These included exile proper (*ssylka*, the obligation to live in a given locality), banishment (*vysylka*, the obligation not to live in a given locality or localities, often the six main cities of the country), and 'special settlement'. The 'special settlers' (*spetsial'nyye pereselentsy*, abbreviated to *spets-pereselentsy*) are people who have been deported, generally in large groups, and are obliged to live in a given locality, either in settlements set up for them, or among the local inhabitants. Peasants

[1] Gosudarstvennyy plan (1951), pp. 13, 141, 484.

who refused to join collective farms, supposedly unreliable elements in the Baltic states, and whole peoples from the Caucasus and the Crimea during the Second World War, became 'special settlers'. In addition, it has been common for those completing a sentence in a corrective labour camp to be designated 'special settlers' and obliged to remain in the same area. It is likely that all these categories have been present in the north, but the predominant ones seem to have been corrective labour camps and 'special settlers'.

The period during which all this flourished seems to have been roughly the 30 years between 1929 and 1958. This falls neatly between the two effective censuses, but these would not have been much help anyway because, as noted earlier, convicts are not discernible in the census results. Collectivisation of the peasants, started in 1929, provided the first large contingents of prisoners, and the first five-year plan (1928–32) provided the economic incentive for using them. The peak was probably reached in the 1930's, and since Stalin's death in 1953 there has been a gradual reduction. Many corrective labour camps were converted to corrective labour colonies in 1956, and they were abolished as a separate category in 1958. The institution is certainly not dead, but there seems good reason to suppose that it is on a much smaller scale than it was.[1] Evidence that this is so comes not only from the legislative changes just mentioned, and from official announcements of amnesties. There are also such indirect indications as a falling off in numbers between the early and late 1950's at certain of the industrial settlements, and advertisements in the Soviet press for labour to go to these places. Further, if it is true, as seems likely, that convicts are not included in the census returns of the district in which they are living, but that released convicts are so included, then it would follow that release of a number of prisoners who afterwards remain in the district will result in an apparent rise in the population of that district as shown in certain official returns. It can be demonstrated[2] that a rise greater than the national average did take place in some northern areas in 1950–55 and 1955–60, while the increase in industrial production was below the national average. This is true of Yakutskaya ASSR, Magadanskaya Oblast'

[1] This section is based on information in Forced labour (1952), Utechin (1961), and Sbornik zakonov (1961), pp. 727–45.
[2] Newth (1962).

and Kamchatskaya Oblast', and probably of other areas too. The argument is by no means conclusive, but could be another indication of the reduction of camps. Finally, publication for the first time in the Soviet Union of a story of life in the camps (Solzhenitsyn's 'One day in the life of Ivan Denisovich', which appeared in the journal *Novyy Mir* in 1962) would scarcely have been permitted if they had still been common. On the other hand, evidence that they still exist, or at least are popularly supposed to in the Soviet Union, can be found in the casual use in Soviet newspapers of the phrase 'sent to the Arctic' or 'sent to the Kolyma'.[1] The fact that foreign visitors have not yet (early 1963) been permitted to visit the major camp areas, such as Vorkuta, Noril'sk and the Kolyma, is a further indication.

The actual distribution of camps and associated centres of forced labour in the north is the point at which one has to start relying on the recollections of what prisoners heard from other prisoners. There are three major centres, however, of which the existence is beyond doubt because some who escaped and told the tale were there themselves: the Vorkuta coal-mining region, the Noril'sk non-ferrous metal mining region, and the network of enterprises on the Kolyma and in that vicinity operated by Dal'stroy. Of these three more will be said below. But in addition to them there are many reports of other centres. These reports have been summarised by Dallin and Nicolaevsky.[2] At first (1928–30) the only camps in the north as defined on Map 1 were in Kol'skiy Poluostrov. They had grown from the original Soviet northern penal settlement on the Solovet-skiye Ostrova, a group of islands in the White Sea—which also had a long history as a place of confinement under the Tsars. In 1935 Igarka, Bodaybo, Novaya Zemlya and Vaygach are mentioned as well; and in 1945–47 Zemlya Frantsa-Iosifa, the Yenisey estuary, Turukhansk, Aldan, the lower Lena, Chukotka, and Kamchatka are added. Another summary relating to 1953–54[3] lists even more, but the main groups coincide with those already mentioned. Of these, the mainland sites are all credible, because mining or lumbering is known to go on in the vicinity. But the islands of Vaygach, Novaya Zemlya and Zemlya Frantsa-Iosifa are less so, because there is no known economic activity there, at least of a sort

---

[1] For instance, in a news item about an embezzler in *Izvestiya*, 13 September 1961.
[2] 1958, pp. 52–72.   [3] Yakovlev (1955), pp. 65–207.

which could use forced labour. It is unlikely that they were purely punitive, for it would be quite unnecessary to go to the expense of building and maintaining camps in such remote places when equally severe punishment can be inflicted closer at hand. But it is possible that the labour could be used for such jobs as airfield construction. At any rate, almost all the major industrial areas in the north are listed, and there seems little reason to question the existence of camps at these places on a long-term basis.

Of the three areas which have been described by former inmates, the best covered is the Kolyma. The population of the area reached the hundreds of thousands—some reports say millions—and there is no doubt that the camps accounted for almost all this. The enormous scale of this forced labour empire and the cruelty with which its operations were conducted, are perhaps best conveyed by Elinor Lipper, a Dutch-born woman who spent seven years there (1939–46).[1] Confirmation is plentifully available from other accounts. In the section above on miners, Dal'stroy was considered as a mining organisation. Here it must be emphasised that the entire structure of Dal'stroy, many-sided as it became, rested on a basis of forced labour and was administered, not by a mining ministry, but by the NKVD. Certain technical staff were not under sentence, and nor, of course, were the administrators. But the enterprise as a whole could never have started to function if it had not been on that basis.

On a smaller scale, but nevertheless still impressively large, was the network of mines at Vorkuta in the Pechora basin. The employment of forced labour here appears to date from the construction of the railway in 1941–42. This was itself a major and notorious undertaking, on which many Poles were employed, since the occupation of eastern Poland in 1939 had provided this readily available labour force. It was also an interesting parallel to the Murmansk railway, constructed in the same kind of war-time emergency and with the same ruthless disregard of human life. The mines were greatly expanded once the railway was completed, and their operation was largely ensured by forced labour. In this German prisoners of war were at one time a significant component. The most informative account of life here is provided by a German doctor, Joseph Scholmer, who was there from 1950 to 1953.[2] A reliable total for

[1] Lipper (1951).   [2] Scholmer (1954).

the number of prisoners cannot be obtained. One source gives 130,000 in 1953,[1] but even if this is true, there were no doubt considerable fluctuations.

Noril'sk is the third centre on which there is some first-hand information. The decision to start mining there was taken in 1935, and forced labour was used right from the start. This is made clear by a report by a foreign journalist who visited the area in 1936, and who is almost certainly the only foreign journalist to visit an Arctic labour camp.[2] That the subsequent astonishing growth of the town was essentially due to an influx of prisoners cannot be doubted. No later eye-witness account of Noril'sk itself is available; but in the period 1950–54 a Finn was in detention at Dudinka, the river port to which Noril'sk is connected by rail, and from his story much can be inferred about conditions at Noril'sk.[3] The free population at both towns cannot have been more than a small proportion of the total.

The pattern at all these places has many common features: severe hardship, low productivity of labour, gross inefficiency of management. There is no reason to suppose that conditions were substantially different in the other regions for which no first-hand accounts are yet available. The work undertaken by the prisoners, it should perhaps be explained, was not restricted to operating the mines. All the other jobs required for the building and maintenance of the settlement were done too. Most of them were unskilled, like forest clearance, road making and hut building, but some were both skilled and responsible, like medical services. The free population filled the remaining responsible positions, which could sometimes be surprisingly few.

Vorkuta and Noril'sk have a further common feature. They were the site of strikes among the prisoners after Stalin's death in 1953.[4] These strikes were badly organised and achieved few immediate local results, but subsequent improvements in prisoners' conditions should certainly be ascribed to them. The fact that they took place at all, however, is of the highest importance. The long-term political results, in the sense of showing the Kremlin where it had to stop, must have been great, and concerned far more than just the Arctic.

[1] Yakovlev (1955), p. 96.
[2] Smolka (1937), pp. 146–62.
[3] Parvilahti (1959).
[4] Barton (1959), pp. 319–50, 467–83.

In fact, these strikes may prove ultimately to have been the most important contribution of the Arctic to the life of the country.

It is quite clear, then, that many, probably most, Soviet Arctic mines could not have started to function unless there had been forced labour available. The labour camps were sited with these considerations in mind. Since soon after the death of Stalin, there has been a reduction in the number of prisoners. But this does not necessarily imply a proportionate reduction in output. Forced labour may have been essential to starting an enterprise, but even if all the prisoners were released (and this is not likely to be the case), the enterprise would not come to a complete halt. The main reason for supposing this to be so is the classification of many time-expired prisoners as 'special settlers' obliged to live in the same region. In this way a quasi-free labour force was built up when the camps were flourishing. Even without such classification, there could be reasons for prisoners remaining in the vicinity: the physical difficulty of getting elsewhere (from the Kolyma to European Russia is well over 7000 km.), and the psychological difficulty of taking up the old life after being possibly presumed dead for a decade or even two. In addition, there would be the volunteers who had responded to appeals and advertisements in the press.

The movement towards free labour is obviously a desirable one for all concerned, the state gaining no less than the individual because productivity rises. But the crucial question is whether northern settlement on the scale demanded by the economic undertakings built up under Soviet rule can be maintained without recourse to large-scale compulsion. The answer to this is not yet clear, but more will be said about it below in connection with government policy and the use of the carrot rather than the stick. But it might have been argued in Moscow that compulsion was necessary to start up the industrialisation of the north, and then, once the wilderness was somewhat tamed, less ruthless measures would be enough to carry it on. Events seem to lend some support to such a view.

9

GOVERNMENT POLICY

Once the Soviet government had established itself firmly and had overcome the multifarious and urgent problems facing it to the extent of having the leisure to contemplate the whole of its northern territory, it was relatively consistent in its view of the use it expected to make of the north. In words attributed to Stalin by a Deputy Chairman of the Council of Peoples Commissars in 1936: 'The Arctic and our northern regions have colossal wealth. We must create a Soviet organisation which can in the shortest period include this wealth in the general resources of our socialist structure.'[1] In this, Stalin was following Lenin's ideas. Much has been made in the Soviet Union of the fact that Lenin signed a decree in 1921 setting up a scientific institute to study the Arctic—the Floating Marine Scientific Institute (Plavuchiy Morskoy Nauchnyy Institut). He was closely associated with other legislation concerning the north in those early years. Much of it, in fact, did not achieve its object. But a recent analysis of the drafts of certain early decrees and of the events leading up to them shows that Lenin and the Council of Peoples Commissars constantly urged a broadening of the scope of the matter under discussion, in the direction of wider investigations which would lead to more effective utilisation of resources.[2] The same insistence on exploitation of resources has been reiterated in another recent work, an authoritative survey of northern development.[3] The main emphasis, therefore, seems always to have been on the economic exploitation of the north.

Since the middle 1930's strategic aims have also appeared to exert an influence, but strategy and economics are really two sides of the same question when seen from the highest level, and in a totalitarian state they can be more easily treated as such. Their close connection in the Soviet Union is often apparent, as for instance in the secrecy which has surrounded certain economic information for over 25 years. Another motive which was certainly present was the desire to re-educate the northern peoples in the principles of Marxism-

[1] Na priyeme (1936), p. 25.
[2] Belov (1961).
[3] Slavin (1961a), pp. 4, 297.

Leninism. But although it was the cause of the earliest manifestation of Soviet interest in the region, and has always had great ideological significance, its importance as a factor affecting settlement has not been great, because the numbers required for implementing any politico-cultural programme of this sort are quite small.

It is thus fair to say that the Soviet government has shown greatest interest in the north for the practical use that could be made of it, and the exigencies of the historical situation—'socialism in one country', and the increased need, as a consequence, to build up industrial and military strength—have concentrated attention on the mineral wealth. Most other activities, such as transport and agriculture, have been regarded largely as complementary to the extractive industries. To implement this policy, the government had to tackle a number of problems, of which the chief were provision of a labour force, development of building techniques, and supply of food.

In finding labour, the guiding principle for a Soviet government, obviously, was that there should be no movement of settlers which was not planned.[1] There were three approaches to the problem. One, compulsion, has just been described, and accounted for an unknown, but clearly large, proportion of the incoming workers. The second was to appeal to young people to go out to remote areas as their contribution to the building of communism. Again it is not possible to determine how many may have responded, but it would be unwise to underestimate the reserve of idealism on which the government could call. Such appeals were particularly numerous after the Second World War. The third approach was supplementary to the second, and it was the capitalist method of attraction by incentives. It was used at the same time as the others, there being always, presumably, certain grades of worker who could not be acquired in any other way. There has been legislation on this subject in force continuously since 1932, with the exception of three years during the Second World War, 1942–45, when incentives to work far from the front were no doubt thought inappropriate. The first relevant decree, issued on 10 May 1932, set the pattern which has been adhered to ever since.[2] The main points are an increase of basic rate of pay, longer annual

[1] Voshchinin (1932), pp. 267–70.
[2] Quoted in English translation in Taracouzio (1938), pp. 491–5.

leave, increased pension rights, and certain privileges in education and housing. The decree was amended by another of 1 August 1945, in which the incentives were somewhat increased,[1] and that in turn was superseded by another of 10 February 1960, in which they were, on balance, somewhat reduced again. The main provisions of this last are as follows.[2] The north is divided, as it has been since 1945, into two zones—the 'far north', and 'regions equated to the far north', the former being the more remote. The boundary between the two is evidently determined by other factors besides the climate (see Map 7). The north as defined for this book includes almost the whole of the former and about half the latter. For the far north, the increase of basic pay is 10 per cent per year in most areas, or per six months in distant regions like Chukotka, up to a maximum increase of 80 per cent. For regions equated, it is 10 per cent per two years, up to a maximum of 50 per cent. The addition to annual leave is 18 days for the far north, and 12 days for regions equated. Leave may be held over and accumulated for up to three years, and travel time is not included in the leave period once every three years. Persons transferred, directed (but not by a court of law), or invited to work in the north for a period of five years or more get their fares paid, may retain their former accommodation until their return, and have their pension rights either doubled, if working in the far north, or increased by 50 per cent, if working in regions equated. Persons going north on their own initiative qualify for some but not all these privileges. To give examples of how this worked in practice: the authorities calculated that a building worker in Noril'sk in 1960 got, on average, if a cash equivalent of the associated privileges is included, 2·4 times as much pay as he would have had in the central regions of the country; and for Magadanskaya Oblast', which is still more remote, it was calculated at about the same time that the cost to the state of maintaining a worker was 3·5 times as much as it would be in a central region.[3]

There are no figures at all to show how many people were attracted by the terms of these decrees. Evidence that the incentives were set at about the right level is provided by the fact that only relatively

---

[1] Sbornik vazhneyshikh (1958), pp. 114–15.
[2] Sbornik zakonov (1961), pp. 575–8.
[3] Kushnev (1961), p. 33; Slavin (1961 *b*), p. 17.

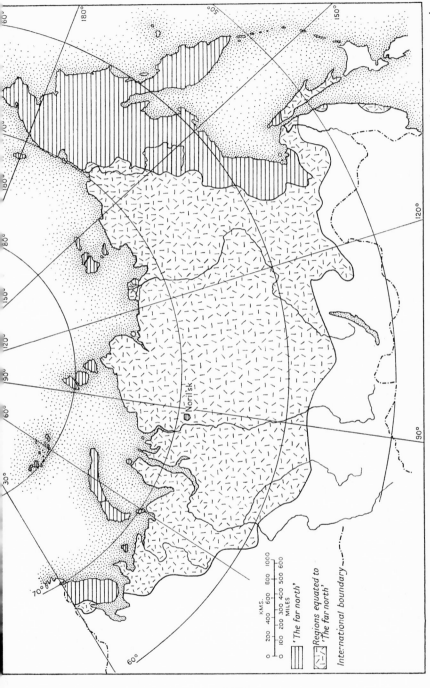

Map 7. 'The far north' and 'Regions equated to the far north' for certain legal purposes. This map shows these two main subdivisions as defined by the labour law of 1 August 1945, with subsequent amendments. Source: Sbornik vazhneyshikh (1958), pp. 114–27, translated in part in Armstrong (1961).

small adjustments have been necessary over nearly 30 years. On the other hand, it has to be remembered that deficiencies could be eased by using whatever degree of compulsion might be thought appropriate, from the directed labour of school and university leavers to the forced labour of long-term convicts. In spite of all this, there has been evidence of labour shortages. Examples quoted in literature referring to Yakutskaya ASSR in the early 1950's mostly show deficiencies of only 10–20 per cent,[1] and it may be that this proportion is virtually inevitable in very remote regions. It is also known that the mobility of labour has been high.[2] Although some specialists have been persuaded to spend long periods, even their whole working lives, in the north, the majority come for the money and leave as soon as they have it.

It is this attitude which efforts are now being made to combat. The most hopeful approach, it is thought, is the improvement of working and living conditions. Khrushchev, speaking at Vladivostok in 1959, emphasised that it was this sort of improvement, rather than high rates of pay, which would attract people to remote areas. He was speaking of Primorskiy Kray, but the principle can clearly be of general application.[3] The idea in a northern context was at once taken up by others,[4] and even carried a little further; conditions should be not just as good as those in more southerly regions, but better.[5] Grandiose futuristic plans, not very common in recent Soviet literature, were published, showing a town of 10,000–12,000 inhabitants, built on piles and covered by a plastic dome, so that blizzards would pass underneath and the population would enjoy air conditioning and heating in total insulation from its environment.[6] There is no suggestion that such constructions are imminent, but perhaps the knowledge that they are even being thought about is helpful to recruiting. Less spectacularly, there has been some useful work in planning lay-out of northern settlements, Noril'sk in particular; although these plans are not as sophisticated as those by Ralph Erskine in northern Sweden. The Leningrad branch of the

[1] Vasyutin (1958), p. 420.
[2] Vasyutin (1958), p. 422; Slavin (1961 a), p. 291; Pokshishevskiy (1962), pp. 59–60.
[3] *Pravda*, 8 October 1959.
[4] Slavin (1961 a), p. 291; Pokshishevskiy (1962), pp. 27, 61; Shishkin (1962), pp. 23–4.
[5] Alampiyev (1962), p. 61.
[6] *Soviet News*, 12 February 1962; *Trud*, 11 January 1962.

Academy of Building and Architecture (Akademiya Stroitel'stva i Arkhitektury) has been the pioneer in this field.[1] Development of secondary industries was recognised as a desirable way of making settlements more permanent, for it was hoped that not only would their products be welcome, but they would provide employment for women. Whether such measures as all these will be a sufficient attraction without the addition of pay increases remains to be seen. It is certainly a move in the right direction. In this connection one may note that the Soviet government has an easier task than the Canadian or United States governments have, in so far as the drop in the standard of living which the Soviet northern settler must expect is relatively less, since his starting level is in many cases a good deal lower. Nevertheless, the success or failure of this approach of improving living conditions rather than directly increasing pay deserves to be followed closely in North America, for high labour turnover is one of the major unsolved problems there also. The incentive of high wages in the American Arctic, while it has attracted the necessary numbers, has made little progress towards the solution of this longer-term problem. Nor is it ever likely to do so, because high wages and hard conditions will always tend to attract the sort of man who comes for a short time.

The health of the inhabitants of northern settlements, and measures to protect it, are other matters which have an obvious bearing on the labour position. It is clear that medical services are active and aware of the problems. One of the few public health reports that have been published quotes the results of surveys made in the Noril'sk and Murmansk regions in the late 1950's, and compares the results with those from comparable groups in the central regions.[2] A sample of 3060 schoolchildren at Noril'sk, for instance, showed an abnormally high percentage (11·6) with malnutrition, and bad eyesight was also significantly greater than in the south. Vitamin C deficiency, the most expectable condition in such settlements, was noted in as many as 80 per cent of a sample of over 500 persons of various ages and occupations, although the great majority of these (84 per cent) were practically healthy. Again,

---

[1] Kushnev (1961). See also several papers in *Problemy Severa*, vyp. 6, 1962.

[2] Arnol'di & Belousova (1962), pp. 35, 37, 61–2, 93. Some of the points made here are amplified in papers in *Problemy Severa*, vyp. 6, 1962.

neuromuscular disease was found to occur among heavy manual workers more frequently at Noril'sk than in the south. It must be assumed that some knowledge of these facts, probably exaggerated, is widespread, and acts as a deterrent. On the evidence of this report, however, the situation does not seem desperately serious, and the report itself is evidence of the intention to bring about improvements.

The decision to develop the north on any considerable scale at once posed problems of permafrost engineering. No substantial building whose foundations rest on permanently frozen soil will remain serviceable unless precautions are taken. A specialised scientific body was therefore created in 1930 to determine what these were—the Commission for the Study of Permafrost, now renamed the V. A. Obruchev Institute of Permafrost Studies (Institut Merzlotovedeniya imeni V. A. Obrucheva). Its findings have been used in the construction of all the major townships and industrial sites. From photographs of, for instance, Noril'sk,[1] it is clear that, while mistakes have been made, some remarkable results have been achieved. The main problem is to prevent settlement of foundations due to differential thawing of the subsoil. This has been overcome, apparently even in large buildings (see Pls. XV and XVI) of five stories or more, mainly by particular methods of ventilation, whereby the subsoil is preserved in its frozen state. Water and sewage systems, on the other hand, have to be prevented from freezing, while at the same time their warmth must not be communicated to building foundations. The solution to this is largely a matter of careful planning. There are a few cases in which frozen soil, or ice, is an advantage from the constructional point of view. In certain mines, for example, pit props are not necessary, provided the temperature is kept low; and ice can be used as an engineering material, especially in building winter roads. The Russian experience in this sort of work is also great.

The problem of food supply is important, in so far as the balance between imported and locally grown food could influence profoundly the scale of settlement. The big sea fisheries in the North Atlantic and the North Pacific have national importance, but their product satisfies northern demand presumably only to a limited

[1] Dunayev (1960); Kushnev (1961).

extent and in the area round their shore bases. Of greater importance in the north is the fishery on the lower reaches of Siberian rivers,
which produced 25,000 metric tons in 1955, and must help the supply
situation on the lower Ob' and Yenisey. Locally grown crops and
vegetables seem to be effective in Khanty-Mansiyskiy National'nyy
Okrug, but not elsewhere. The small amount of cultivated land in
the north, and the insufficient use of glasshouses, have recently been
emphasised.[1] Whatever has been done, and however remarkable the
achievement is, this source of food clearly comes nowhere near to
satisfying the demand. Considerable efforts have also been made,
evidently with some success, to increase the supply of fresh milk to
northern settlements, but the relation of supply to demand is probably similar to that in the case of crops and vegetables.

There remains the reindeer industry. The total number of domesticated reindeer, living in a region which largely coincides with the
north as defined for this book, has fluctuated around the figure of
2,000,000 animals over the last 20 years.[2] The meat yield from this
herd is reported by Andreyev[3] to be at the level of 10,000–12,000
metric tons per year. This is sufficient, at the national nutritional
norm of 62 kg. per person per year, for 160,000–195,000 people, and
would thus meet rather less than 10 per cent of the demand. The
resolutions adopted at the end of a conference on problems of
acclimatisation and nutrition in the far north, held in Moscow in
1960,[4] make it clear that half this production goes to the reindeer-
herding peoples themselves, who undoubtedly eat more meat than
the norm lays down and therefore number less than half the totals
above. The contribution of the reindeer industry to the immigrant
population probably satisfies about 80,000 people. Some regions are
likely to be better provided than others in this respect, and the indications are that western Yakutskaya ASSR, Magadanskaya Oblast'
and Kamchatskaya Oblast' are the best.[5]

The reason behind the application of these policies to the north
has been, in the last analysis, the desire to make the country strong
and independent in a mainly hostile world. In other words, government policy for the north in the Soviet period has been strongly

[1] Ivanovskiy (1960, 1962); Artem'yev (1962).
[2] Narodnoye khozyaystvo RSFSR (1961), p. 281.
[3] Andreyev (1962), p. 230.   [4] Rezolyutsiya (1962), p. 263.
[5] Konovalenko (1961), p. 27; Naumov (1962), p. 102.

influenced by external pressures, in contrast to the Tsarist period when these were largely absent. They were threats to the whole state, and were not directed specifically against northern territory. At first the threats were more imagined than real, although the hostility of the victorious powers after the First World War was plain enough, but later Japan and Germany gave cause for serious alarm. But within that framework, there were particular threats to the north, and these are relevant to this inquiry, because they must have played a part in shaping settlement policy.

FOREIGN INFLUENCES

The most dangerous period for the Soviet state was, of course, its infancy. Weak and thoroughly disorganised, it knew that it offered a tempting target. There were threats to both eastern and western ends of the territory. In the west, there was the intervention by allied forces (mainly British, French, and American, numbering 18,000 men) at Murmansk and Arkhangel'sk in 1918–19. This confused incident, which started as a necessary and legitimate measure towards defeating the central powers in the First World War, became, after the Armistice, a conflict of an essentially different character, easily represented as, at best, interference in the affairs of another state, or, at worst, an attempt to win and colonise territory. This last was never remotely considered as a possibility by the allies, and was often disclaimed in their public pronouncements,[1] but nevertheless it is easy to see how it could come to be believed. Important among their motives, on the contrary, was a feeling of loyalty towards brothers-in-arms who had refused to make a separate peace. It is plausible to suppose that the intervention as a whole played a part in stimulating Soviet activity in the frontier regions, and in Kol'skiy Poluostrov in particular, as an insurance against any possible future assault on that part of Soviet territory.

The White Sea region was only one theatre of war out of many in which the Soviet state was then engaged. The other one which is relevant here is the far eastern. There the situation was even more confused. The leading Russian anti-Bolshevik, Admiral Kolchak, was operating in southern Siberia, and there was allied intervention

[1] Strakhovsky (1944).

by British, American, French and Japanese troops in Vladivostok and its hinterland. After Kolchak's execution and the evacuation of the allied forces early in 1920, a nominally independent but in fact Bolshevik-controlled 'Far Eastern Republic' was set up to rule the territory between Baykal and the Pacific. The Japanese again intervened, establishing a puppet 'Amur Government' in 1921, but they were finally constrained to withdraw, and the 'Far Eastern Republic' joined the Soviet state in 1922. None of these activities was specifically directed against the north, but their influence was felt there.

In Kamchatka, Soviet rule was established in 1917–18, but ousted in 1918. There was fighting at intervals, particularly when Bochkarev and Birich, emissaries from the Japanese-sponsored 'Amur Government', arrived in 1921. Soviet power was re-established in 1922. Similarly in Chukotka, the Bolsheviks seized power in 1918, lost it in 1920 and returned in 1923.[1] It was on the shores of the Sea of Okhotsk that the last armed resistance against the Bolsheviks was finally crushed. Bochkarev was killed at Nayakhan in April 1923, together with General Polyakov, another anti-Bolshevik leader; and General Pepelyayev and his Siberian volunteer company were captured at Ayan in June of that year, after sporadic fighting during the winter in Yakutiya.[2] Behind some of these incidents, particularly in Kamchatka, the hand of Japan was clearly discernible. Japan had acquired fishing rights along the Kamchatka coasts (but not in the rivers) after the Russo-Japanese War, and not only were there shore installations, but Japanese warships came into Petropavlovsk often in 1921 and 1922 to protect Japanese fishing interests there.[3] The Amur Government even proposed to rent Chukotka to Japan for three years.[4] Japan was thus the most deeply implicated of the foreign powers active in the North Pacific, and her expansionist aims were clear, but there is also some evidence of American activity. Scientists aboard the U.S. Revenue cutter *Bear* carried out magnetic observations at Bukhta Emma on the north coast of Chukotka in 1920, and unwisely left the standard station notice stating 'For disturbing this mark $250 fine or imprisonment'.

[1] Gapanovich (1933), vol. I, pp. 75–9; Preobrazhennyy kray (1956), p. 101; Zhikharev (1961), pp. 10–112.
[2] Strod (1961), p. 183.
[3] Bergman (1927), pp. 28, 60, 86, 148.
[4] Zhikharev (1961), p. 76.

When the notice was brought to Soviet official attention four years later, this action was construed as a gross violation of sovereignty. This it perhaps was, although permission to take observations had been obtained from the local authorities. But the action does not merit the interpretation put on it by later Soviet writers, that it amounted to proclaiming American jurisdiction over the peninsula.[1] Also in 1920 the American industrialist Washington B. Vanderlip tried to obtain (and thought he succeeded) immense concessions in Kamchatka, including, he hoped, an option on renting or buying the whole peninsula; but they were contingent upon American recognition of the Soviet state, and therefore came to nothing.[2] All these events, whether genuine threats to the territory or not, undoubtedly stimulated the Soviet government into taking greater notice of the far north-east.

They were closely followed by another, more overt, claim to territory, this time inside the Arctic Circle. Ostrov Vrangelya is a bleak island, then uninhabited, off the north coast of Chukotka. It was first sighted by Captain Kellett of the Royal Navy in 1849 during the search for Franklin, and later by American whalers. F. P. Vrangel', the Russian explorer, had postulated the existence of land in this region in 1824, but never saw it, and the first Russian party to land on it was one from the *Taymyr* and *Vaygach* expedition in 1911. In the summer of 1914, the shipwrecked party from the Canadian explorer Stefansson's expedition ship *Karluk* lived on the island until they were rescued. It therefore seemed to Stefansson in 1921 that sovereignty over the island was by no means a settled issue, and that the British could rest a good claim on both first discovery and occupation. He accordingly organised and sent an expedition to the island that autumn, intending its five members to stay there for two years and thereby buttress the claim. The end was tragic, however, for all but one of the party, an Eskimo woman, died before the arrival of the relief ship; and on the political side, neither the Canadian, the British nor the United States governments were inclined to take up the claim. In 1924, the Soviet government sent an armed party in the *Krasnyy Oktyabr'*, an icebreaker converted into a gunboat, to assert Soviet sovereignty and to remove the group of

---

[1] Papers relating (1939), vol. 2, pp. 682–3; Belov (1959), p. 216; Gotskiy (1962), p. 187.
[2] White (1950), pp. 327–8; Zhikharev (1961), p. 80.

twelve Eskimo and one American who were there.[1] This threat was, perhaps, never a very serious one, for it would have been extremely difficult for any foreign power, especially Britain, to assert sovereignty over an island in that position, but it undoubtedly stimulated Soviet activity, and led directly to the setting up of a station on the island in 1926, since when it has never been unoccupied. It is worth mentioning in this connection that the Soviet assertion of sovereignty was rather less of a stern eviction of foreign interlopers than later Soviet accounts would like to have people believe. In fact, there was mention in the press of a Soviet offer to lease the island to the United States for development, but this was not followed up.[2]

During this same period there was a continuation of the American trading activities mentioned earlier.[3] Schooners from Nome continued to visit settlements in Chukotka until the late 1920's. During the Civil War, the Hudson's Bay Company also carried on a successful business at a number of points along the north coast as far as the Kolyma. The action of the *Krasnyy Oktyabr'* no doubt had a discouraging effect, but the Soviet Government found it convenient to encourage some American traders to continue, because the Government's own communications with Chukotka were so uncertain.[4]

These were pressures which arose because the Soviet state was still weak. Since it has become strong, there has been only one serious threat to its northern territory, and that was the German attack from Finland in the Second World War. German troops advanced on Murmansk in the summer of 1941, and on many occasions in the next three years attempted to capture the port, or at least cut the railway to the south of it. The Red Army withstood these attacks, and in 1944 itself advanced and drove the Germans out of northern Scandinavia. For three years the threat was very real, but it was held to a stalemate.[5] Behind the Russian lines, however, there was much activity stimulated directly by it.

[1] Stefansson (1926); Mineyev (1946), pp. 7–42.
[2] *New York Evening Post*, 20 September 1924, quoted in Stefansson (1926), p. 276.
[3] See p. 110.
[4] Belov (1959), pp. 217–20; Swenson (1944), pp. 173–270.
[5] Blyth (1955).

10

RELATIONS WITH THE NATIVES

Before the revolution of October 1917 was a fortnight old, the 'Declaration of Rights of the Peoples of Russia' was issued, proclaiming the equality of all peoples and the free development of national minorities.[1] The first Commissar of Nationalities, responsible for seeing that this was put into effect, was Stalin. Soviet policy towards the native peoples was therefore clear and deliberate from the start. The forms of exploitation which had been common for centuries were to be ended. A committee was set up in 1924 to supervise the application of the policy to the northern peoples, whose problems were somewhat different from those of other minorities. This was the Committee of Assistance to the Peoples of the North (Komitet sodeystviya narodnostyam severnykh okrain), later known simply as the Committee for the North. It was an influential body with executive powers, and it did much to improve the material conditions of these peoples during the decade or so of its active life (1924–35).[2] Help of many kinds—education, training, medical services, equipment for hunting and fishing—was provided on a generous scale. Special attention was paid to devising systems of government which would permit the natives the greatest share in their own administration, and to training natives to hold positions of responsibility. Here an important part was played by the Institute of the Peoples of the North (Institut Narodov Severa), founded in 1930, and its successors, of which the most important is the northern faculty at Leningrad University. At a lower level, some natives became highly qualified workers in industrial undertakings: first in fields with which they were familiar, such as fisheries and reindeer husbandry, and later in other industries.[3] Thus the Soviet government, like its predecessor, had a humane policy towards these peoples, but it was better able than its predecessor to ensure that the policy was carried out effectively.

There is plenty of evidence to show that the Soviet government,

[1] See Appendix IV.
[2] Sergeyev (1962).
[3] Sergeyev (1955), pp. 407–8.

at various times, did much towards providing essential services. To quote just one example, which is certainly typical: in 1959 there were 40 schools in Taymyrskiy Natsional'nyy Okrug, with 4589 pupils, contrasting with none before 1917 (when, admittedly, the population was much smaller). Russians and natives attended the same schools, but in practice village schools were largely native and town schools largely Russian. The native children were boarders, presumably because their parents were still nomads, and their curriculum was beginning to include practical instruction in such things as reindeer husbandry, hunting, and fishing.[1] All this was a notable achievement, and every credit must be given. This impression of the helpfulness of the central authorities is a general one derived from not uncritical study of the Soviet literature, but it must not be taken to mean that conditions were always good in the north. On the contrary, civil war, famine, and other convulsions which caused such hardship to most Soviet citizens undoubtedly had repercussions also in the north.

But if it be granted that the native peoples were rescued from dangers to which they had been so long exposed, they were nevertheless threatened by new ones. It would be wrong to give the impression that Soviet improvements were always accepted unquestioningly by the natives themselves. The introduction of collectivisation caused upheavals in the north, as it had in the rest of the country. The number of domesticated reindeer in the Soviet Union fell by 30 per cent between 1929 and 1933 as a direct result of attempts at collectivisation.[2] These were later officially admitted to have been over-zealous and badly planned. The human tragedy behind this deliberate killing-off of the most valuable possession can be imagined. Collectivisation was in fact not fully introduced until later, and then native reindeer herders, like the peasants of other parts of the country, had to learn to like what was judged to be good for them. Associated with collectivisation was the drive to encourage nomads to settle, another process not always welcomed by the natives, and which is by no means complete yet. Further, the Soviet government, in the interests of what it believed to be social justice, incited the poorer members of a group against the richer and more successful. This was a reflection of the drive against the better-off peasants, or kulaks, in

---

[1] Faynberg (1962).   [2] Gul'chak (1954), p. 26.

more southerly regions, and it naturally led to violence. It is not unlikely that the feeling engendered by these sorts of action led in places to armed clashes; one is thought to have taken place in Yakutskaya ASSR in about 1928.

Yet besides these events involving constraint and violence—events which may be seen, perhaps, as the inevitable accompaniment of a revolution such as that of 1917—there was another and more subtle danger. A man might perhaps no longer exploit his fellows, but there was nothing to prevent the state from doing what it pleased with its subjects. The state had no cause to behave more harshly towards the northern peoples than towards any others of its subjects, for they constituted no possible danger to it, real or potential, by reason of their small numbers and retarded development. Rather was there everything to be gained from treating them in the way communist theory required, and this it did. But the state was interested in making a useful and productive citizen out of the Siberian tribesman, and was not unduly worried about the survival of his national culture. The danger to which he was now exposed, therefore, at a time of massive immigration into the north, was the loss of his national identity by assimilation into a larger national group, the Russian being the likeliest.

This process has been described in the Taymyr region, and, more fully, in northern Yakutskaya ASSR,[1] and there can be no doubt that it is happening in many other parts of the north also. The Soviet view is that assimilation of small groups into large ones is, at least in these cases, a 'progressive' phenomenon, being associated with a rise in economic and cultural standards brought about by, for instance, the introduction of collective farming. There is therefore no reason to wish to arrest the process, supposing this were possible.[2] It does not cause physical suffering. But it will, surely, lead to the disappearance of the northern people as separate national entities. It may even be that this process is inevitable, and the Soviet regime should not be held responsible for the results. But in that case the regime's claims to have found a successful solution to an admittedly very difficult problem must also be discounted.

A particular aspect of assimilation which deserves special attention is the linguistic one. The history of the Soviet attitude towards the

[1] Dolgikh (1949); Gurvich (1960, 1962).   [2] Sergeyev (1955), pp. 522–8.

northern native languages has been interesting. In the 1920's and early 1930's, Russian-born linguists recorded the languages, often for the first time, and produced school books for the instruction of the natives in their own language. The alphabet in which the languages were written was a modified roman one. But in about 1936 the policy was changed, and all native languages were thenceforth written in cyrillic, the alphabet used by Russian. The introduction of Russian loan words was thus facilitated, and this process has continued apace, many of the languages having had, of course, a poor vocabulary to start with. The native languages have been, and are still being, used in the schools, but there is evidence that in 1958–59 there were non-Russian Soviet citizens who bitterly resented attempts to boost Russian at the expense of their own languages.[1] No specific examples of this came from the north, however.

It is difficult not to see in all this a policy of deliberate russianisation, albeit by slow stages. There is much evidence that this is the policy which has been applied for some time towards larger national groups.[2] In the case of the smaller and very harmless groups in the north, it is perhaps still just possible to hold that the process was inevitable, and that the state, by its silence or by its actions, merely hastened it. But the trend in the country as a whole makes this increasingly hard to do.

The point was made above that the Soviet state paid special attention to devising systems of government by which the natives would play the greatest part in their own administration. But the constitutional arrangements, which gave the impression, as intended, that the minority peoples had full control of their own affairs, were entirely misleading. The 'Autonomous Republics', such as the Yakut and the Komi, and the 'National Districts', such as the Chukchi and six others in the north,[3] had less autonomy than an English county. The difference between the appearance and the reality has several causes. The most important is that real power in the Soviet Union resides not in the constitutionally established organs of government, although these do exist and function, but in the communist party, and this is a highly centralised body. It is also true that many of the largest economic undertakings in the territory

[1] Bilinsky (1962). [2] Kolarz (1952, 1954); Barghoorn (1956).
[3] See Map 11, p. 191.

of the autonomous and national regions—mining trusts, transport agencies, and so forth—have in any case been run straight from Moscow and have been quite independent of the local government. The way in which this has affected both the local situation and the aspirations of the natives has been made clear in Kolarz's two complementary volumes.[1] In fact, with the enormous influx of Russians during the Soviet period, it would be unreal to expect any genuine autonomy to have survived, even if it had existed in the first place. How could 20,000 or so Khanty and Mansi, for instance, be expected to retain the initiative when nearly 100,000 Russians were living in their territory? Russian domination in almost all areas does not have to be imposed any more. It has become inevitable. The threat to the national identity of the northern peoples is thus increased. Yet the fiction of their national autonomy is still preserved.

As far as numbers are concerned, it will be recalled that there was little change in the strength of the northern peoples between the census of 1926 and that of 1959.[2] In the space of one generation one would have expected a substantial rise, especially in view of the Soviet government's boasts, which could scarcely all have been empty, of the favourable treatment these peoples were getting. The population of the country as a whole, after adjustment for frontier changes, increased by over 20 per cent during the period. No explanation of the apparent failure of this policy has yet been offered on the Soviet side. But two conjectures may be offered. One is that the peoples are indeed not flourishing in the way they should be and the way the government would like. The other is that many individuals among them have become russianised to the extent of calling themselves Russian, for the 1959 census regulations permitted each person to determine his own nationality.[3] Both explanations may contain some truth, but the second seems likely to be the more important. The merging process happens in many other parts of the world where conditions are similar. It is true that in the Soviet Union the law has conferred on the northern peoples certain advantages, such as tax concessions.[4] But their appeal may now be less.

---

[1] Kolarz (1952, 1954).   [2] See Appendix I, Table 2.
[3] *Soviet News* (London), 23 January 1959.
[4] Taraconzio (1938), pp. 283–5; Sbornik zakonov (1961), p. 682.

Finally, there is the question of the role which the Soviet government expected or desired the natives to play. Although scattered, they are sufficiently numerous to be a useful addition to the industrial labour force. One piece of evidence quoted earlier indicates that they have been so employed—up to 1600 Yakut at the Aldan gold mines in 1931–32. This could be regarded as implying that quite a large proportion of the labour force might be, or have at any time been, native; but it does not seem likely. In his detailed work on the peoples of the north under Soviet rule, Sergeyev states that only a small proportion were employed in industry: natives constituted 2·3 per cent of the labour force in 1935.[1] He is not concerned in this book with the two largest groups, the Yakut and the Komi. But neither of the most recent economic surveys of these two republics[2] makes anything of this point, and it is likely that they would if there had been any substantial movement of natives into industry. The same impression is given by a population study of three mining settlements in southern Yakutskaya ASSR.[3] Furthermore, there is some realisation of the importance of not making an industrial labour force out of these peoples. A paper given to the conference on the geography of population at Moscow in 1962 stresses the point that they should be permitted to continue to exercise their skill at hunting and fishing. If they stopped doing this, the effect on the economy would be great, whereas if they were used in other capacities, the gain to the economy would not be commensurate.[4]

In summary, Soviet policy towards the northern peoples has been to promote their material well-being, as judged by Soviet standards, and if necessary using force, but to inhibit their political development, and their cultural development, too, in so far as it affects political development. The result seems to be one which the authorities may find satisfactory. Numbers are in the aggregate maintained, but any possibly embarrassing increase quietly syphons itself off by merging with the majority people.

[1] Sergeyev (1955), p. 408.   [2] Mityushkin (1960); Shishkin (1959).
[3] Pokshishevskiy (1962), pp. 96–101.
[4] Gurvich (1961), p. 15.

CONCLUSION

The events described have been part of a process referred to in this book as settlement, rather than as colonisation, because practical rather than political considerations were the more important. Yet it would not be wrong to use the word colonisation. It is true that the word has come recently to have a pejorative sense, especially in Soviet usage, with the implication that the settlers exploit or otherwise oppress the original inhabitants of the colony. Thus in the Soviet Union the word colonisation has been dropped in reference to Soviet territory, although it was used quite freely until well into the Soviet period in connection with Siberia.[1] But it was not for that reason that the term has been avoided in this book, and it is relevant to recall the term now because the political aspect must not be forgotten.

Apart from her Alaskan venture, Russia played no part in the colonisation of overseas territories by European powers during the great period of expansion in the fifteenth to early nineteenth centuries. She colonised Siberia instead; a territory that happened to be adjacent to the motherland. The motive for its acquisition was the same as that which impelled the Western European powers to go overseas—the search for wealth. Fur replaced precious metals. Thus the first stage of Russian colonisation of the north was carried out certainly with the approval of the central government, and, as it progressed, actually by the agents of that government. The *sluzhilyye lyudi* provided the framework within which the *promyshlenniki* operated. In this way, the whole of the north of Eurasia was colonised. Great numbers of people were not required. It was only necessary to have sufficient to extract the maximum quantity of fur, and to control the small number of natives, and for this a few thousand sufficed. It was a model of Girault's *colonie d'exploitation*, in which a small number of colonists employs native labour to develop the riches of the territory.[2]

Then, after the initial colonisation, two things happened which had the effect of not only preventing further growth, but even of diminishing in some places the number of colonists. One was the exhaustion of stocks of fur bearers, a state of affairs which was

---

[1] For example, Anson (1928), pp. 151–6.   [2] Girault (1943), pp. 26–7.

generally only temporary, but of long enough duration to oblige hunters to move on. The other was the occupation of more southerly areas, and the resulting shift to the south of the main routes through Siberia. This period of stagnation lasted for most of the eighteenth century in the western and central parts of northern Siberia, extending into the nineteenth further east. It is perhaps to be wondered at that settlements remained in being at all, for it might be supposed that a colony which brought in little income, and was not a sufficiently attractive place in other ways to draw settlers, might have collapsed entirely and been abandoned. This did happen in a few places, Mangazeya being the most notable example, but it is remarkable that there were not many more. One reason for the continuance of the colonies seems to have been, quite simply, inertia. For the individual, it was a major undertaking to get back from the lower Yenisey or Lena, and in any case there may have been nowhere better for him to go. For the authorities, the force of administrative inertia is always strong, and the worse the administration—Siberia was always a byword for that—the stronger the inertia. The continuing presence of cossacks in the north for decades and even centuries after their real usefulness had ended could be interpreted in this way, even if some measure of official awareness of their colonising function be conceded.

But inertia was not the only factor. It is an oversimplification to imagine the period of stagnation to be complete, or well defined. For it was in this period that peasants started to arrive in the north. They were by no means numerous, but once they came, they stayed. Although they did not penetrate to the most northerly regions, seldom crossing the 62nd parallel, in the end it was they who constituted the most stable element, in fact the mainstay, of the Russian colonisation, just as they did in southern Siberia. Their numbers included people under sentence and religious dissenters, and those who came of their own free will were often refugees. Here again is a close parallel with Western European colonisation, where political and religious discontent explained much of the emigration, and penal settlements became important colonial centres. By this means the number of colonists gradually grew.

There was a notable increase in the second half of the nineteenth century. This was brought about partly by the opening of gold mines in the Yenisey and Lena basins. There was also a marked increase in the number of exiles and convicts in the north. This was related to the growth of mining, because the miners were largely drawn from their ranks, but at the same time there were many exiles who were not miners. This period was one of massive immigration into Siberia as a whole, and some at least of the free immigrants found their way to the north. As a result of all this, there were between 50,000 and 100,000 Russian colonists in the north as defined for this book by the time of the 1917 revolution. They were a small minority in the total population, which was largely made up of native peoples. These had been exploited and maltreated for centuries, by individual Russians, and in spite of an apparently benevolent government, yet their numbers, it seems, grew rather than diminished.

From this modest, but solid, beginning, the most spectacular advance occurred in the Soviet period. The number of Russians increased to 1,600,000, easily outstripping the natives. The colony may thus be said to have changed from a *colonie d'exploitation* to a *colonie de peuplement* (to continue Girault's usage), and to have become, as it were, a Soviet Australia or Canada. But with one tremendous difference: the greater part of the colonists were under constraint. Without compulsion, there would no doubt have been some growth, but nothing like what in fact took place. The terrible multiplication of labour camps in the Arctic was one of the worst excesses of the Stalin era, and happily now, it would seem, a thing largely of the past. The Soviet official attitude would no doubt be to deny this interpretation as at best grossly exaggerated, and to point to the paucity of data supporting it. But until the Soviet government itself publishes credible figures on Siberian detention and exile, there is no alternative to accepting deductions from the evidence available. Penal colonisation, however, was not the whole story, even at the height of Stalin's repression. The incentives of a capitalist economy were used too, and with success, for they helped to build up most valuable cadres of enthusiastic and devoted Arctic workers in many branches of specialisation.

The main motive for this growth is to be found in the effort to make a large centralised economy self-sufficient. Complementary to it was the need for foreign currency, now met by gold rather than fur. It was these that caused the minerals to be sought and then exploited, the communication network to be created or improved. The mainstay of the Russian colonisation was no longer the peasant, but the mine-worker.

The motive was sufficiently strong for the government to accept the very great burden of bringing in sufficient food for this greatly increased number of settlers. For despite the advances of agriculture, no settlement of any size was able to support itself wholly on local resources, nor is it likely that this will be the case in the foreseeable future. The danger of basing northern settlement on mineral exploitation has been pointed out in Canada:[1] exhaustion of the ore body removes the *raison d'être* of the settlement. But in the Soviet Union, the situation is different. The reserves at the major mining centres such as Noril'sk and Vorkuta are great enough to guarantee long-term exploitation. Furthermore, the Soviet Government has deliberately pursued a policy of building up secondary industries in northern towns. And finally, a 'command economy' of the Soviet type permits those in control to disregard, within certain limits, considerations of profit and loss.

Meanwhile, the natives of the northern lands played the part allotted to them as Soviet citizens. Now a minority in their own territories, they took little part in the major economic developments of the region, but contributed to the economy through pursuit of their traditional way of life, modified to conform to the Soviet pattern. Their feelings at this change in their fortunes are not known, for none have had the opportunity to give them free expression. But, denied effective political rights, they seem to be starting to merge into the Russian majority.

Now that some, perhaps most, of the compulsion has been removed, it will be interesting to see the effects on settlement of the north. It seems that there has been a certain drop in numbers, but not a very big one. There are signs that improvements in living conditions are having some of the desired effect. It may be that once again Russians will live in the north freely and happily, as they did three centuries ago, and will really tame an environment which their ancestors, with such remarkable endurance, had been able only to tolerate. If they can do this, it will be largely because they have had such ancestors. It is not possible to fight such a battle with nature,

[1] Bladen (1962), pp. 80–117.

175

and on such a scale, without much experience. The importance in this regard of the Russian settlers of long standing (*russkiye starozhily*) is specifically recognised.[1] Before the revolution, quite a lot had been accomplished. The manner in which it was done may have been primitive and to some extent haphazard, but a point was nevertheless reached from which, to borrow an economist's phrase, take-off was possible. Many fundamental lessons had been learnt. Using them, the Soviet settlers could undertake the impressive projects that have been described. The manner in which they were carried through has in some major aspects been far from praiseworthy, but the results have been remarkable, and are unequalled in similar environments elsewhere. The Soviet Union has, or will shortly have, something of which it can be proud. Let it open its northern gates, so that the rest of us may see, admire, and learn.

[1] Gurvich (1961), pp. 14–15.

APPENDIX I

PEOPLES OF THE NORTH

The following brief notes are intended as a guide to the language, occupation and numbers of the various peoples with whom the Russians came into contact as they settled in the north. The information has been taken largely from Czaplicka (1914), Dolgikh (1960), Itogi (1963), Jochelson (1928), Levin & Potapov (1956), Matthews (1951), Sergeyev (1955), and the second edition of the Great Soviet Encyclopaedia (1949–58). For those who wish to study these peoples further, a good source in a language other than Russian is given at the end of each entry, where this is possible; beyond that, the reader is referred to the bibliography, arranged by peoples, given in Levin & Potapov (1956), pp. 993–1016, or, for the Palaeosiberian peoples, to Jakobson et al. (1957).

There is no detailed racial classification of these peoples on the basis of physical characters, and it may well be that the task of making one is impossible. Various broad classifications include these peoples, but do not agree with each other. Thus Jochelson (1928) sorts them into two large divisions—Mongoloids (the majority), and Americanoids (those in the far north-east)—and leaves two peoples (Ainu and Ket) in undetermined positions. Haddon (1929) includes them all in the Leiotrichi, or straight-haired peoples, and then classifies them by skull size. Another broad classification, by Deniker, groups them all under Mongoloid. It has not therefore seemed worthwhile including remarks on racial classification in the notes which follow.

Nomenclature of the peoples is another difficult matter, since in the early 1930's the Soviet authorities renamed many of them, often replacing the old name with a self-designation. Some of the new names eliminate ambiguities, or permit more accurate identification, and so are useful, but others have failed to gain acceptance, even in the Soviet Union. While both old and new names are given below, and in the index, it has been necessary to prefer one for ordinary use in the text. The choice has been determined by common sense, and without seeking to impose consistency. Names are given in the singular, except in a few cases where the plural is better known (for instance, Chukchi).

The numbers of these peoples living in the area with which this book is concerned are given in Table 2 at the end of this appendix.

The Ainu (in Russian Ayny), a people speaking a language of the Palaeo-siberian, or Palaeoasiatic, complex (which is not a family of languages, but a group of those which will not fit into the Uralian or Altaic families). They were living in the area with which this book is concerned only in the seventeenth and eighteenth centuries, when there were a few at the southern tip of Kamchatka. Today there are 16,000 Ainu, and they are found largely in Japan and southern Sakhalin, which was called Karafuto when under Japanese sovereignty. The Kamchatkan Ainu were fishers and hunters. They are the 'hairy Ainu' of English nursery tales, and were so called because of their luxuriant body hair which contrasted strongly with that of their neighbours.

The Aleut, sometimes called in Soviet usage by their self-designation Unangan, live mainly on the Aleutian Islands, which became United States territory in 1867. Some, however, were introduced to the uninhabited Komandorskiye Ostrova (Commander Islands) by the Russian-American Company in 1825 or 1826, in order to exploit fur resources, and these islands remained Russian. The descendants of the original settlers, augmented by further importations of Aleut, Eskimo, and others, are still there. The Aleut physical type predominates, but the language, which is closely related to Eskimo, does not, for in 1959 over three-quarters of the Aleut regarded Russian as their native language. The Aleut were primarily sea-mammal hunters, but terrestrial fur bearers were also hunted. Both occupations continue today, together with some agriculture. The Aleuts were converted to Russian Orthodoxy in the nineteenth century, and those now in United States territory (5600 in 1939, and apparently fewer now) have remained faithful to it.

Further reading: Hřdlicka (1945).

The Chukchi, or as they have occasionally been called in Soviet usage, Luorovetlan, have lived in the extreme north-east tip of Asia for as long as there has been any contact with the Russians. Their language is one of the Palaeosiberian group, and is related to those of their neighbours, the Eskimo and the Koryak. Most of them are reindeer herders, following their herds in the tundra as far west as the Alazeya, but about a third of the people have always lived a settled life on the coast, fishing and hunting sea mammals. The Chukchi offered more resistance to the Russians than most northern peoples, and for this reason, as well as their remoteness, they became Russian subjects only in 1789, nearly a century and a half after the first contacts. Their religion was shamanistic, and there was little even nominal conversion to Christianity. In Soviet times, most Chukchi have been persuaded to join reindeer or fishing collectives. There are a number of books in the Chukchi language, and one Chukchi writer, Rytkheu, is well known in the Soviet Union.

Further reading: Bogoras (1904–9).

Chuvantsy, see *Yukagir*.

Dolgan, see *Tungus*.

Entsy, see *Samoyed*.

Peoples of the North

The Eskimo (Eskimos in Russian) are the most widespread Arctic people, stretching from north-east Siberia across North America to Greenland. In Russia there is only the small group of Asiatic Eskimo living in settlements on the shore of Bering Strait. Their language is related to those of all the other Eskimo, but most closely with those of the south Alaskan Eskimo groups. The Asiatic Eskimo were, and remain, sea-mammal hunters.

Further reading: Bogoras (1913).

The Kamchadal are the aboriginal inhabitants of Kamchatka, speaking a language of the Palaeosiberian group related to Koryak and Chukchi. They are usually called Itel'men in Soviet usage, but the correspondence is not always exact, since Kamchadal is used by some ethnologists to denote the Russian-aboriginal half-breeds, who now greatly outnumber those of pure native stock. Kamchadal was also sometimes used in the eighteenth and nineteenth centuries to mean the descendants of early Russian settlers, so caution is needed. The aboriginals were a true fishing people, and had no domestic animals except the dog. Their religion was animistic. Under Soviet rule they have become hard to distinguish from the Russian 'old settlers', with whom they work in fishing collectives. In 1959 nearly two-thirds of them regarded Russian as their native language. The attempt to create a literary language was abandoned after publication of two school books.

Kazakh, see *Kirgiz*.

The Ket, also known as the Yenisey Ostyak or Yeniseian, live on the middle Yenisey. They have no ethnic link with their neighbours (their supposed relationship to one of them, the Ostyak, gave rise to the name), and their language is now classed in the Palaeosiberian group, the rest of the members of which live much further east. They are the only survivors of a group of peoples speaking related languages, the others—Kot, Asan and Arin—having been assimilated by their neighbours. The ancestors of the Ket probably came from the south. They were primarily hunters and secondarily fishers. Reindeer were used for transport. Under Soviet rule, most Ket have been organised into collectives, and fur farming has been introduced. The attempt to create a literary language was abandoned after publication of one book in 1934.

Further reading: Donner (1933).

The Khanty (or Ostyak) are probably the descendants of the Yugrians of the early Russian accounts, who lived in the Pechora basin and later moved eastwards across the Ural mountains to the lower Ob' region where the Khanty are found today. Their language is one of the Ugrian group, which also includes Magyar, and which is often hyphenated to the related Finnic languages as Finno-Ugrian. The people were originally

12-2

Appendix I

hunters and fishers, and they acquired an interest in reindeer herding from their northern neighbours, the Samoyed. They were for long not distinguished from their closer neighbours, the *Mansi* or Vogul, to whom they are related and with whom they share many aspects of their culture.

Further reading: Manninen (1932), pp. 321–67.

The Kirgiz are one of the most ancient peoples of Central Asia, inhabiting the valleys of the Tien Shan mountains and speaking a Turkic language. They are concerned with the subject matter of this book only in so far as an outlying group, the Yenisey Kirgiz, energetically opposed Russian advance into their territory, and raided Russian settlements at Tomsk, Achinsk and Krasnoyarsk under their prince Irenak Isheyev in the seventeenth century. By their action, they forced the Russian advance across Siberia into more northerly regions. The Kirgiz are Sunnite Moslems, and have until recently led a nomadic or semi-nomadic life tending herds of cattle, sheep, goats, horses and camels. Most of their territory was incorporated into the Russian Empire in the second half of the nineteenth century, while some Kirgiz remained, and remain, in China. Under Soviet rule they have been granted the status of a Union Republic—Kirgizskaya SSR.

There has been much confusion in the past between the Kirgiz, who were formerly known as Kara-Kirgiz, and the *Kazakh*, who were formerly known as the Kirgiz-Kaisak, or Kazak Kirgiz, or even Kazak (which also means cossack). The Kazakh are a related people in language, customs and mode of life, but not in origin. It may be that the Yenisey Kirgiz were of the group now called Kazakh, but this is not very likely.

The Koryak, for a short period called by their self-designation Nymylan in Soviet literature, speak a language of the Palaeosiberian group related to Chukchi and Kamchadal, the languages of their neighbours to north and south. They have lived on and about the isthmus of the Kamchatka peninsula since first contact with the Russians, but were wider spread along the shores of the Okhotsk and Bering Seas in the seventeenth and eighteenth centuries than they are now. They are reindeer herders, hunters of sea mammals, fishermen, and fur hunters, different groups specialising in one or other of these pursuits. The sedentary groups, mainly in coastal settlements, have been skilled dog drivers. In Soviet times, collectivisation was introduced, not without a struggle. A number of books have been published in the Koryak language.

Further reading: Jochelson (1905–8).

Lamut, see *Tungus*.

The Lapps, called in Russian Lopari, or more recently Saami, have lived throughout the period of Russian settlement in Kol'skiy Poluostrov, the peninsula of Kola. The Lapps in Russian territory are of course related to those in northern Finland, Sweden and Norway, but they are the smallest

of the four groups, who number altogether some 30,000. The Lappish
language is one of the West Finnic family. The Russian Lapps are either
reindeer herders, or fishers, or both, and have tended to keep in the
interior of the peninsula. In Soviet times there has been a great increase
of Russian population in the peninsula, and little is now heard of the small
Lapp community, of whom nearly 30 per cent regarded Russian as their
native language in 1959.

Mansi, see *Khanty*.

Nentsy, see *Samoyed*.

Nganasan, see *Samoyed*.

Samoyed is the name now given in the Soviet Union to the language group
which includes four northern peoples: the *Nentsy, Entsy, Nganasan* and
Sel'kup. Before these four names were introduced in the 1930's, the Nentsy
were called Yurak, or simply Samoyed, the Entsy were called Yenisey
Samoyed, the Nganasan were called Tavgi Samoyed, and the Sel'kup were
called Ostyak Samoyed, but the correspondence was not always exact.
The Samoyed languages make up, together with the Finno-Ugrian
languages, the Uralian family. The peoples hunt, fish, and herd reindeer
in the tundra along the coast from the White Sea to Taymyr. They were
nomads, but the Soviet Government has tried to induce them to settle,
evidently with some success, and has organised collective farms which often
act as a base for settlement. The Nganasan, living on Taymyr, and thus
the most northerly inhabitants of the country, apart from groups at
scientific stations, hunt wild reindeer in addition to the other pursuits.
The Entsy, a very small group, are being rapidly assimilated by their
neighbours. The Sel'kup, although Samoyed linguistically, are more like
the Khanty in their way of life, reindeer herding being known only among
some of them, and in those cases learnt from their northern neighbours.
Half the Sel'kup regarded Russian as their native language in 1959.
    Further reading: Donner (1915).

Sel'kup, see *Samoyed*.

Tatar is the name given to a number of peoples in Tsarist Russia, and now
the Soviet Union, who are Sunnite Moslems by religion and speak Turkic
languages. Originally the Tatars were apparently a single ethnic group,
perhaps of Kipchak stock, living in the west Siberian plain, and they
achieved prominence when Jenghiz Khan organised them into fighting
groups ('hordes') for his tremendous conquests in the thirteenth century.
By the sixteenth century they had fragmented into a number of geo-
graphically distinct groups, and some were mixed with other peoples. The
Tatars of the Crimea and the Caucasus are of no direct concern here.
Those of the Volga, who were defeated when Ivan the Terrible took

Kazan' in 1552, were the descendants of the Golden Horde of the Mongol conquests, the name Golden Horde also being used for the state which they established over a large area of southern Russia.

It was the west Siberian Tatars whom Yermak encountered. They were the people of the Siberian Khanate under Kuchum, and were descended, with Mongol admixture, from the White Horde, a fighting formation of Jenghiz Khan's grandson Batu. Suffering defeat by the Russians at the end of the sixteenth century, some Tatars of the Siberian Khanate fled eastwards and settled in the Tomsk and Chulym regions, where they are still to be found. At first the west Siberian Tatars were cattle nomads, but with the advent of the Russians settled to crop growing. None live in the north as defined for this book.

The Tungus, called in Soviet usage Evenk, are a very wide-ranging people, found also in Manchuria and Outer Mongolia. The word Tungus is retained in Soviet literature for the language group of the Tungus and related peoples, a group which forms, with Manchu, one of the main sub-divisions of the Altaic language family. The Tungus peoples are spread thinly over an enormous area between Taymyr on the Arctic Ocean, the Sea of Okhotsk, and the Amur River. Those with whom this book is concerned are nomadic reindeer herders and hunters, while the southern group farm cattle and horses. Their religion was shamanistic, and although most Tungus were converted to Russian Orthodoxy, this was often nominal. In the 1959 census, a third of all Tungus in the Soviet Union considered Yakut their native language. The culture and language of the *Lamut* (Even in Soviet usage) are closely similar to those of the Tungus, and some ethnologists have felt that the two should not be separated. The Lamut live on the shores of the Sea of Okhotsk and the Arctic Ocean, their name being derived from the Tungus word for sea. The *Dolgan* are another small group of Tungus origin, and are also reindeer herders and hunters. They live in the southern part of Taymyr, and have adopted the Yakut language, a fact which has caused them to be confused with the Yakut at times. As elsewhere in the Soviet north, collectivisation was introduced in the 1930's, and it is probable that most of these peoples have now joined.

Further reading: Shirokogoroff (1933).

The Yakut are the most numerous of the northern peoples of the Soviet Union. Their self-designation, Sakha, is not commonly used. They speak a Turkic language. It has generally been thought that they moved northwards into their present territory on the middle Lena not long before the Russians arrived, but recent archaeological evidence casts some doubt on this. They have apparently for long had horses and cattle, and only a minority in the north have been reindeer herders. They have always done well as traders. Originally shamanists, by the nineteenth century all Yakut were members of the Russian Orthodox

Church, and the conversion was often genuine. Under Soviet rule the Yakut territory is administered as an Autonomous Republic, the Yakut-skaya ASSR. In this, Yakut have until now predominated, but Russians nearly equalled them in 1959. There is a considerable literature in the Yakut language, based on the important linguistic studies commenced in the second half of the nineteenth century.

Further reading: Jochelson (1933).

The Yukagir, sometimes called in Soviet usage by their self-designation Odul, speak a Palaeosiberian language. When the Russians first reached their lands, they occupied a wide belt of tundra between the Lena and the Anadyr'. Similarities between their language and those of certain North American Indians have been noticed. The numbers and territory of the Yukagir shrunk, and now the people have no longer an ethnic unity. There has been much assimilation into neighbouring Lamut, Yakut and Russian groups, and of those who still called themselves Yukagir in 1959, a third regarded Russian as their native language. The Yukagir were chiefly hunters and fishers when the first Russians arrived, but reindeer herding was also practised, this evidently being an innovation borrowed from the Lamut, and it gained in importance. Under Soviet rule collective farms were established, and most Yukagir now live settled lives in them. No attempt has been made to create a Yukagir literary language, and the people's continued existence as a separate entity does not seem likely to last long.

The Chuvantsy, or Etel, had a culture and language closely similar to the Yukagir, but their language disappeared in the nineteenth century, and they have all been assimilated into Russian, Chukchi and Koryak groups. Some Soviet ethnologists argue that the Chuvantsy should not have been regarded as a separate people, but as a part of the Yukagir people.

Further reading: Jochelson (1910–26).

Appendix I

Table 2. *Numbers of native peoples living in the north as defined on Map 1*

	People	Seventeenth-century estimates based largely on fur-tribute returns	1897 census	1926 census	1959 census
1	Lapp (Saam)	1,600	1,738	1,720	1,760
2	Nentsy (Samoyed, Yurak)	10,430, including Nganasan and Entsy	9,427	16,375	22,845
3	Nganasan (Tavgi, Tavgiyskiy Samoyed)	Ancestors included as Nentsy; estimated to number 1,030	876	867	721
4	Entsy (Yenisey Samoyed)	Ancestors included as Nentsy; estimated to number 3,100	500	1,445	Not listed
5	Khanty (Ostyak)	9,420, including Mansi	22,700 Including Mansi	16,270	17,000
6	Mansi (Vogul)	Included as Khanty	Included as Khanty	5,700	6,318
7	Sel'kup (Ostyak Samoyed)	645	1,450	1,500	1,250
8	Ket (Yenisey Ostyak, Yeniseian)	1,525	1,000	1,250	1,000
9	Tungus (Evenk)	17,100, including Lamut and Dolgan	20,700	15,700	13,000
10	Lamut (Even)	Included as Tungus; estimated to number 6,710	Included as Tungus	7,000	9,023
11	Dolgan	Included as Tungus; estimated to number 1,030	1,224	1,445	Not listed
12	Yakut	28,470	226,000	235,926	236,125
13	Yukagir	4,775, including Chuvantsy	1,200	443	440
14	Chuvantsy (Etel)	Included as Yukagir; estimated to number 600	506	704	Not listed
15	Chukchi (Luorovetlany)	2,400	11,800	12,364	11,680
16	Koryak (Nymylan)	10,785	7,300	7,434	6,168
17	Kamchadal (Itel'men)	12,680	2,800	814	1,096
18	Eskimo	4,000	1,300	1,294	1,111
19	Ainu (Ayny)	270	None	None	None
20	Aleut	None	Not known	345	339
	Totals	104,100	310,521	328,596	330,936

This table is intended to be a rough guide and no more. Although the information is believed to be the best available, reliability is by no means uniform. Detailed comment on the figures would therefore be out of place. But the most astonishing change of all—the increase of the Yakut people by a factor of eight between the seventeenth century and 1897—perhaps requires the assurance that it is believed to be the truth by Dolgikh, who supports his seventeenth-century figure with 200 pages of argument.

In arriving at the figures given above for 1897, 1926 and 1959, it has been necessary in some cases to make adjustments for the geographical area with which this book is concerned. Numbers of native peoples are often given as a total of that national or tribal group for the whole country, without subdivision by region. This causes no difficulty when a people is known to live wholly, or very nearly wholly, within the area, and this is fortunately the case with most of those listed. But when the national or tribal home

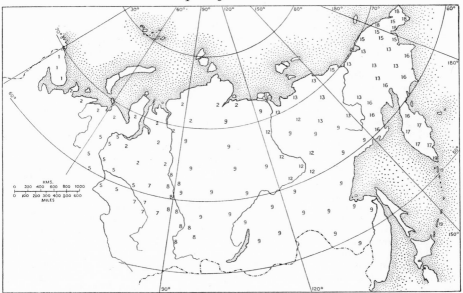

Map. 8. Distribution of native peoples in the seventeenth century. The numbers
refer to column 1 of Table 2, p. 184. Source: Dolgikh (1960*a*).

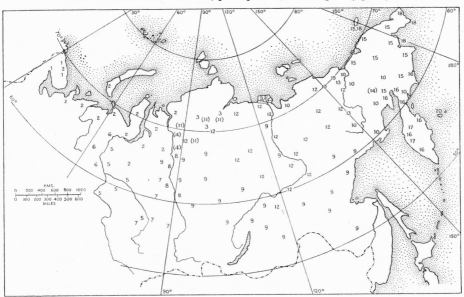

Map 9. Distribution of native peoples in 1959. The numbers refer to column 1 of
Table 2, p. 184. Numbers in brackets signify the last known locations of peoples
no longer listed in the census returns. Source: Karta narodov (1962).

spreads across the southern boundary of the area, it becomes necessary to estimate how many live in the northern part. This is the case for the Khanty, Tungus, Sel'kup and Ket. Certain sources do offer information on a regional basis. Thus Patkanov (1906) provides evidence for a figure for the Tungus in 1897, Levin & Potapov (1956) for the Sel'kup and Ket in 1926, Terletskiy (1930) for the Khanty and Tungus in 1926, and Itogi (1963) for the Khanty, Tungus and Sel'kup in 1959. This makes it possible to calculate what percentage of the group lived in the area at those times. The remaining uncertain cases— Khanty, Sel'kup and Ket in 1897, and Ket in 1959—can then be estimated on the broad supposition that the proportion living in the north had been, or remained, the same. The Komi have been omitted altogether owing to the difficulty of determining how many lived within the area. The 1959 census records 12,681 Komi living in the national districts to the north and east of Komi ASSR, and therefore within the area, but there is no way of knowing how many more there may have been in, for instance, the north-eastern tip of Komi ASSR itself.

The peoples listed in Table 2 form the bulk of the 'Small peoples of the north', a term in Soviet administrative usage since 1925. The term excludes the Yakut, who are too numerous, and the Ainu, who no longer live in the USSR, but includes eight more peoples living further south: Negidal'tsy, Tofalar, Nanay or Gol'd, Ul'ch, Orok, Oroch, Ude, and Nivkh or Gilyak. The continued inclusion of the Chuvantsy seems to be due to administrative oversight.

Sources: seventeenth century, Dolgikh (1960a); Kolycheva (1956), p. 76, for Nentsy in Europe; Hallström (1911), pp. 266–7, for Lapp. 1897 and 1926, Levin & Potapov (1956). 1959, Itogi (1963), pp. 300–2, 312–37.

APPENDIX II

Aldan 12,100

Amderma 2,200

Anadyr' 5,600

Apatity 19,938

Batagay 5,800

Berezov 6,800

Bodaybo 17,500

Chul'man 6,000

Deputatskiy 1,900

Dikson 2,000

Dudinka 16,400

Ege-Khaya 3,200

Igarka 14,300

Kandalaksha 37,045

Khandyga 4,100

Khanty-Mansiysk 20,677

Kirovsk 39,047

Kola 8,000

Korf 2,100

Labytnangi 5,200

Magadan 62,225

Mirnyy 5,640

Monchegorsk 45,523

Mukhtuya 7,834

Murmansk 221,874

Nar'yan-Mar 13,000

Nikel' 16,305

Noril'sk 109,442

Nyurba 6,448

Okhotsk 8,500

Olekminsk 7,900

Olenegorsk 12,100

Palana 900

Pechenga 3,500

Peleduy 4,995

Petropavlovsk-na-Kamchatke 85,582

Pevek 5,800

Pokrovsk 5,000

Polyarnyy 11,300

Provideniya 4,800

Salekhard 16,567

Severomorsk 32,234

Seymchan 4,100

Srednekolymsk 2,100

Tiksi 6,000

Tommot 5,400

Tura 2,000

Ust'-Kamchatsk 10,900 (1963)

Ust'-Nera 9,800 (1963)

Verkhoyansk 1,400

Vilyuysk 4,500

Vitim 2,877

Vorkuta 55,668

Yakutsk 74,330

Zyryanka 4,200

Note. All population figures are believed to be derived from the 1959 census, unless another date is shown. Most sources quote figures to the nearest hundred, or sometimes thousand.

Sources: Grigor'yev (1960–); Pokshishevskiy (1962), pp. 22– ; Gladkov (1961); Itogi (1963), pp. 30–8.

APPENDIX III

TOTAL POPULATION OF THE NORTH, 1926 AND 1959

Table 3. *Total population, in 1926 and 1959, of areas approximating to that shown on Map 1*

Administrative area (See Maps 10 and 11, pp. 190–1)	Total population	Russians (including Ukrainians and Belorussians)
1926		
Murmanskaya Guberniya	22,800	16,700
Arkhangel'skaya Guberniya:		
Pechorskiy Uyezd	21,800	15,600
Izhmopechorskiy Uyezd	30,700	500
Tobol'skiy Okrug:		
Berezovskiy, Obdorskiy, Samarovskiy and Surgutskiy Rayony, towns of Surgut and Berezov	49,300	18,900
Turukhanskiy Kray	23,600	7,900
Yakutskaya ASSR	273,000	30,200
Kamchatskiy Okrug	34,700	6,800
Nikolayevskiy Okrug:		
Ol'skiy and Okhotskiy Rayony, town of Okhotsk	6,200	1,400
Total	462,100	98,000
1959		
Murmanskaya Oblast'	567,672	536,579
Nenetskiy Natsional'nyy Okrug	45,534	33,886
Vorkuta mining area	170,000	150,000 (estimate)
Yamalo-Nenetskiy Natsional'nyy Okrug	62,334	30,098
Khanty-Mansiyskiy Natsional'nyy Okrug	123,926	95,457
Taymyrskiy Natsional'nyy Okrug	33,382	23,398
Noril'sk (town only)	109,442	100,000 (estimate)
Evenkiyskiy Natsional'nyy Okrug	10,320	6,171
Yakutskaya ASSR	487,343	230,058
Kamchatskaya Oblast'	193,228	173,004
Chukotskiy Natsional'nyy Okrug	46,689	32,439
Koryakskiy Natsional'nyy Okrug	27,525	17,984
Magadanskaya Oblast'	188,889	169,521
Total	2,066,284	1,598,595

Total Population of the North

This table should not be regarded as more than a rough guide, although the figures are believed to be the best available. The total for 1959 accords well with an estimate of 2,000,000 given by Slavin (1961 a, pp. 7–26, 290–1) for an area he terms 'the far north', which very roughly approximates to that defined on Map 1.

It should be noted that for 1926, the difference between the total population and the number of Russians is 364,100 (462,100 less 98,000) whereas the table in Appendix I shows the northern peoples as numbering 328,600 at that date. This discrepancy is too big to be explained by difference in the size of area under consideration, and must therefore be largely due to the presence in the north of immigrants other than Russians, although the latter have been taken to include Ukrainians and Belorussians for this purpose. This group of non-Russian immigrants was larger in 1959. The census records the presence of 12,681 Komi, 3766 Karelians, 6740 Koreans (in Kamchatka), 3075 Mordvinians (also in Kamchatka), 3040 Jews (in Murmanskaya Oblast'), and 23,570 Tatars (scattered throughout). These total over 50,000, and another 75,000 must be accounted for by groups too small to be listed in currently available results.

Sources: for 1926, Vsesoyuznaya perepis' (1928), tom 1, pp. 52, 58, 124; tom 4, pp. 134, 254–5; tom 6, p. 48; tom 7, pp. 24–6, 130, 167–71. For 1959, Itogi (1963), pp. 24–9, 37, 312–37; Korovitsin (1961), p. 55.

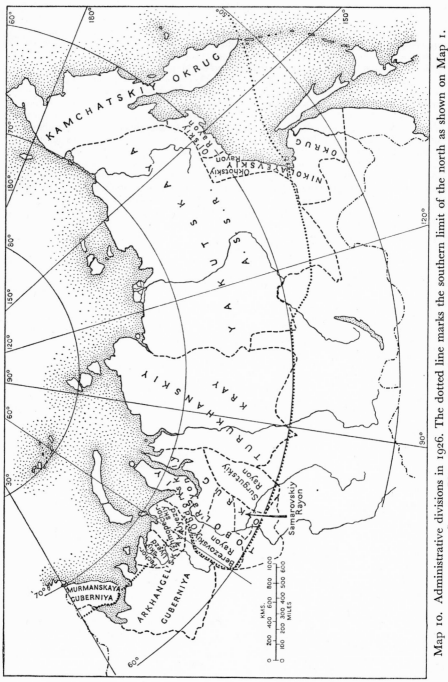

Map 10. Administrative divisions in 1926. The dotted line marks the southern limit of the north as shown on Map 1.
Source: Vsesoyuznaya perepis (1928), maps at the end of vols. 1, 4, 6, 7.

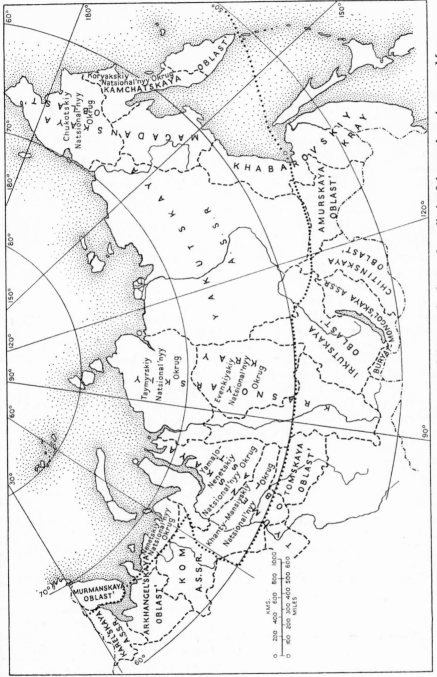

Map 11. Administrative divisions in 1959. The dotted lines marks the southern limit of the north as shown on Map 1.
Source: Atlas SSSR (1962).

APPENDIX IV

On the rights of the peoples of Russia.

The October Revolution of workers and peasants began from a general desire for liberation.

The peasants are freeing themselves from the power of the landlords, since the landlords no longer have a right to land—it has been taken away. The soldiers and sailors are freeing themselves from the power of the autocratic generals, since generals henceforth will be elected and replaced. The workers are freeing themselves from the caprices and arbitrariness of the capitalists, since henceforth workers' control will be established in the factories. Everything alive and viable is freeing itself from hated yokes.

There remain only the peoples of Russia, who have endured and are enduring oppression and arbitrary rule, liberation from which should be undertaken without delay, and the freeing of whom should be carried out decisively and irreversibly.

In the epoch of Tsarism the peoples of Russia were systematically set against each other. The results of this policy are known: slaughter and massacre on the one hand, slavery of the peoples on the other.

There is not and should not be a return to this shameful policy of setting one against the other. From henceforth this should be replaced by a policy of the voluntary and honourable union of the peoples of Russia.

In the period of imperialism, after the February revolution, when power went to the bourgeois Cadet Party, the open policy of setting one against another yielded to a policy of cowardly distrust of the peoples of Russia, a policy of cavilling and of provocations, masked by verbal declarations on the 'freedom' and 'equality' of the peoples. The results of this policy are known: the strengthening of national enmity, the collapse of mutual trust.

This unworthy policy of lies and distrust, cavilling and provocation, should be ended. From henceforth it should be replaced by an open and honourable policy leading to full mutual trust among the peoples of Russia.

Only as a result of such trust can an honourable and lasting union of the peoples of Russia be built.

Only as a result of such a union can the workers and peasants of the peoples of Russia be forged into a single revolutionary force, able to stand up against any onslaughts of the aggressive imperialist bourgeoisie.

The Congress of Soviets in June of this year proclaimed the right of the peoples of Russia to free self-determination.

The Second Congress of Soviets in October of this year confirmed this inalienable right of the peoples of Russia more decisively and exactly.

Appendix IV

Fulfilling the will of these Congresses, the Council of Peoples Commissars decided to adopt the following principles as the basis for their actions on the question of the nationalities of Russia:

1. Equality and sovereignty of the peoples of Russia.

2. Right of the peoples of Russia to free self-determination, up to the point of secession and the formation of an independent state.

3. Abolition of each and every national and national-religious privilege and limitation.

4. Free development of national minorities and national groups inhabiting the territory of Russia.

Concrete decrees following from these principles will be worked out without delay after the establishment of a commission for nationality affairs.

In the name of the Russian Republic,

V. Ul'yanov (Lenin)
Chairman of the Council of
Peoples Commissars
Iosif Dzhugashvili Stalin
Peoples Commissar for
Nationality Affairs

2 November (old style) 1917
Source: Deklaratsiya (1917–18).

APPENDIX V

Ivan III (the Great) 1462–1505
Vasiliy III 1505–33
Ivan IV (the Terrible) 1533–84
Fedor Ivanovich 1584–98
Boris Godunov 1598–1605
"Time of troubles" 1605–13
Mikhail Fedorovich Romanov 1613–45
Aleksey Mikhaylovich 1645–76
Fedor Alekseyevich 1676–82
Peter I (the Great) 1682–1725
Ivan V 1682–96
Catherine I 1725–27
Peter II 1727–30
Anna 1730–40
Ivan VI 1740–41
Elizabeth 1741–62
Peter II 1762
Catherine II (the Great) 1762–96
Paul 1796–1801
Alexander I 1801–25
Nicholas I 1825–55
Alexander II 1855–81
Alexander III 1881–94
Nicholas II 1894–1917

GLOSSARY OF RUSSIAN TERMS

Avtozimnik, pl. *avtozimniki*: winter motor road, without an all-weather surface and therefore usable only when the ground is frozen hard.

Guberniya, pl. *gubernii*: see *Okrug*.

Oblast', pl. *oblasti*: see *Okrug*.

Okrug, pl. *okrugi*: an administrative district in both Tsarist and Soviet Russia. Before 1917, it was inferior to a *Guberniya*, which is generally translated as a Government and which was the largest of the administrative divisions in the eighteenth and nineteenth centuries, and to an *Oblast'*; and roughly of equal standing with an *Uyezd*. *Guberniya*, *Oblast'* and *Uyezd* all lasted into the Soviet period, but only *Oblast'* remains in use today. In Soviet times *Okrug* is chiefly used in the phrase *Natsional'nyy Okrug*, National District, a subdivision designed for small minority peoples.

Ostrog, pl. *ostrogi*: a fortress consisting of an outer wall, with towers at intervals, forming a rectangle within which were houses, church, barracks and stores. It was essentially a frontier fortification. In the eighteenth and nineteenth centuries the word acquired the meaning of prison, no doubt because an *ostrog* might be used for that purpose after its usefulness as a frontier post was over. Many settlements in Siberia were *ostrogi* early in their history, and the word formed part of the place-name (e.g. Yeniseyskiy Ostrog, which became Yeniseysk). See Pl. II (*a*) and (*b*).

Posad, pl. *posady*: that part of an early Russian settlement lying outside the walls of the fortified place (probably an *ostrog*) which formed the core of the original settlement. The officials and the soldiers lived in the *ostrog*, while the traders and the artisans lived in the *posad*. Thus the *posad* was the true ancestor of any town which grew up at that place. See Pl. II (*a*) and (*b*).

Promyshlennik, pl. *promyshlenniki*: in Siberia in the seventeenth and eighteenth centuries, a person who practised a craft for his living, the craft being normally connected with hunting or fishing. The word connoted more than the idea of hunter (which was *okhotnik*, or *okhochiy chelovek*), including something of the sense of a trader as well. In the nineteenth and twentieth centuries the word came to mean industrialist.

Pyatidesyatnik: cossak commander of 50 men.

Raskol'nik, pl. *raskol'niki*: a religious sect which broke away from the Russian Orthodox Church in the seventeenth century over revision of the liturgical books, and has remained independent ever since. There have been many adherents, who have from time to time suffered persecution. Generally translated as Old Believers.

Glossary of Russian Terms

Skopets, pl. *Skoptsy*: a small religious sect which existed in Russia from the late eighteenth to the early twentieth centuries. Adherents believed that castration was a necessary condition for salvation. For much of the sect's existence, membership was punishable with exile to Siberia.

Sloboda, pl. *slobody*: a large village in pre-Revolutionary Russia, originally one without serfs and tax obligations, often located close to a town or monastery (from *svoboda* = freedom).

Sluzhilyye lyudi, sing. *sluzhilyy chelovek*: servants of the Russian state in the fifteenth to seventeenth centuries. The translation as 'service people' or 'service men' used in this book is inadequate, but hard to improve. It is a general term embracing the nobility, who owed service to the crown, the armed forces, and civilian employees. Among the nobility were the *deti boyarskiye*, singular *syn boyarskiy* (= esquires, literally children of noblemen), a rank which had lost its hereditary character in Siberia at this time and was conferred on any thought deserving, whatever their origins. The second group, the armed forces, included the *strel'tsy*, singular *strelets*, who were the regular infantry, and also the *kazaki*, singular *kazak*, the cossacks, who constituted the irregular forces employed in Siberia (see pp. 65–7). All these terms, except cossacks, disappeared in the early eighteenth century when the army and civil service were re-organized by Peter the Great.

Sotnik: cossack commander of 100 men.

Spetspereselenets, pl. *spetspereselentsy*: abbreviation of *spetsial'nyy pereselenets*, meaning special settler, a person deported by the Soviet government and obliged to live in a given locality under supervision of the Ministry of Internal affairs (NKVD, later MVD). A category of punishment common from the 1930's to the 1950's.

Strelets, pl. *strel'tsy*: see *Sluzhilyye lyudi*.

Syn boyarskiy, pl. *deti boyarskiye*: see *Sluzhilyye lyudi*.

Uyezd, see *Okrug*.

Voyevoda: an old Slavonic term for a military leader. In Siberia in the seventeenth and eighteenth centuries the word was more commonly used to mean the military governor of a town or a region. The area of his jurisdiction was called a *voyevodstvo*.

Yamshchik, pl. *yamshchiki*: peasant employed by the Russian Government in the time of horse transport to man post stations on the trunk roads. *Yamshchiki* were responsible for the horses provided for travellers.

Yasak: a word of Turkic origin meaning tribute, but in Siberia it came to mean fur tribute. *Yasak* had been levied in furs by Tatars and Mongols before the arrival of the Russians, who took over many points in the existing collection system. The Russian levy was on all able-bodied males among the native peoples, and was never payable by Russian settlers. It was of two kinds: *okladnoy*, which required a fixed number of skins annually, generally between five and ten; and *neokladnoy*, when the collector took what he could get. In order to emphasise that this was tribute, and not a tax, the Russians at first used to make gifts to the natives when the *yasak* was collected. But later this ceased, and *yasak* came to be paid often in money, and became very like other taxes. It remained in force in certain parts of the north until 1917. For a full account, see Bakhrushin (1955 *b*), pp. 49–85, and also Fisher (1943), pp. 49–61.

Yurta, pl. *yurty*: a hut, generally circular in plan and a truncated cone in elevation, consisting of an outer covering supported by a wooden framework. It is used by many Turkic and Mongol tribes. Among the Yakut the covering is generally of turf and earth. The word yourt has found some acceptance in English.

Zimov'ye, pl. *zimov'ya*: a wintering cabin in the forest used by traders and hunters. Generally strongly built of logs, and designed to withstand attack, with heavy doors and slits for shooting through. It was common for a settlement to begin as a *zimov'ye*, become an *ostrog*, and finally drop both appellations (e.g. Nizhnekolymskoye Zimov'ye, Nizhnekolymskiy Ostrog, Nizhnekolymsk).

REFERENCES

This is primarily a list of works consulted, and not a bibliography. Almost all the entries are referred to from the text. The few which are not so referred to are included because they are useful works.

ABRAMOV, N. A. (1857). Opisaniye Berezovskogo Kraya [Description of the Berezov region]. *Zapiski Imperatorskogo Russkogo Geograficheskogo Obshchestva*, kniga 12, pp. 327–48.

ALAMPIYEV, P. M. (1962). Krupnyye ekonomicheskiye rayony SSSR po novomu rayonirovaniyu i problemy ikh razvitiya [Large economic regions of the USSR according to the new zoning and problems of their development]. *Izvestiya Akademii Nauk SSSR. Seriya Geograficheskaya*, no. 1, pp. 57–71.

ALEKSANDROV, V. A. (1960). Russkoye naseleniye Mangazeysko-Turukhanskogo kraya v XVII–pervoy chetverti XVIII veka [Russian population of the Mangazeya-Turukhansk region in the seventeenth and first quarter of the eighteenth centuries]. *Akademiya Nauk SSSR. Institut Etnografii imeni N. N. Miklukho-Maklaya. Kratkiye Soobshcheniya*, no. 35, pp. 14–24.

ALEKSANDROV, V. A. (1961). Cherty semeynogo stroya u russkogo naseleniya Yeniseyskogo kraya XVII–nachala XVIII v. [Features of family structure among the Russian population of the Yenisey region in the seventeenth and early eighteenth centuries]. *Trudy Instituta Etnografii imeni N. N. Miklukho-Maklaya. Novaya Seriya*, tom 64, pp. 3–26.

ALEKSEYENKO, YE. A. (1961). Sredstva peredvizheniya ketov [Means of transport of the Ket]. *Trudy Instituta Etnografii imeni N. N. Miklukho-Maklaya. Novaya Seriya*, tom 64, pp. 64–97.

ALEKSEYEV, A. I. (1961). *Uchenyy chukcha Nikolay Daurkin [Nikolay Daurkin, the Chukchi scientist]*, 88 pp. Magadan: Knizhnoye Izdatel'stvo.

ALEKSEYEV, M. P. (1941). *Sibir' v izvestiyakh zapadno-yevropeyskikh puteshestvennikov i pisateley...*, 2-oye izdaniye [*Siberia in reports of west European travellers and writers...*, 2nd edition], lxii, 612 pp. Irkutsk: Oblastnoye Izdatel'stvo. (Annotated excerpts from writings of 49 non-Russian authors.)

ALISOV, B. P. (1956). *Klimat SSSR [Climate of the USSR]*, 127 pp. Moscow: Izdaniye Moskovskogo Universiteta.

AL'KOR, YA. P. & GREKOV, B. D. (eds.) (1936). Kolonial'naya politika moskovskogo gosudarstva v Yakutii XVII v. [Colonial policy of the Moscow state in Yakutiya in the seventeenth century]. *Trudy Istoriko-Arkheograficheskogo Instituta Akademii Nauk SSSR*, tom 14; also *Nauchno-Issledovatel'skaya Assotsiatsiya Instituta Narodov Severa. Trudy po Istorii*, tom 1, 281 pp. (Collection of archive materials, with introduction and commentary.)

References

ANDREYEV, V. N. (1962). Nauchno-prakticheskiye rekomendatsii po proizvodstvu olen'yego myasa [Scientific and practical recommendations for producing reindeer meat]. *Problemy Severa*, vyp. 6, pp. 229–33.

ANDRIYEVICH, V. K. (1889). *Sibir' v XIX stoletii (1796–1819)* [*Siberia in the nineteenth Century (1796–1819)*], 2 vols. St Petersburg: Tipografiya V. V. Komarova.

ANSON, A. A. (1928). *Ekonomicheskaya geografiya Sibiri* [*Economic Geography of Siberia*], 303 pp. Novosibirsk: Sibirskoye Krayevoye Izdatel'stvo. (Standard textbook of its time.)

ARGENTOV, A. V. (1876). Ocherk Nizhnekolymskogo kraya [Outline of the Nizhnekolymsk region]. *Sbornik Gazety Sibir'*, tom 1, pp. 387–96.

ARMSTRONG, TERENCE E. (1960). *The Russians in the Arctic. Aspects of Soviet Exploration and Exploitation of the Far North, 1937–57* (reprinted with minor corrections), 182 pp. London: Methuen.

ARMSTRONG, TERENCE E. (1961). Soviet terms for the north of the USSR. *Polar Record*, vol. 10, no. 69, pp. 609–13.

ARMSTRONG, TERENCE E. (1962). The population of the north of the USSR. *Polar Record*, vol. 11, no. 71, pp. 172–8.

ARMSTRONG, TERENCE E. (1963). Oil and gas in the Soviet Arctic. *Polar Record*, vol. 11, no. 73, pp. 431–4.

ARNOL'DI, I. A. & BELOUSOVA, A. Z. (1962). *Hygienic problems of acclimatization of the population of the far north*, 94 pp. Washington: U.S. Department of Commerce Office of Technical Services. (Translation of parts of *Gigiyenicheskiye voprosy akklimatizatsii naseleniya na kraynem severe*, Moscow, 1961.)

ARSEN'YEV, V. K. & TITOV, YE. I. (1928). *Byt i kharakter narodnostey Dal'nevostochnogo kraya* [*Way of Life and Character of the Peoples of the Far Eastern Region*], 84 pp. Vladivostok: 'Knizhnoye Delo'.

ARTEM'YEV, G. V. (1962). Osnovnyye voprosy razvitiya ovoshchevodstva zashchishchennogo grunta na kraynem severe [Main questions of the development of vegetable growing in protected ground in the far north]. *Problemy Severa*, vyp. 6, pp. 164–71.

ATLAS SSSR (1962). *Atlas SSSR* [*Atlas of the USSR*], 185 pp. Moscow: Glavnoye Upravleniye Geodezii i Kartografii. (Includes many useful distribution maps, both physical and economic.)

BADDELEY, JOHN F. (1919). *Russia, Mongolia, China. Being some Record of the Relations between them from the Beginning of the XVIIth Century to the Death of the Tsar Alexei Mikhailovich A.D. 1602–1676...*, 2 vols. London: Macmillan. (A magnificent and erudite work, of which only 250 copies were ever printed.)

BAER, K. E. VON (1845). Nachrichten aus Ost-Sibirien. *Beiträge zur Kenntnis des Russischen Reiches*, bd. 7, pp. 41–272.

BAGROW, LEO (1947). Sparwenfeld's map of Siberia. *Imago Mundi*, no. 4, pp. 65–70.

References

BAKHRUSHIN, S. V. (1955a). *S. V. Bakhrushin. Nauchnyye trudy.* III. *Izbrannyye raboty po istorii Sibiri XVI–XVII vv.* Chast' pervaya. *Voprosy russkoy kolonizatsii Sibiri v XVI–XVII vv.* [*S. V. Bakhrushin. Scientific Works.* III. *Selected Works on the History of Siberia in the Sixteenth and Seventeenth Centuries.* First Part. *Questions of Russian Colonisation of Siberia in the Sixteenth and Seventeenth Centuries*], 376 pp. Moscow: Izdatel'stvo Akademii Nauk SSSR.

BAKHRUSHIN, S. V. (1955b). *S. V. Bakhrushin. Nauchnyye trudy.* III. *Izbrannyye raboty po istorii Sibiri XVI–XVII vv.* Chast' vtoraya. *Istoriya narodov Sibiri v XVI–XVII vv.* [*S. V. Bakhrushin. Scientific Works.* III. *Selected Works on the History of Siberia in the Sixteenth and Seventeenth Centuries.* Second part. *History of the Peoples of Siberia in the Sixteenth and Seventeenth Centuries*], 299 pp. Moscow: Izdatel'stvo Akademii Nauk SSSR.

BAKHRUSHIN, S. V. (1959). *S. V. Bakhrushin. Nauchnyye trudy.* IV. *Ocherki po istorii Krasnoyarskogo uyezda v XVII v. Sibir' i Srednyaya Aziya v XVI–XVII vv.* [*S. V. Bakhrushin. Scientific Works.* IV. *Outlines in the History of Krasnoyarskiy Uyezd in the Seventeenth Century. Siberia and Central Asia in the Sixteenth and Seventeenth Centuries*], 258 pp. Moscow: Izdatel'stvo Akademii Nauk SSSR.

BARGHOORN, FREDERICK C. (1956). *Soviet Russian Nationalism,* 330 pp. London: Oxford University Press.

BARTENEV, V. (1896). *Na kraynem severo-zapade Sibiri. Ocherki Obdorskogo Kraya* [*In the Far North-West of Siberia. Outlines of the Obdorsk Region*], 154 pp. St Petersburg: Tipo-Litografiya M. F. Paykina.

BARTON, PAUL (1959). *L'institution concentrationnaire en Russie (1930–1957),* 519 pp. Paris: Plon. (Supplements Dallin and Nicolaevsky (1948).)

BASHARIN, G. P. (1956). *Istoriya agrarnykh otnosheniy v Yakutii (60-ye gody XVIII–seredina XIX v.)* [*History of Agrarian Relations in Yakutiya (60's of the Eighteenth–Middle of the Nineteenth Centuries',* 428 pp. Moscow: Izdatel'stvo Akademii Nauk SSSR.

BELOV, M. I. (ed.) (1952). *Russkiye morekhody v Ledovitom i Tikhom okeanakh* [*Russian Seafarers in the Arctic and Pacific Oceans*], 385 pp. Moscow, Leningrad: Izdatel'stvo Glavsevmorputi. (Archive materials with introduction and notes.)

BELOV, M. I. (1956). *Istoriya otkrytiya i osvoyeniya Severnogo morskogo puti.* Tom 1. *Arkticheskoye moreplavaniye s drevneyshikh vremen do serediny XIX veka* [*History of the Discovery ond Utilisation of the Northern Sea Route.* Tom 1. *Arctic Seafaring from Ancient Times to the Middle of the Nineteenth Century*], 592 pp. Moscow: Izdatel'stvo 'Morskoy Transport'. (This, with the next entry, forms part of a 4- or 5-volume history now in preparation. The scope is wider than the title suggests, and covers activities over a large part of the mainland.)

BELOV, M. I. (1959). *Istoriya otkrytiya i osvoyeniya Severnogo morskogo puti.* Tom 3. *Sovetskoye arkticheskoye moreplavaniya 1917–1932 gg.* [*History of*

References

the Discovery and Utilisation of the Northern Sea Route. Tom 3. *Soviet Arctic Seafaring, 1917–32*], 510 pp. Leningrad: Izdatel'stvo 'Morskoy Transport'.

BELOV, M. I. (1961). Leninskiy dekret o kompleksnom izuchenii Arktiki [Lenin's decree on the complex study of the Arctic]. *Izvestiya Vsesoyuznogo Geograficheskogo Obshchestva*, tom 93, vyp. 5, pp. 377–83.

BERGMAN, STEN (1927). *Through Kamchatka by Dog-sled and Skis*, 284 pp. London: Seeley, Service and Co. (Narrative of a Swedish expedition undertaken in 1920–22.)

BIBIKOV, S. D. (1912). *Arkhangel'skaya guberniya, yeye bogatstva i nuzhdy* [*Arkhangel'skaya Guberniya, Its Riches and Needs*]. Arkhangel'sk.

BILINSKY, Y. (1962). The Soviet education laws of 1958–59 and the Soviet nationality policy. *Soviet Studies*, vol. 14, no. 2, pp. 138–57.

BLADEN, V. W. (ed.) (1962). *Canadian Population and Northern Colonization*, x, 158 pp. Toronto: University of Toronto Press. (Royal Society of Canada Symposium.)

BLYTH, J. D. M. (1955). The war in Arctic Europe, 1941–45. *Polar Record*, vol. 7, no. 49, pp. 278–301.

BODNARSKIY, M. S. (1958). *Slovar' geograficheskikh nazvaniy* [*Dictionary of Geographical Names*], 391 pp. Moscow: Gosudarstvennoye Uchebno-Pedagogicheskoye Isdatel'stvo.

BOGORAS, W. (BOGORAZ-TAN, V. G.) (1904–9). The Chukchee. *Memoirs of the American Museum of Natural History*, vol. 11, xvii, 733 pp.

BOGORAS, W. (BOGORAZ-TAN, V. G.) (1913). The Eskimo of Siberia. *Memoirs of the America Museum of Natural History*, vol. 12, pp. 417–56.

BOULITCHOFF, J. DE (BULYCHOV, I.) (1856). *Voyage dans la Sibérie Orientale....* Première partie. *Voyage au Kamtchatka*. St Petersburg. (Collection of prints. The accompanying text, published at the same time, has the same title in Russian.)

BRÄNDSTRÖM, ELSA (1929). *Among Prisoners of War in Russia and Siberia*, 284 pp. London: Hutchinson. (By the daughter of the Swedish Ambassador to Russia.)

BUTSINSKIY, P. N. (1889). *Zaseleniye Sibiri i byt pervykh yeye nasel'nikov* [*The Settlement of Siberia and the Mode of Life of its First Settlers*], 345 pp. Khar'kov: Tipografiya Gubernskogo Pravleniya.

CASTRÉN, M. A. (1853). *Nordische Reisen und Forschungen*. 1. *Reiseerinnerungen aus den Jahren 1838–1844*, xiv, 308 pp. St Petersburg: Eggers et Comp. (The first of twelve volumes containing the results of his linguistic and ethnographic researches in northern Europe and Asia.)

CHERNYSHEVSKIY, M. N. (ed.) (1913). *Chernyshevskiy v Sibiri. Perepiska s rodnymi*. Vyp. 3. (*1878–1883*) [*Chernyshevskiy in Siberia. Correspondence with relatives*. No. 3. (*1878–1883*)], l, 247 pp. St Petersburg: Tipografiya B. M. Vol'fa. (Letters from N. G. Chernyshevskiy to his wife and other relatives, from Vilyuysk.)

CHUDNOVSKIY, S. (1885). *Yeniseyskaya guberniya k 300-letnemu yubileyu*

References

[*Yeniseyskaya Guberniya on its 300th Anniversary*], 200 pp. Tomsk: Tipografiya 'Sibirskoy Gazety'.

COCHRANE, JOHN DUNDAS (1824). *Narrative of a Pedestrian Journey through Russia and Siberian Tartary...*, 2nd edition, 2 vols. London: Charles Knight. (By a retired British naval officer who crossed Siberia in 1820–23.)

COTTRELL, CHARLES HERBERT (1842). *Recollections of Siberia in the Years 1840 and 1841*, 410 pp. London: John W. Parker. (Journey along the Siberian road.)

CZAPLICKA, MARIE ANTOINETTE (1914). *Aboriginal Siberia. A Study in Social Anthropology*, xvi, 376 pp. Oxford: Clarendon Press. (Written before visiting Siberia.)

CZAPLICKA, MARIE ANTOINETTE (1916). *My Siberian Year*, xii, 315 pp. London: Mills and Boon. (Describes her visit in 1914–15.)

CZAPLICKA, MARIE ANTOINETTE (1918). The evolution of the cossack communities. *Journal of the Royal Central Asian Society*, vol. 5, pt. 2, pp. 43–58.

DALLIN, DAVID J. & NICOLAEVSKY, B. I. (1948). *Forced Labour in Soviet Russia*, xv, 331 pp. London: Hollis and Carter. (Summary of evidence from escapers and defectors.)

DAL'STROY (1956). *Dal'stroy. K 25-letiyu* [*Dal'stroy. On its 25th Anniversary*], 240 pp. Magadan: Knizhnoye Izdatel'stvo. (Popular account of its achievements.)

DANILEVSKIY, V. V. (1959). *Russkoye zoloto. Istoriya otkrytiya i dobychi do serediny XIX v.* [*Russian Gold. The History of its Discovery and Mining up to the Middle of the Nineteenth Century*], 380 pp. Moscow: Gosudarstvennoye Nauchno-Tekhnicheskoye Izdatel'stvo po Chernoy i Tsvetnoy Metallurgii.

DARWIN, CHARLES (1890). *Journal of Researches into the Natural History and Geology of the Countries Visited During the Voyage of H.M.S. 'Beagle' round the World*, xx, 381 pp. London: Ward Lock.

DEKLARATSIYA (1917–18). Deklaratsiya prav narodov Rossii [Declaration of rights of the peoples of Russia]. *Sobraniye Uzakoneniy i Rasporyazheniy Rabochego i Krest'yanskogo Pravitel'stva RSFSR*, paragraph 18, pp. 21–2.

DITMAR, K. VON (1890). Reisen und Aufenthalt in Kamtschatka in den Jahren 1851–1855. *Beiträge zur Kenntnis des Russischen Reiches. Dritte Folge*, bd. 7, 867 pp.

DITMAR, K. VON (1900). Reisen und Aufenthalt in Kamtschatka in den Jahren 1851–1855. Zweiter Teil. Allgemeines über Kamtschatka. Erster Abteilung. *Beiträge zur Kenntnis des Russischen Reiches. Dritte Folge*, bd. 8, 273 pp.

DMITRIYEV, N. A. (1959). *Murmanskaya oblast' v poslevoyennyye gody* [*Murmanskaya Oblast' in the Post-War Years*], 160 pp. Murmansk: Knizhnoye Izdatel'stvo.

References

DOBELL, PETER (1830). *Travels in Kamchatka and Siberia...*, 2 vols. London: Colburn and Bentley. (Notes by an official of the Russian Government during his travels, 1812–28.)

DOLGIKH, B. O. (1949). Kolkhoz im. Kirova Taymyrskogo natsional'nogo okruga [Kirov collective farm of Taymyrskiy Natsional'nyy Okrug]. *Sovetskaya Etnografiya*, no. 4, pp. 75–93.

DOLGIKH, B. O. (1960a). Rodovoy i plemennoy sostav narodov Sibiri v XVII v. [Clan and tribal composition of the peoples of Siberia in the seventeenth century]. *Trudy Instituta Etnografii imeni N. N. Miklukho-Maklaya. Novaya Seriya*, tom 55, 622 pp.

DOLGIKH, B. O. (1960b). Yezda na sobakakh u russkogo starozhil'cheskogo naseleniya nizov'yev Yeniseya [Dog transport among the old Russian population of the lower Yenisey]. *Akademiya Nauk SSSR. Institut Etnografii imeni N. N. Miklukho-Maklaya. Kratkiye Soobshcheniya*, no. 35, pp. 25–37.

DONNER, K. (1915). *Bland Samoyeder i Sibirien, åren 1911–1914*, 235 pp. Helsingfors. English translation of later German edition: *Among the Samoyed in Siberia*, xx, 176 pp. New Haven: Human Relations Area Files Press, 1954.

DONNER, K. (1933). Ethnological notes about the Yenisey Ostyak. *Mémoires de la Société Finno-Ougrienne*, vol. 66, 104 pp.

DREW, R. F. (1961). The Siberian fair: 1600–1750. *Slavonic and East European Review*, vol. 39, no. 93, pp. 423–39.

DUNAYEV, V. P. (1960). *Samyy severnyy (geograficheskiy ocherk o zapolyarnom gorode Noril'ske) [The Most Northerly (Geographical Outline of the Polar Town of Noril'sk)]*, 72 pp. Moscow: Gosudarstvennoye Izdatel'stvo Geograficheskoy Literatury.

D'YACHKOV (1893). Anadyrskiy kray. Rukopis' zhitelya sela Markova [The Anadyr' region. Manuscript of an inhabitant of the village of Markovo]. *Zapiski Obshchestva Izucheniya Amurskogo Kraya*, tom 2.

ENGELHARDT, ALEXANDER P. (1899). *A Russian Province of the North*, xix, 356 pp. London: Archibald Constable. (Provincial Governor describes his territory and activities.)

ERMAN, ADOLPH (1848). *Travels in Siberia...*, 2 vols. London: Longman. (Journey by German naturalist in 1828–29.)

FAYNBERG, L. A. (1962). Politekhnizatsiya shkoly na Taymyre [Polytechnicisation of a school in Taymyr]. *Letopis' Severa*, tom 3, pp. 91–2.

FISCHER, J. E. (1774). *Sibirskaya istoria s samogo otkrytiya Sibiri do zavoyevaniya sey zemli Rossiyskim oruzhiyem [Siberian History from the Discovery of Siberia to its Conquest by Russian Arms]*, 631 pp. St Petersburg: Imperatorskaya Akademiya Nauk.

FISHER, RAYMOND H. (1943). The Russian fur trade, 1550–1700. *University of California Publications in History*, vol. 31, xi, 275 pp.

FORCED LABOUR (1952). *Forced Labour in the Soviet Union*, 69 pp. Washing-

References

ton: Department of State (publication no. 4716). (In some respects supplements Dallin & Nicolaevsky (1948).)

GAGEMEYSTER (1854). *Statisticheskoye obozreniye Sibiri* [*Statistical summary of Siberia*], 3 vols. St Petersburg.

GAPANOVICH, I. I. (1933). *Rossiya v severo-vostochnoy Azii* [*Russia in North-Eastern Asia*], 2 vols. Peking.

GIRAULT, A. (1943). *Les colonies françaises avant et depuis 1815. 6e édition,* 202 pp. Paris: Sirey.

GLADKOV, V. (1961). *Monchegorsk,* 87 pp. Murmansk: Knigoizdat.

GLINKA, G. V. (ed.) (1914). *Aziatskaya Rossiya.* Tom pervyy. *Lyudi i poryadki za Uralom* [*Asiatic Russia.* Tom I. *People and Customs beyond Ural*], viii, 576 pp. St Petersburg: Izdaniye Pereselencheskogo Upravleniya.

GMELIN, J. G. (1751–52). *Reise durch Sibirien von dem Jahr 1733 bis 1743,* 4 vols. Göttingen: Abram Vandenhoeck. (Report on Great Northern Expedition by a member representing the Academy of Sciences.)

GOLOVACHEV, P. (1902). *Sibir'. Priroda, lyudi, zhizn'* [*Siberia. Nature, People, Life*], 300 pp. Moscow: Tipografiya I. N. Kushnerev.

GOSUDARSTVENNYY PLAN (1951). Gosudarstvennyy plan razvitiya narodnogo khozyaystva SSSR na 1941 god [State Plan for Development of the National Economy of the USSR in 1941]. Reprinted as *American Council of Learned Societies Reprints. Russian Series,* no. 30. (A secret document, published after its capture.)

GOTSKIY, M. V. (1962). Morskoy torgovyy put' na Kolymu i Dobrovol'nyy Flot [Sea trade route to the Kolyma and the Volunteer Fleet]. *Letopis' Severa,* tom 3, pp. 176–87.

GRANIK, G. I. (1962). Letopis' sudokhodstva na rekakh Yakutii [Chronicle of shipping on the rivers of Yakutiya]. *Letopis' Severa,* tom 3, pp. 211–22.

GREENWOOD, G. (1955). *Australia. A Social and Political History,* xiii, 445 pp. Sydney: Angus and Robertson.

GREKOV, V. I. (1960). *Ocherki iz istorii russkikh geograficheskikh issledovaniy v 1725–1765 gg.* [*Outlines from the History of Russian Geographical Investigations in 1725–1765*], 426 pp. Moscow: Izdatel'stvo Akademii Nauk SSSR.

GRIGOR'YEV, A. A. (ed.) (1960–). *Kratkaya geograficheskaya entsiklopediya* [*Short geographical encyclopaedia*], 5 vols. Moscow: 'Sovetskaya Entsiklopediya'. (Only 4 vols. published at time of going to press, reaching 'Yugoslavia'.)

GRINER, D. A. (1949). Iz istorii Murmana i Murmanskoy (Kirovskoy) zheleznoy dorogi [From the history of Murman and the Murmansk (Kirov) railway]. *Letopis' Severa,* tom 1, pp. 175–88.

GUL'CHAK, F. YA. (1954). *Severnoye olenevodstvo* [*Reindeer Industry*], 216 pp. Moscow: Gosudarstvennoye Izdatel'stvo Sel'skokhozyaystvennoy Literatury.

References

GURVICH, I. S. (1953). Etnograficheskaya ekspeditsiya v basseyn r. Indigirki [Ethnographic expedition to the basin of the Indigirka]. *Akademiya Nauk SSSR. Institut Etnografii imeni N. N. Miklukho-Maklaya. Kratkiye Soobshcheniya*, no. 19, pp. 28–42.

GURVICH, I. S. (1960). Sovremennyye etnicheskiye protsessy, protekayushchiye na severe Yakutii [Present ethnic processes happening in the north of Yakutiya]. *Sovetskaya Etnografiya*, no. 5, pp. 3–11.

GURVICH, I. S. (1961). Voprosy ratsional'nogo ispol'zovaniya traditsionnykh trudovykh navykov narodov Sovetskogo Soyuza [Questions of the rational use of traditional labour patterns of the peoples of the Soviet Union]. *Materialy i Mezhduvedomstvennogo Soveshchaniya po Geografii Naseleniya*, vyp. 5, pp. 14–17.

GURVICH, I. S. (1962). K voprosu ob etnicheskoy prinadlezhnosti korennogo naseleniya Bulunskogo rayona [On the ethnic affiliation of the native population of the Bulun region]. *Akademiya Nauk SSSR. Institut Etnografii imeni N. N. Miklukho-Maklaya. Kratkiye Soobshcheniya*, no. 36, pp. 55–9.

HADDON, A. C. (1929). *The Races of Man and their Distribution*, revised edition, viii, 184 pp. Cambridge University Press.

HAKLUYT, RICHARD (1809). *Hakluyt's Collection of the Early Voyages, Travels and Discoveries of the English Nation*, vol. 1. London: Evans, Mackinlay and Priestley.

HALLSTRÖM, GUSTAF (1911). Kolalapparnas hotade existens. *Ymer*. hft. 3, pp. 239–316.

HARRISON, JOHN A. (1953). *Japan's Northern Frontier. A Preliminary Study in Colonisation and Expansion with Special Reference to Relations of Japan and Russia*, xii, 202 pp. Gainesville: University of Florida Press.

HILL, S. S. (1854). *Travels in Siberia*, 2 vols. London: Longman, Brown, Green and Longmans.

HRDLIČKA, A. (1945). *The Aleutian and Commander Islands and Their Inhabitants*, x, 630 pp. Philadelphia: Wistar Institute of Anatomy and Biology.

INFANT'YEV, P. (1912). *Kamchatka, yeya bogatstva i naseleniye [Kamchatka, its wealth and population]*, 96 pp. St Petersburg: Izdaniye E. I. Blek.

INNIS, HAROLD A. (1956). *The Fur Trade in Canada. An Introduction to Canadian Economic History*, revised edition, 463 pp. Toronto: University of Toronto Press.

ITOGI (1962). *Itogi vsesoyuznoy perepisi naseleniya 1959 goda. SSSR (Svodnyy tom) [Results of the All-Union Census of 1959. U.S.S.R. (Summary volume)]*, 284 pp. Moscow: Gosstatizdat.

ITOGI (1963). *Itogi vsesoyuznoy perepisi naseleniya 1959 goda. RSFSR [Results of the All-Union Census of 1959. RSFSR]*, 456 pp. Moscow: Gosstatizdat. (This volume is preferred to Itogi (1962), both because it is fuller and because its figures for native peoples, being restricted to RSFSR, eliminate those living in certain southerly areas.)

References

Ivanovskiy, A. I. (1960). Zemledeliye na kraynem severe vostochnoy Sibiri [Agriculture in the far north of eastern Siberia]. In Rostovtsev, N. F. (ed.) *et al. Razvitiye proizvoditel'nykh sil vostochnoy Sibiri. Sel'skoye khozyaystvo [Development of the Productive Forces of Eastern Siberia. Agriculture]*, pp. 208–20. Moscow.

Ivanovskiy, A. I. (1962). Nauchno-prakticheskiye rekomendatsii po vyrashchivaniyu sel'skokhozyaystvennykh rasteniy na kraynem severe [Scientific and practical recommendations for growing agricultural plants in the far north]. *Problemy Severa*, vyp. 6, pp. 158–63.

Jakobson, Roman et al. (1957). *Paleosiberian Peoples and Languages. A Bibliographical Guide*, by Roman Jakobson, Gerta Hüttl-Worth & John Fred Beebe, vii, 222 pp. New Haven: Human Relations Area Files Press.

Jochelson, Waldemar (Iokhel'son, Vladimir) (1905–8). The Koryak. *Memoirs of the American Museum of Natural History*, vol. 10, pts. 1 and 2, xv, 842 pp.

Jochelson, Waldemar (Iokhel'son, Vladimir) (1910–26). The Yukaghir and the Yukaghirized Tungus. *Memoirs of the American Museum of Natural History*, vol. 12, xvi, 469 pp.

Jochelson, Waldemar (Iokhel'son, Vladimir) (1928). *Peoples of Asiatic Russia*, 277 pp. New York: American Museum of Natural History.

Jochelson, Waldemar (Iokhel'son, Vladimir) (1933). The Yakut. *Anthropological Papers of the American Museum of Natural History*, vol. 33, pt. 2, pp. 37–225.

Kabo, R. M. (1949). *Goroda zapadnoy Sibiri. Ocherki istoriko-ekonomicheskoy geografii (XVII–pervaya polovina XIX vv.) [Towns of Western Siberia. Outlines in Historical and Economic Geography (Seventeenth–first half of the Nineteenth Century]*, 219 pp. Moscow: Geografgiz.

Karnilov (1828). *Zamechaniya o Sibiri [Notes on Siberia]*, 105 pp. St Petersburg: Tipografiya Karla Kraya.

Karta Narodov (1962). *Karta narodov SSSR [Map of the Peoples of the USSR]*, 1:10 million. Moscow: Glavnoye Upravleniya Geodezii i Kartografii.

Kazanskiy, N. N. (1960). Razvitiye perevozok lesnykh gruzov transportom v svyazi s osvoyeniyem lesnykh bogatstv [Development of timber transport in connection with utilising timber resources]. In T. S. Khachaturov, (ed.). *Razvitiye proizvoditel'nykh sil Vostochnoy Sibiri. Transport [Development of the Productive Forces of Eastern Siberia. Transport]*, pp. 110–21. Moscow.

Kennan, George (1891). *Siberia and the Exile System*, 2 vols. London: Osgood and McIlvaine.

Kennan, George (1910). *Tent-life in Siberia. A New Account of an Old Undertaking*, xix, 482 pp. New York and London: Putnam. (Author's participation in planning the New York to Paris telegraph line, 1865–67.)

Khachaturov, T. S. (ed.) (1960). *Razvitiye proizvoditel'nykh sil vostochnoy Sibiri. Transport [Development of the Productive Forces of Eastern Siberia.*

References

Transport], 204 pp. Moscow: Izdatel'stvo Akademii Nauk SSSR. (Papers of a major conference held in 1958.)

KLOCHKOV, M. (1911). *Naseleniye Rossii pri Petre Velikom po perepisyam togo vremeni*. Tom pervyy. *Perepisi dvorov i naseleniya (1678–1721)* [*Population of Russia under Peter the Great from Censuses of that Time*. Tom 1. *Censuses of Households and Population (1678–1721)*], 435 pp. St Petersburg: Senatskaya Tipografiya.

KOLARZ, WALTER (1952). *Russia and her colonies*, 335 pp. London: George Philip.

KOLARZ, WALTER (1954). *The Peoples of the Soviet Far East*, 194 pp. London: George Philip.

KOLYCHEVA, YE. I. (1956). Nentsy yevropeyskoy Rossii v kontse XVII–nachale XVIII veka [Nentsy of European Russia at the end of the seventeenth and beginning of the eighteenth centuries]. *Sovetskaya Etnografiya*, no. 2, pp. 76–88.

KONOVALENKO, V. G. (1961). Zemel'nyye fondy natsional'nykh okrugov kraynego severa i ikh ispol'zovaniye [Land resources of the national districts of the far north and their use]. *Voprosy Geografii*, Sbornik 54, pp. 20–40.

KOROL, ALEXANDER (1952). *Gold Resources and Gold Mining in the U.S.S.R.*, iv, 142 pp. New York: unpublished M.A. thesis for Columbia University.

KOROL'KOV, N. F. (1908). *Trifono-Pechengskiy monastyr', osnovannyy prepodobnym Trifonom, prosvetitelem loparey, yego razoreniye i vozobnovleniye* [*The Trifono-Pechengskiy Monastery, Founded by the Holy Trifon, Enlightener of the Lapps, its Destruction and Revival*], 162 pp. St Petersburg.

KOROVITSIN, V. P. (1961). Sdvigi v geografii gorodskikh naseleniy SSSR (1926–1959 g.) [Movements in the geography of urban populations of the USSR (1926–59)]. *Izvestiya Akademii Nauk SSSR. Seriya Geografwhencheskaya*, no. 6, pp. 47–58.

KRASHENINNIKOV, S. P. (1949). *Opisaniye zemli Kamchatki* [*Description of the Land of Kamchatka*], 841 pp. Ed. L. S. Berg, A. A. Grigor'yev and N. N. Stepanov. Moscow and Leningrad: Izdatel'stvo Glavsevmorputi.

KRASOVSKIY, M. A. (1895). Russkiye v Yakutskoy oblasti v XVII v. [Russians in the Yakut province in the seventeenth century]. *Izvestiya Obshchestva Arkheologii, Istorii i Etnografii Kazanskogo Universiteta*, tom 12, vyp. 2, pp. 143–76.

KUSHNEV, A. P. (1961). *Proyektirovaniye zdaniy dlya rayonov Kraynego Severa* [*Planning Buildings for Regions of the Far North*], 196 pp. Leningrad and Moscow: Gosudarstvennoye Izdatel'stvo Literatury po Stroitel'stvu, Arkhitekture i Stroitel'nym Materialam.

LATKIN, N. V. (1892). *Yeniseyskaya guberniya, yeya proshloye i nastoyashcheye* [*Yeniseyskaya Guberniya, its Past and Present*], ii, iii, 467 pp. St Petersburg: Tipografiya Tikhanova.

References

LEVIN, M. G. & POTAPOV, L. P. (ed.) (1956). *Narody Sibiri. Etnograficheskiye ocherki* [*Peoples of Siberia. Ethnographic Outlines*], 1083 pp. Moscow and Leningrad: Izdatel'stvo Akademii Nauk SSSR. (English translation, *The Peoples of Siberia*, published by University of Chicago Press in 1964.)

LEVIN, M. G. & POTAPOV, L. P. (ed.) (1961). *Istoriko-etnograficheskiy atlas Sibiri* [*Historical and Ethnographic Atlas of Siberia*], 498 pp. Moscow and Leningrad: Izdatel'stvo Akademii Nauk SSSR.

LIPPER, ELINOR (1951). *Eleven Years in Soviet Prison Camps*, 310 pp. London: Hollis and Carter. (Refers mainly to Kolyma.)

LOGINOV, V. P. (1962). *Puti povysheniya effektivnosti razvitiya gornoy promyshlennosti severo-vostoka SSSR* [*Ways of Increasing the Effectiveness of Development of the Mining Industry of the North-east of the USSR*], 183 pp. Moscow: Izdatel'stvo Akademii Nauk SSSR.

LORIMER, FRANK (1946). *The Population of the Soviet Union: History and Prospects*, xiv, 289 pp. Geneva: League of Nations.

LUBIMENKO, INNA (1914). A project for the acquisition of Russia by James I. *English Historical Review*, vol. 24, pp. 246–56.

MAKARIY [BULGAKOV] (1887). *Istoriya russkoy tserkvi* [*History of the Russian Church*], tom 6, kniga 1. St Petersburg: Tipografiya R. Golike.

MANNINEN, I. (1932). *Die Finnisch-ugrischen Völker*, 384 pp. Leipzig; Otto Harrassowitz.

MATHISEN, TRYGVE (1951). *Svalbard i internasjonal politikk, 1871–1925*, xi, 320 pp. Oslo: Aschehoug.

MATTHEWS, W. K. (1951). *Languages of the U.S.S.R.*, x, 179 pp. Cambridge University Press.

MAYDEL', G. (1893–96). Reisen und Forschungen im Jakutischen Gebiet Ostsibiriens in den Jahren 1861–1871. *Beiträge zur Kenntnis des Russischen Reiches. Vierte Folge*, bd. 1–2.

MAYNOV, I. I. (1912). Russkiye krest'yane i osedlyye inorodtsy Yakutskoy oblasti [Russian peasants and settled natives of Yakutskaya Oblast']. *Zapiski Imperatorskogo Russkogo Geograficheskogo Obshchestva. Otdeleniye Statistiki*, tom 12, xvi, 357, 29 pp.

MAYNOV, I. I. (1927). Naseleniye Yakutii [Population of Yakutiya]. In P. V. Vittenburg (ed.). *Yakutiya. Sbornik statey* [*Yakutiya. Collected papers*], pp. 323–420.

MATERIALY DLYA ISTORII (1861). Materialy dlya istorii russkikh zaseleniy po beregam Vostochnogo okeana [Materials for a history of Russian settlements on the shores of the Eastern Ocean]. *Morskoy Sbornik*, nos. 1–4, appendix.

MEINSHAUSEN, K. (1871). Nachrichten über das Wilui-Gebiet in Ostsibirien. *Beiträge zur Kenntnis des Russichen Reiches*, bd. 26, 246 pp.

MIKHAYLOV, S. V. (1958). Rybnyye i zverinyye promysly sovetskogo zapolyar'ya [Fishing and hunting industries of the Soviet polar regions]. *Problemy Severa*, no. 2, pp. 238–52. (Summarised in *Polar Record*, no. 63, 1959, pp. 578–9.)

References

MINEYEV, A. I. (1946). *Ostrov Vrangelya*, 432 pp. Moscow and Leningrad: Izdatel'stvo Glavsevmorputi. (General description and history of exploration of Wrangel Island, by leader of polar station on the island, 1929–34.)

MITYUSHKIN, V. V. (1960). *Sotsialisticheskaya Yakutiya* [*Socialist Yakutiya*], 360 pp. Yakutsk: Knizhnoye Izdatel'stvo. (Economic growth, especially since 1917.)

MÜLLER, G. F. (MILLER, G. F.) (1750). *Opisaniye Sibirskogo tsarstva i vsekh proizshedshikh v nem del.* . . [*Description of the Siberian Kingdom and of all that Happened in it.* . .], 2 vols. St Petersburg: Imperatorskaya Akademiya Nauk. (The 'official' history which resulted from the work of the Great Northern Expedition.)

MURAV'YEV-APOSTOL, M. I. (1922). *Vospominaniya i pis'ma* [*Recollections and Letters*], 96 pp. Petrograd: Izdatel'stvo 'Byloye'.

NA PRIYEME (1936). Na priyeme v Kremle [At a reception in the Kremlin]. *Sovetskaya Arktika*, no. 3, pp. 6–27.

NANSEN, FRIDTJOF (1911). *In Northern Mists. Arctic Exploration in Early Times*, 2 vols. London: Heinemann.

NARODNOYE KHOZYAYSTVO RSFSR (1957). *Narodnoye khozyaystvo RSFSR. Statisticheskiy sbornik* [*National Economy of the RSFSR. Statistical Handbook*], 371 pp. Moscow: Gosstatizdat.

NARODNOYE KHOZYAYSTVO RSFSR (1961). *Narodnoye khozyaystvo RSFSR v 1960 godu. Statisticheskiy yezhegodnik* [*National Economy of the RSFSR in 1960. Statistical Yearbook*], 572 pp. Moscow: Gosstatizdat.

NARODNOYE KHOZYAYSTVO SSSR (1956). *Narodnoye Khozyaystvo SSSR. Statisticheskiy sbornik* [*National Economy of the USSR. Statistical Handbook*], 262 pp. Moscow: Gosstatizdat.

NASELENIYE GORODOV (1897). *Naseleniye gorodov po perepisi 28-go yanvarya 1897 goda* [*Population of Towns According to the Census of 28 January 1897*], 42 pp. St Petersburg: Tsentral'nyy Statisticheskiy Komitet.

NASELENIYE IMPERII (1897). *Naseleniye Imperii po perepisi 28-go yanvarya 1897 goda po uyezdam* [*Population of the Empire According to the Census of 28 January 1897, by Provinces*], 29 pp. St Petersburg: Tsentral'nyy Statisticheskiy Komitet.

NAUMOV, G. V. (1962). *Zapadnaya Yakutiya (ekonomiko-geograficheskaya kharakteristika)* [*Western Yakutiya (Characteristics of Economic Geography)*], 142 pp. Moscow: Izdatel'stvo Akademii Nauk SSSR.

NAZAROV, V. S. (1947). Istoricheskiy khod ledovitosti Karskogo morya [Historical fluctuation of ice cover in the Kara Sea]. *Izvestiya Vsesoyuznogo Geograficheskogo Obshchestva*, tom 79, vyp. 6, pp. 653–5.

NEWTH, J. A. (1962). Private communication dated 6 October.

[NOVOSILTSOV] (1902). Lower course of the Pechora. *Scottish Geographical Magazine*, vol. 18, no. 7, p. 378.

NUTTONSON, M. Y. (1950). *Agricultural Climatology of Siberia, Natural Belts,*

References

and *Agro-Climatic Analogues in North America*, 64 pp. Washington: American Institute of Crop Ecology.

OGORODNIKOV, V. I. (1920). *Ocherk istorii Sibiri do nachala XIX stoletiya. Chast' 1 [Outline of the History of Siberia before the Nineteenth Century. Part 1]*, 4, 289 pp. Irkutsk: Tipografiya Shtaba Voyennogo Okruga.

OGRYZKO, I. I. (1953). Otkrytiye Kuril'skikh ostrovov [Discovery of Kuril'skiye Ostrova]. *Uchenyye Zapiski Leningradskogo Gosudarstvennogo Universiteta*, tom 157, pp. 167–207.

OKLADNIKOV, A. P. & PINKHENSON, D. M. (ed.) (1951). *Istoricheskiy pamyatnik russkogo arkticheskogo moreplavaniya XVII veka [Historical Memorial of Russian Arctic Seafaring in the Seventeenth Century]*, 252 pp. Leningrad and Moscow: Izdatel'stvo Glavsevmorputi.

OKUN', S. B. (1935). *Ocherki po istorii kolonial'noy politiki tsarizma v Kamchatskom kraye [Outlines in the History of the Colonial Policy of Tsarism in the Kamchatka District]*, 150 pp. Leningrad.

OKUN', S. B. (1951). *The Russian-American Company*. Translated by Carl Ginsburg. 311 pp. Cambridge, Mass.: Harvard University Press.

OLIVER, PASFIELD (ed.) (1893). *The Memoirs and Travels of Mauritius Augustus Count de Benyowsky*, 399 pp. London: Unwin.

OLSUF'YEV, A. V. (1896). Obshchiy ocherk Anadyrskoy okrugi, yeya ekonomicheskago sostoyaniya i byta naseleniya [General outline of the Anadyr' region, its economic condition and the way of life of its inhabitants]. *Zapiski Priamurskago Otdela Imperatorskago Russkago Geograficheskago Obshchestva*, tom 2, vyp. 1, 245 pp.

OPISANIYE MURMANSKOGO POBEREZH'YA (1909). *Opisaniye Murmanskogo poberezh'ya [Description of the Murman Coast]*. St Petersburg: Tipografiya Morskogo Ministerstva.

ORLOVA, N. S. (ed.) (1951). *Otkrytiya russkikh zemleprokhodtsev i polyarnykh morekhodov XVII veka na severo-vostoke Azii. Sbornik dokumentov [Discoveries of Russian Travellers and Polar Seafarers of the Seventeenth Century in the North-East of Asia. Collected Documents]*, 618 pp. Moscow: Geografgiz.

ORLOVA, V. V. (1962). *Klimat SSSR. Vyp. 4. Zapadnaya Sibir' [Climate of the USSR. Vyp. 4. Western Siberia]*, 360 pp. Leningrad: Gidrometeorologicheskoye Izdatel'stvo.

ORLOVA, YE. P. (1962). U aleutov na Komandorskikh ostrovakh [Among the Aleuts of Komandorskiye Ostrova]. *Izvestiya Sibirskogo Otdeleniya Akademii Nauk SSSR*, no. 8, pp. 3–10.

PAMYATNAYA KNIZHKA (1895). *Pamyatnaya knizhka Yakutskoy oblasti na 1896 god. Vyp. 1 [Notebook for Yakutskaya Oblast' for 1896. Vyp. 1]*. Yakutsk. (Statistical compilation.)

PAPANIN, I. D. (1939). Rech' tov. I. Papanina na XVIII s'yezde VKP (b) [Speech of comrade I. Papanin at the 18th congress of the All-Union Communist Party (bolsheviks)]. *Sovetskaya Arktika*, no. 4, pp. 89–94.

PAPERS RELATING (1939). *Papers Relating to the Foreign Relations of the United States, 1924*, 2 vols. Washington: Government Printing Office.

References

PARVILAHTI, UNTO (1959). *Beria's Gardens. Ten Years Captivity in Russia and Siberia*, 286 pp. London: Hutchinson. (Concerns Dudinka region.)

PATKANOV, S. (1906). Opyt geografii i statistiki tungusskikh plemen Sibiri na osnovanii dannykh perepisi naseleniya 1897 g. i drugikh istochnikov. Chast' 1. Tungusy sobstvenno. Vyp. 1 [An essay in the geography and statistics of the Tungus tribes of Siberia on the basis of data from the 1897 census and other sources. Part 1. The Tungus themselves. Vyp. 1]. *Zapiski Imperatorskogo Russkogo Geograficheskogo Obshchestva po Otdeleniyu Etnografii*, tom 31, chast' 1, xii, 175 pp.

PATKANOV, S. (1911). *O priroste inorodcheskago naseleniya Sibiri. Statisticheskiye materialy dlya osveshcheniya voprosa o vymiranii pervobytnykh plemen [Growth of the Native Population of Siberia. Statistical Material throwing light on the question of the Dying-out of Primitive Tribes]*, 210 pp. St Petersburg: Imperatorskaya Akademiya Nauk.

PESTEL', I. B. (1926). Istoricheskaya zapiska o Kamchatke [Historical note on Kamchatka]. *Izvestiya Obshchestva Arkheologii, Istorii i Etnografii Kazanskogo Universiteta*, tom 33, vyp. 2–3, pp. 175–87.

PESTOV (1831). Svedeniya o Yeniseyskoy gubernii [Information on Yeniseyskaya Guberniya]. *Zhurnal Ministerstva Vnutrennykh Del*, chast' 5, kniga 4, pp. 75–113.

PIROZHNIKOV, P. L. (1962). Promyslovyye ryby krupnykh rek Sibirskogo severa, sostoyaniye zapasov i vozmozhnyye ulovy [Commercial fish of the great rivers of Siberia, state of stocks and possible catches]. *Problemy Severa*, vyp. 6, pp. 222–8.

PLATONOV, S. F. (1924). *Proshloye russkogo severa: ocherki po istorii kolonizatsii Pomor'ya [The Past of the Russian North: Outlines in the History of Colonisation of Pomor'ye]*, 107 pp. Berlin: Obelisk.

POKSHISHEVSKIY, V. V. (1951). *Zaseleniye Sibiri (istoriko-geograficheskiye ocherki) [Settlement of Siberia (Outlines in Historical Geography)]*, 208 pp. Irkutsk: Oblastnoye Gosudarstvennoye Izdatel'stvo.

POKSHISHEVSKIY, V. V. (1957). *Yakutiya. Priroda—lyudi—khozyaystvo [Yakutiya. Nature—People—Economy]*, 199 pp. Moscow: Izdatel'stvo Akademii Nauk SSSR.

POKSHISHEVSKIY, V. V. & VOROB'YEV, V. V. (ed.) (1962). *Geografiya naseleniya Vostochnoy Sibiri [Population Geography of Eastern Siberia]*, 163 pp. Moscow: Izdatel'stvo Akademii Nauk SSSR.

PREOBRAZHENNYY KRAY (1956). *Preobrazhennyy kray. Sbornik [Transformed Region. A Handbook]*, 400 pp. Magadan: Oblastnoye Knizhnoye Izdatel'stvo. (Popular impressions of recent economic growth of Magadanskaya Oblast'.)

PRIKLONSKIY, V. L. (1890). Tri goda v Yakutskoy oblasti. Etnograficheskiye ocherki [Three years in Yakutskaya Oblast'. Ethnographic sketches]. *Zhivaya Starina*, vyp. 1, pp. 63–83; vyp. 2, pp. 24–54.

PRIKLONSKIY, V. L. (1896). *Letopis' Yakutskogo kraya, sostavlennaya po offitsial'nym i istoricheskim dannym [Chronicle of the Yakutsk Region, Compiled*

References

from Official and Historical Data], 205, xvi pp. Krasnoyarsk: Yeniseyskaya Gubernskaya Tipografiya.

PYPIN, A. N. (1892). *Istoriya russkoy etnografii*. Tom 4. *Belorussiya i Sibir'* [*History of Russian ethnography*. Tom 4. *Belorussia and Siberia*], xi, 488 pp. St Petersburg.

RAEFF, MARC (1956). *Siberia and the Reforms of 1822*, xvii, 210 pp. Seattle: University of Washington Press.

REZOLYUTSIYA (1962). Rezolyutsiya soveshchaniya po problemam akklimatizatsii i pitaniya naseleniya na kraynem severe [Resolution of the conference on problems of acclimatisation and nutrition of the population in the far north]. *Problemy Severa*, vyp. 6, pp. 248–66.

RICH, E. E. (1958). *The History of the Hudson's Bay Company, 1670–1870*, 2 vols. London: Hudson's Bay Record Society.

ROMANOV, N. V. (ed.) (1904). *Statisticheskiye issledovaniya Murmana*. Tom 1. Vyp. 2. *Kolonizatsiya (po materialam 1899, 1900 i 1902 gg.)* [*Statistical Studies of Murman*. Tom 1, Vyp. 2. *Colonisation (on Material of 1899, 1900 and 1902)*], 297 pp. St Petersburg: Tipografiya Gol'dberg.

RYABOV, A. (1960). Sever — kray industrial'nyy [The north is an industrial region]. In *30 let Chukotskogo Natsional'nogo Okruga. Sbornik* [*Thirty Years of Chukotskiy Natsional'nyy Okrug. A Handbook*], pp. 30–8. Magadan.

SARYCHEV, G. A. (1952). *Puteshestviye po severo-vostochnoy chasti Sibiri, Ledovitomu moryu i Vostochnomu okeanu* [*Voyage to the North-East Part of Siberia, the Arctic Sea and the Eastern Ocean*], 326 pp. Moscow: Geografgiz. (Reprinted narrative of expedition led by Joseph Billings, 1785–93.)

SAUER, MARTIN (1802). *An Account of a Geographical and Astronomical Expedition to the Northern Parts of Russia...*, xxiii, 332, 58 pp. London: T. Cadell and W. Davies. (Narrative of expedition led by Joseph Billings, 1785–93.)

SBORNIK ISTORIKO-STATISTICHESKIKH SVEDENIY (1875–76). *Sbornik istoriko-statisticheskikh svedeniy o Sibiri i sopredel'nykh yey stranakh*. Tom 1 [*Handbook of Historical and Statistical Information on Siberia and Adjacent Countries. Tom 1*]. St Petersburg: Russkaya Skoropechatnya.

SBORNIK VAZHNEYSHIKH (1958). *Sbornik vazhneyshikh zakonov i postanovleniy o trude* [*Handbook of the Most Important Laws and Decrees on Labour*], 232 pp. Moscow: Izdatel'stvo VTsSPS.

SBORNIK ZAKONOV (1961). *Sbornik zakonov SSSR i ukazov Prezidiuma Verkhovnogo Soveta SSSR, 1938–1961 g.* [*Handbook of Laws of the USSR and Decrees of the Presidium of the Supreme Soviet of the USSR, 1938–61*], 976 pp. Moscow: Izdatel'stvo 'Izvestiya Sovetov Deputatov Trudyashchikhsya SSSR'.

SCHOLMER, JOSEPH (1954). *Vorkuta*, 264 pp. London: Weidenfeld and Nicolson. (By a German political prisoner.)

SERGEYEV, M. A. (1955). Nekapitalisticheskiy put' razvitiya malykh narodov severa [Non-capitalist path of development of the small peoples of the north]. *Trudy Instituta Etnografii imeni N. N. Miklukho-Maklaya. Novaya Seriya*, tom 27, 569 pp.

References

SERGEYEV, M. A. (1962). Komitet sodeystviya narodnostyam severnykh okrain [Committee of assistance to peoples of the northern marches]. *Letopis' Severa*, tom 3, pp. 72–81.

SGIBNEV, A. (1869). Okhotskiy port s 1649 po 1852 g. (istoricheskiy ocherk) [The port of Okhotsk from 1649 to 1852 (historical sketch)]. *Morskoy Sbornik*, tom 105, no. 11, pp. 1–92; no. 12, pp. 1–64.

SHAKHOVSKOY, A. (1822). Izvestiya o Gizhiginskoy kreposti [News of the fortress of Gizhiga]. *Severnyy Arkhiv*, chast' 4, pp. 283–312.

SHASKOL'SKIY, I. P. (1962). O vozniknovenii goroda Koly [On the revival of the town of Kola]. *Istoricheskiye Zapiski*, tom 71, pp. 270–9.

SHCHEGLOV, I. V. (1883). *Khronologicheskiy perechen' vazhneyshikh dannykh Sibiri (1032–1882 g.)* [*Chronological List of the Most Important Data on Siberia (1032–1882)*], 778 pp. Irkutsk: Tipografiya Shtaba Vostochnogo Sibirskogo Voyennogo Okruga.

SHCHERBAKOVA, YE. YA. (1961). *Klimat SSSR. Vyp. 5. Vostochnaya Sibir'* [*Climate of the USSR. Vyp. 5. Eastern Siberia*], 300 pp. Leningrad: Gidrometeorologicheskoye Izdatel'stvo.

SHIROKOGOROFF, S. M. (1933). *Social Organisation of the Northern Tungus*, xvi, 428 pp. Shanghai: Commercial Press.

SHISHKIN, N. I. (1959). *Komi ASSR. Ekonomiko-geograficheskaya kharakteristika* [*Komi ASSR. Characteristics of its Economic Geography*], 224 pp. Moscow: Geografgiz.

SHISHKIN, N. I. (1962). O sozdanii postoyannykh kadrov v severnykh rayonakh strany [On creating permanent cadres in the northern regions of the country]. *Problemy Severa*, vyp. 6, pp. 18–24.

SHUNKOV, V. I. (1946). *Ocherki po istorii kolonizatsii Sibiri v XVII–nachale XVIII vekov* [*Outlines in the History of the Colonisation of Siberia in the Seventeenth and Early Eighteenth Centuries*], 228 pp. Moscow and Leningrad: Izdatel'stvo Akademii Nauk SSSR.

SHUNKOV, V. I. (1956). *Ocherki po istorii zemledeliya Sibiri (XVII vek)* [*Outlines in the History of Agriculture of Siberia (Seventeenth Century)*], 432 pp. Moscow: Izdatel'stvo Akademii Nauk SSSR.

SHVETSOV, S. (1888). Ocherk Surgutskogo kraya [Outline of the Surgut region]. *Zapiski Imperatorskogo Russkogo Geograficheskogo Obshchestva. Zapadno-Sibirskiy Otdel*, kniga 10, pp. 1–87.

SLAVIN, S. V. (1949a). Amerikanskaya ekspansiya na severo-vostoke Rossii v nachale XX veka [American expansion in the north-east of Russia at the beginning of the twentieth century]. *Letopis' Severa*, tom 1, pp. 136–53.

SLAVIN, S. V. (1949b). Avantyura Loyk de Lobelya i tsarskiy dvor [The adventure of Loïcq de Lobel and the Tsar's court]. *Letopis' Severa*, tom 1, pp. 227–41.

SLAVIN, S. V. (ed.) (1960). *Problemy razvitiya proizvoditel'nykh sil Kamchatskoy oblasti* [*Problems of the Development of Productive Forces of Kamchatskaya Oblast'*], 421 pp. Moscow: Izdatel'stvo Akademii Nauk SSSR.

References

SLAVIN, S. V. (1961*a*). *Promyshlennoye i transportnoye osvoyeniye severa SSSR* [*Industrial and Transport Utilisation of the North of the USSR*], 302 pp. Moscow: Ekonomgiz.

SLAVIN, S. V. (ed.) (1961*b*). *Problemy razvitiya proizvoditel'nykh sil Magadanskoy oblasti* [*Problems of Development of the Productive Forces of Magadanskaya Oblast'*], 303 pp. Moscow: Izdatel'stvo Akademii Nauk SSSR. (Offprints of the opening and concluding chapters only have been seen, through the courtesy of their author, S. V. Slavin.)

SLOVTSOV, P. A. (1886). *Istoricheskoye obozreniye Sibiri*, Izdaniye 2-oye [*Historical Survey of Siberia*, 2nd edition], 2 vols. St Petersburg: Tipografiya I. N. Skorokhodova.

SMIRNOV, V. A. (1928). *Istoricheskiy ocherk Priyeniseyskogo kraya*. Chast' 2-ya [*Historical Outline of the Yenisey Region*. Part 2], 47 pp. Krasnoyarsk: Izdaniye Byuro Krayevedeniya pri Sredne-Sibirskom otdele Russkogo Geograficheskogo Obshchestva.

SMOLITSCH, IGOR (1953). *Russisches Mönchtum. Entstehung, Entwicklung und Wesen, 988–1917*, 556 pp. Würzburg: Augustinus Verlag.

SMOLKA, H. P. (1937). *Forty Thousand Against the Arctic. Russia's Polar Empire*, 288 pp. London: Hutchinson. (Describes a visit made in 1936 to lower Yenisey region.)

STATISTICHESKOYE OBOZRENIYE (1810). *Statisticheskoye obozreniye Sibiri, sostavlennoye na osnovanii svedeniy, pocherpnutykh iz aktov pravitel'stva i drugikh dostovernykh istochnikov* [*Statistical Survey of Siberia, Compiled on the Basis of Information Obtained from Official Government Documents and Other Reliable Sources*]. St Petersburg.

STEFANSSON, V. (1926). *The Adventure of Wrangel Island*, 416 pp. London: Jonathan Cape.

STEFANSSON, V. (1958). *Northwest to Fortune. The Search of Western Man for a Commercially Practical Route to the Far East*, xix, 356 pp. New York: Duell, Sloan and Pearce.

STEPANOV (1835). *Yeniseyskaya guberniya*, 2 vols. St Petersburg.

STRAKHOVSKY, LEONID I. (1944). *Intervention at Archangel. The Story of Allied Intervention and Russian Counter-Revolution in North Russia, 1918–20*, ix, 336 pp. Princeton: University Press.

STROD, I. YA. (1961). *V Yakutskoy tayge* [*In the Yakut Tayga*], 187 pp. Moscow: Voyennoye Izdatel'stvo. (Red Army officer's reminiscences of campaign against Whites, 1922–23.)

SWENSON, OLAF (1944). *Northwest of the World. Forty Years Trading and Hunting in Northern Siberia*, 270 pp. New York: Dodd, Mead and Co.

TARACOUZIO, T. A. (1938). *Soviets in the Arctic*, xiv, 563 pp. New York: Macmillan. (Detailed general description of Soviet activities up to 1937.)

TARASENKOV, G. N. (1930). *Turukhanskiy kray. Ekonomicheskiy obzor s istoricheskim ocherkom* [*The Turukhansk Region. An Economic Survey with a Historical Outline*], 477, xviii pp. Krasnoyarsk: Izdaniye Turukhanskogo RIKa.

References

TERLETSKIY, P. YE. (1930). Natsional'noye rayonirovaniye Kraynego Severa [National zoning of the far north]. *Sovetskiy Sever. Obshchestvenno-Nauchnyy Zhurnal*, nos. 7–8, pp. 5–28, map opp. p. 134.

TIKHOMIROV, B. A. (1956). Ob okhrane lesov na ikh severnom predele i o zashchitnom lesorazvedenii v tundre [On preserving forests at their northern limit and on protective tree planting in the tundra]. *Rastitel'-nost' Kraynego Severa SSSR i yeye osvoyeniye*, vyp. 1, pp. 5–15.

TIKHOMIROV, M. N. (1962). *Rossiya v XVI stoletii [Russia in the Sixteenth Century]*, 583 pp. Moscow: Izdatel'stvo Akademii Nauk SSSR.

TOKAREV, S. A. (ed.) ET AL. (1957). *Istoriya Yakutskoy ASSR*. Tom 2. *Yakutiya ot 1630-kh godov do 1917 [History of Yakutskaya ASSR. Tom 2. Yakutiya from the 1630's to 1917]*, 419 pp. Moscow: Izdatel'stvo Akademii Nauk SSSR.

TOMILOV, F. S. (1947). *Sever v dalekom proshlom. Kratkiy istoricheskiy ocherk. [The North in the Distant Past. A Short Historical Outline]*, 96 pp. Arkhangel'sk: Arkhangel'skoye Izdatel'stvo. (Refers only to Russia in Europe.)

TREADGOLD, DONALD W. (1957). *The Great Siberian Migration: Government and Peasant in Resettlement from Emancipation to the First World War*, xiii, 278 pp. Princeton: University Press.

TRET'YAKOV, P. (1869). Turukhanskiy kray [The Turukhansk region]. *Zapiski Imperatorskogo Russkogo Geograficheskogo Obshchestva po Obshchey Geografii*, tom 2, pp. 217–530.

TROFIMOV, P. M. (1961). *Ocherki ekonomicheskogo razvitiya yevropeyskogo severa Rossii [Outlines in the Economic Development of the European North of Russia]*, 264 pp. Moscow: Izdatel'stvo Sotsial'no-Ekonomicheskoy Literatury.

TROYNITSKIY, N. A. (ed.) (1899). *Pervaya vseobshchaya perepis' naseleniya rossiyskoy imperii 1897 g. [First General Census of the Population of the Russian Empire, 1897]*. No. 1, Arkhangel'skaya Guberniya; No. 76, Primorskaya Oblast'.

TROYNITSKIY, N. A. (ed.) (1905). *Obshchiy svod po imperii rezul'tatov razrabotki dannykh pervoy vseobshchey perepisi naseleniya, proizvedennoy 28 yanvarya 1897 goda [General Summary for the Empire of the Results of Working up the Data of the First General Census of the Population Carried Out on 28 January 1897]*, 2 vols. St Petersburg.

TRUDY VYSOCHAYSHE (1885). *Trudy vysochayshe uchrezhdennoy kommissii dlya razsmotreniya predlozheniy po ustroystvu Severnogo kraya v administrativnom i ekonomicheskom otnosheniyakh [Transactions of the Commission Established by Imperial Order for Considering Suggestions for the Reconstruction of the Northern Region in Administrative and Economic Respects]*, 232 pp. St Petersburg: Tipografiya V. Kirshbauma.

UTECHIN, S. V. (1961). *Concise Encyclopaedia of Russia*, 623 pp. London: J. M. Dent.

VAGIN, V. (1872). *Istoricheskiye svedeniya o deyatel'nosti grafa M. M. Speran-*

References

skogo v Sibiri, s 1819 po 1882 god [*Historical Information on the Activity of Count M. M. Speranskiy in Siberia, from 1819 to 1822*], 2 vols. St Petersburg: Tipografiya 2-go Otdeleniya Sobstvennoy Ye. I. V. Kantselyarii.

VASYUTIN, V. F. ET AL. (1958). *Problemy razvitiya promyshlennosti i transporta Yakutskoy ASSR* [*Problems in the Development of Industry and Transport of Yakutskaya ASSR*. By V. F. Vasyutin, S. V. Slavin, M. A. Vilenskiy], 459 pp. Moscow: Izdatel'stvo Akademii Nauk SSSR.

VOLENS, N. V. (1926). Kolonisty Murmana i ikh khozyaystvo. Materialy statistiko-ekonomicheskogo issledovaniya 1921–1922 g. [Colonists of Murman and their economy. Materials of the statistical and economic studies of 1921–22]. *Trudy Nauchno-Issledovatel'skogo Instituta po Izucheniyu Severa*, vyp. 28, 112 pp.

VOSHCHININ, V. P. (1932). History, present policies and organisation of internal colonisation in the USSR. *American Geographical Society Special Publication*, no. 14, pp. 261–72.

VOYEVODSKIY NAKAZ (1842). Voyevodskiy nakaz o dolzhnosti Yakutskogo tamozhennogo i zastavnogo golovy [*Voyevoda's* decree on the duty of the Yakutsk tax and excise head]. *Akty Istoricheskiye Sobrannyye i Izdannyye Arkheograficheskoy Kommissiyey*, tom 5, no. 124, pp. 202–13.

VRANGEL', F. P. (WRANGELL, FERDINAND VON) (1839). Statistische und ethnographische Nachrichten über die Russischen Besitzungen an der Nordwestküste von Amerika. *Beiträge zur Kenntnis des Russischen Reiches und der angrenzenden Länder Asiens*, bd. 1, 322 pp.

VRANGEL', F. P. (WRANGELL, FERDINAND VON) (1840). *Narrative of an Expedition to the Polar Sea in the Years 1820, 1821, 1822 and 1823*, cxxxvii, 413 pp., ed. E. Sabine. London: J. Madden.

VSESOYUZNAYA PEREPIS' (1928). *Vsesoyuznaya perepis' naseleniya 1926 goda* [*All-Union Census of the Population in 1926*], 56 vols. Moscow: Tsentral'-noye Statisticheskoye Upravleniye.

WHITE, J. A. (1950). *The Siberian Intervention*, xii, 471 pp. Princeton: University Press. (Allied intervention, 1918–25.)

WRIGHT, G. F. (1903). *Asiatic Russia*, 2 vols. London: Eveleigh Nash. (American geographical textbook.)

YADRINTSEV, N. M. (1891). *Sibirskiye inorodtsy. Ikh byt i sovremennoye polozheniye* [*Siberian Natives. Their Way of Life and Present Position*], 308 pp. St Petersburg: Izdaniye A. M. Sibiryakova.

YADRINTSEV, N. M. (1892). *Sibir' kak koloniya v geograficheskom, etnograficheskom i istoricheskom otnoshenii*, Izdaniye 2-oye [*Siberia as a Colony in Geographical, Ethnographic and Historical Respects*, 2nd edition], 720 pp. St Petersburg: Izdaniye A. M. Sibiryakova.

YAKOVLEV, B. (1955). Kontsentratsionnyye lageri SSSR [Concentration Camps of the USSR]. *Institut po Izucheniyu Istorii i Kul'tury SSSR. Issledovaniya i Materialy, Seriya 1-ya*, vyp. 23, 256 pp. Munich.

ZAMECHANIYA (1824). Zamechaniya o severo-zapadnoy Sibiri [Remarks on north-western Siberia]. *Sibirskiy Vestnik*, chast' 3, pp. 273–88.

References

ZENZINOV, V. M. (1913). V Russkom Ust'ye [At Russkoye Ust'ye]. *Zemlevedeniye*, tom 20, vyp. 4, pp. 7–49.

ZENZINOV, V. M. & LEVINE, I. D. (1932). *The Road to Oblivion*, 287 pp. London: Cape. (Exile at Yakutsk and on lower Indigirka, 1912–13.)

ZHIKHAREV, N. A. (ed.) (1959). *Na preobrazhennoy zemle. Iz opyta raboty mestnykh sovetov Magadanskoy oblasti* [*In a Transformed Land. The Work of Local Soviets of Magadanskaya Oblast'*], 191 pp. Magadan: Knizhnoye Izdatel'stvo.

ZHIKHAREV, N. A. (1961). *Ocherki istorii severo-vostoka RSFSR (1917–1953 gg.)* [*Outlines in the History of the North-East of the RSFSR (1917–53)*], 252 pp. Magadan: Knizhnoye Izdatel'stvo.

INDEX

Index

Index

Index

Pacific Ocean, first reached by Russians, 23
Palaeosiberian languages, 177–80, 183
Palana, 187
Panteleyev, 71
Paul, Tsar, 28, 194
Pavlovskoye, 77, 91
Pavlutskiy, D., 115
Peasants as settlers, 72–81
Pechenga (Petsamo), 11, 88, 128, 139, 187
Pechora region, 11, 45–6; coalfield, 129;
  penal settlement, 151–2; railway, 139
Pekarskiy, E. K., 84
Peleduy, 187
Pelym, 73
Pepelyayev, General, 163
Perfir'yev, Il'ya, 23
Perm', 5
Permafrost (permanently frozen ground),
  6, 160
Pestel', I. B., 80
Pet, Arthur, 17
Peter I (the Great), 26, 43, 103, 194
Petrilovets, Sem'yun, 10
Petropavlovsk-na-Kamchatke, 55, 56, 108,
  138, 143, 187, Pl. IX
Petsamo (Pechenga), 11, 88, 128, 139, 187
Pevek, 5, 134, 187
Pinega, 10, 11, 95
Place-names, policy on, xi
Podshiversk, 51, 52
Pokrovsk, 187
Pokrovskiy monastery, Yakutsk region, 75,
  89
Polish citizens, 83, 84, 147
Polyakov, General, 163
Polyarnyy, 187
Pomor'ye (the White Sea littoral), 11, 42,
  95, 107
Ponoy, 44
Population statistics, 41–58, 125–7, 184–5,
  187, 188–9
Port workers, 135–8
Portlock, Nathaniel, 26
Portsmouth, Treaty of, 111
Posad, 195, Pl. II
Post stations, 76
Potapov, Dmitriy, 25
Poyarkov, Vasiliy, 23
Preklonskiy, Ivan, 113
Pribilof Islands, 29
Prisoners of war, 82, 147, 151
Promyshlennik, 61, 195
Providenya, Bukhta, 137, 187
Pulnovatvash, 16
Pushkin, Vasiliy, 82

Pustozersk, 45, 79, 91
Pyatidesyatnik, 195
Pyrkakay, 134

Railways, 85, 139–40
Raskol'niki, 91, 195
Rebrov, Ivan, 23
Reindeer, 38, 141, 161, Pl. XIV
Religious groups, 88–93
Remezov, Semen, Pl. V
Research Institute of Agriculture of the
  Far North, 146
'Revisions' of the population, 41–2
River shipping, 138
Roads, 140
Ross Colony, 29, 30
Russia Company, London, 18
Russian-American Company, 28, 30, 57
Russkoye Ust'ye, 51, 64
Rytkheu, 178

Saami (Lapps, Lopari), 10, 180, 184–5
Sable, 10, 62
Saint Petersburg, Treaty of, 111
Sakha people, 182
Sakhalin, 111
Salekhard, *formerly* Obdorsk, 5, 16, 47, 48,
  64, 137, 187, Pl. VII
Salt, 93
Samoyed people (Nentsy), 17, 34, 46, 113,
  115, 120, 181, 184–5
Sannikov, Ivan, 63
Schools, 106, 167, 169
Sel'kup people (Ostyak Samoyed), 181,
  184–6
Serebryanka, Guba, 46
Serfdom, 74–5
Severnaya Dvina, 11
Severomorsk, 187
Seymchan, 5, 187
Shakhovin, *or* Shakhov Voin, 20
Shalaurov, Nikita, 63
Shelikhov, Grigoriy, 28, 29, 117
Shepanov, 20
Shestakov, Afanasiy, 115
Shmidt, O. Yu., 138
Shmidta, Mys, 137
Sibirskiy Prikaz, 66
Sieroszewski, W., 84
Siktyakh, 51
Silver, 46, 93
Sitka, 28, 29
Skoptsy, 91–3, 196, Pl. XI
Skordin, 51
Skornyakov-Pisarev, General G. G., 82

222

Index

Index